The Olympics

Illinois History of Sports

Series Editors

Benjamin G. Rader
Randy Roberts

The Olympics: A History of the Modern Games (2d ed.)
Allen Guttmann
Baseball: A History of America's Game (2d ed.)
Benjamin G. Rader
The World's Game: A History of Soccer
Bill Murray

THE
OLYMPICS

A History of the Modern Games

ALLEN GUTTMANN

Second Edition

University of Illinois Press
Urbana and Chicago

Library of Congress Cataloging-in-Publication Data
Guttmann, Allen.
The Olympics : a history of the modern games /
Allen Guttmann. — 2nd ed.
p.   cm. — (Illinois history of sports)
Includes bibliographical references (p.   ) and index.
ISBN 0-252-02725-6 (cloth : alk. paper) / ISBN 978-0-252-02725-3
ISBN 0-252-07046-1 (pbk. : alk. paper) / ISBN 978-0-252-07046-4
1. Olympics—History. I. Title. II. Series.
GV721.5.G85   2002
796.48—dc21   2001041383

The University of Illinois Press
is a founding member of the
Association of American University Presses.

University of Illinois Press
1325 South Oak Street
Champaign, IL 61820-6903
www.press.uillinois.edu

For Erika

Contents

Illustrations follow pages 72, 164, and 182

Preface to the Second Edition

Very few cultural phenomena attract as much attention as the Olympic Games. More than one hundred thousand spectators vie for seats in the stadium, the arena, the velodrome, and the other sites of competition. Another two *billion* people follow the games on their television screens. Innumerable Olympic victors have testified that receiving their gold medals meant more to them than setting world records or triumphing in other, less symbolically weighted competitions.

Although there are honorable exceptions, most of the countless journalists who cover the games fawn on the victors, commiserate with the losers, regale their readers, listeners, and viewers with accounts of their own adventures, and manage—despite the plethora of words and images—to avoid critical analysis and serious interpretation. Whenever the games are threatened by political controversy, which they almost always are, most commenators lament the unwelcome intrusion and indulge in speculation about "the end of the Olympic Games." These laments and speculations are, by and large, superficial and uninformed.

On the other hand, while hundreds of historians, anthropologists, sociologists, economists, and media experts have studied the Olympics, few of them have written with the ordinary sports fan in mind. Indeed, some scholars seem to prefer an arcane jargon intelligible only to other specialists. In this book, I have sought to play a mediating role and thereby to bridge the gap between journalism and scholarship by writing for the serious nonspecialist reader. What follows is a history of the Olympic Games as a social movement. Although I have included discussions of the most memorable and significant athletic events of each of these games, from 1896 to 2000, my focus and my emphasis have been elsewhere—on what the games were intended to mean and what they have, in fact, meant.

For this second edition I have updated the bibliographical essay and appendix and added two new chapters. In chapter 12 I focus on Juan Antonio Samaranch, four-term president of the International Olympic Committee, and the impact of his leadership on the games of the late twentieth century, during which the use of drugs became more widespread, the economic structure of the games was transformed, and scandals accompanied the awarding of sites. In chapter 13 I highlight the impressive athletic achievements since the end of the cold war, including the debut of openly professional athletes and the significantly increased role of female athletes.

I have, of course, relied upon the work of hundreds of scholars as well as upon my own previous research. My task of interpretation has been aided by Doris Bargen, Benjamin Rader, and Randy Roberts, who read the original manuscript and offered valuable suggestions. Finally, I offer chagrined but heartfelt thanks to Bill Mallon and other reviewers who spotted factual errors in the first edition.

For the photographs and permission to publish them, I am grateful to the Avery Brundage Collection (University of Illinois at Urbana-Champaign), Corbis Images, the International Olympic Committee, the Nationale Olympische Komitee der DDR, Ronald Smith, and AP/Wide World Photos. For permission to use revised portions of the *The Games Must Go On: Avery Brundage and the Olympic Movement* (1984), I am grateful to Columbia University Press. Portions of chapters 9 and 10 appeared, in earlier versions, in the *International Journal* (Autumn 1988).

The Olympics

The Olympic Games Are More Than Games

Whenever the Olympic Games are threatened by political protests or disrupted by acts of terror, as was the case in 1968 and 1972, whenever the games are diminished by massive boycotts, as was the case in 1976, 1980, and 1984, the International Olympic Committee (IOC) and most of the world's sportswriters lament the intrusion of politics into the domain of sports. Politics, however, in the broadest sense of the term, has *always* been a part of the Olympics. The modern games were, in fact, revived to propagate a political message. In the eyes of Pierre de Coubertin and the men who succeeded him as president of the IOC, the political purpose of the games—the reconciliation of warring nations—was more important than the sports. *They* were merely the competitive means to a cooperative end: a world at peace. The games, wrote Coubertin in his *Mémoires Olympiques*, "are not simply world championships, they are the quadrennial festival of universal youth."

The brighter the dream, the darker the despair when the dream is disappointed. The most horrific episode in Olympic history—the ghoulish murder in the middle of the Olympic village of eleven Israeli athletes and officials by Palestinian terrorists—was obviously the antithesis of what Coubertin wanted, but the horror perpetrated in 1972 has to be understood against the background of idealism. The nightmare of nationalistic hatred was the terrorists' answer to the dream of international harmony.

Since most sports spectators are more interested in the athletes and their performances than they are in Olympism as a social movement, the notion that the games are inherently political might seem odd; but a brief consideration of the symbolism of the Olympics is instructive.

The interlocked Olympic rings were designed by Coubertin in 1914 as a representation of the five continents and the colors of their many national flags. The Olympic torch, lit at the site of the ancient games and carried by thousands of relay runners from Greece to the host city, is intended to dramatize connection and continuity through time and space. The parade of national teams, beginning with Greece and concluding with the host country, is another symbol of international cooperation. The athletes who stand and recite the Olympic oath do so in the name of thousands of male and female athletes who come together from every portion of the globe. The Olympic hymn is still another statement of peaceful internationalism.

Coubertin's vision of a better world was liberal in the sense of classic nineteenth-century liberalism (which should not be confused with its collectivist twentieth-century variant). Individual liberty was the highest good. Like other prophets of nineteenth-century liberalism, however, Coubertin was torn between a belief in individualism and the conviction that nationality is the indispensable core of individual identity. His internationalism was never cosmopolitan. Although the Olympic Charter proclaims that the games are contests between individuals, not between nations, the IOC created an institutional structure based on national representation: no athlete can compete as an individual; every athlete must be selected by his or her country's national Olympic committee; every athlete—even the otherwise irrepressible Florence Griffith-Joyner—must wear a national uniform; when a victor is honored, a national flag is raised and a national anthem is played. There have been many efforts to replace these symbols of nationalism with the Olympic flag and the Olympic hymn, but they have always failed. When a number of European teams marched behind the Olympic banner in 1980 to protest the Soviet Union's invasion of Afghanistan, there were bitter complaints from nationalistic fans who wanted to see the Union Jack and the Tricoleur.

In other words, the political vision institutionalized in the Olympics has always been inconsistent and contradictory. The danger of rabidly nationalistic partisanship was there from the start. No wonder, then, that the history of the Olympics has been a mixed one in which the glories of individual athletic achievement have been accompanied by frenzies of chauvinism. To witness the spectators' emotions when *their* national representative mounts the victor's podium, when *their* flag is raised, when *their* anthem is played, is to wonder if nationalism—or sport—is not the true religion of the modern world.

It all depends, of course, on how one defines religion. In their beliefs, Coubertin and his followers were liberals in the spirit of Thomas Jefferson and John Stuart Mill. Deeply suspicious of conventional theistic religions, they promoted Olympism as a substitute for traditional faith. "For me," Coubertin wrote in his *Mémoires Olympiques,* "sport is a religion with church, dogma, ritual." In a radio address delivered in Berlin on August 4, 1935, he repeated his frequently expressed desire that the games be inspired by "religious sentiment transformed and enlarged by the internationalism and democracy that distinguish the modern age." Nearly thirty years later, Coubertin's most dedicated disciple, Avery Brundage, proclaimed to his colleagues on the International Olympic Committee that Olympism is a twentieth-century religion, "a religion with universal appeal which incorporates all the basic values of other religions, a modern, exciting, virile, dynamic religion."

Coubertin and Brundage were quite serious when they touted Olympism as a religion. They realized that, historically, religious differences have caused as much bloodshed as national differences, and they imagined that the Olympic Games might form the nucleus of a modern secular faith based on "good sportsmanship and fair play." To a surprising degree they succeeded. Adherents of every major faith have put aside their religious differences in order to participate, however briefly, in Olympism. The Olympics have actually been far more successful in damping the flames of religious conflict than in controlling the repercussions of political controversy. The one great exception to this generalization occurred when sports, religion, and politics intersected. Attempting to justify the murders committed at the 1972 Games, a Palestinian spokesman averred that the terrorists recognized "that sport is the modern religion of the western world. . . . So we decided to use the Olympics, the most sacred ceremony of this religion, to make the world pay attention to us."

Although Coubertin and his followers were not immune to the racism of their day, their liberalism was—at least theoretically—color-blind. The Olympic Games were also meant to symbolize the irrelevance of race within the world of sports and, ultimately, within the political realm. The removal of racial barriers was a less explicit goal than the elimination of hostilities based on national and religious differences, but interracial harmony has gradually become a major tenet of Olympism. This tenet was especially salient during the long struggle with the South African National Olympic Committee over its refusal to condemn the government's strict policy of apartheid.

Like most nineteenth-century liberals, the aristocratic Coubertin was so enthralled by the notion of individual liberty that he was insufficiently attentive to the constraints of social class. (Karl Marx was definitely *not* one of Coubertin's intellectual mentors.) Although the Frenchman was highly skeptical about the cult of amateurism, he nonetheless embraced it, at least in public, and he seemed unaware that its central purpose was the exclusion of the lower classes from the sports competitions of their "betters." (Amateurism in the late nineteenth century meant the ineligibility of all those who performed *any kind* of manual work, whether or not the work was sports related.) Although more consistently liberal views have prevailed, so that the disadvantages of class have been lessened, the amateur-professional dichotomy still confuses the rule books.

Coubertin's version of liberal individualism was even more inadequate in its narrowly conventional treatment of women. Nonwhite athletes and athletes from working-class families have been disadvantaged, but their road to Olympia has been straighter and smoother than the rocky path female athletes have been forced to traverse. For Coubertin's generation, the socially constructed distinctions of gender seemed to be the dictates of biological inevitability. The games were definitely *not* meant to minimize the differences between men and women. They were never intended, in those days, as a platform for women's rights. The games began as a sports festival for men, and if Coubertin had had his way, women would have remained forever restricted to the role of admiring spectators.

Needless to say, it has taken nearly a century for some of the internal contradictions of Olympism to be understood and partially eliminated (and for other problems, like commercialism and drug abuse, to have arisen). None of the explicit or implicit values of Olympism has ever been perfectly realized. When the German philosopher (and Olympic victor) Hans Lenk attempted to assess the degree to which the goals of Olympism have been reached, he was left with a complicated list of partial successes and partial failures.

Small wonder. The story of the Olympics is a complex narrative. It is comprised of the stellar sports achievements of the world's most gifted athletes competing among themselves as representatives of the strength, swiftness, endurance, grace, and courage of all humankind. It is also comprised of the bitter political conflicts and petty squabbles of men and women groping their way to what we hope may be a better world. The chronologically organized chapters that follow are an attempt to tell this composite story of sports and politics. Although it is quite impossible in a single volume to report on the thousands of contests and the tens of thousands of athletes who have participated from 1896 to 1988, I have tried to comment briefly on some of the most memorable sports achievements. My primary purpose, however, is to demonstrate that the Olympics have, indeed, been what their founders wanted them to be: political. To lament the "intrusion of politics into the world of sports" is naive. To hope that modern sports can contribute significantly to the cause of a more just and humane political order may be equally naive. But Pierre de Coubertin was surely right about one thing: we need our ideals.

1

The Baron's Dream

Born in Paris on January 1, 1863, the son and heir of Baron Charles Louis Frédy de Coubertin and his Norman wife, Agathe Marie Marcelle Gigault de Crisenoy, Pierre de Coubertin was still a child when France suffered a humiliating defeat at the hands of the Prussians in 1870. At Sedan, Emperor Napoleon III was captured along with most of his army. The victorious Prussians annexed the two eastern provinces of Alsace and Lorraine and temporarily occupied the Palace of Versailles in order to announce the formation of the German Empire (led, of course, by Prussia). Like most Frenchmen, the young Coubertin burned with a desire to avenge the defeat and to recover the lost provinces. As the child of one of France's most aristocratic families, Coubertin may have felt a special responsibility to seek *revanche* for the debacle at Sedan.

Like many young aristocrats whose exalted social position barred them from bourgeois occupations, Coubertin initially considered a military career. A short stay at St. Cyr—the French equivalent of West Point—convinced him that he was not meant to be a soldier. For a time he studied law. Then he began to attend classes at the École Libre des Sciences Politiques, where he came under the influence of a reform-minded faculty. At the École, he realized that his true vocation was to be an educator and a propagandist.

Coubertin's mentors introduced him to the social theories of Frédéric LePlay, a thinker whose influence on the young Frenchman was profound. LePlay, shaken by the class divisions that threatened to destroy French society, dedicated his life to the restoration of social peace and domestic harmony. Strongly attracted to this goal, which he saw as a prerequisite to any French challenge to German power, Coubertin published a number of essays in LePlay's journal, *La Re-*

forme Sociale. In 1883, Coubertin joined the Unions de la Paix, which LePlay had founded in 1871.

In these years, Coubertin was haunted by memories of the Franco-Prussian War. He attributed the defeat not to the arrogance of Napoleon III, who fancied himself to have inherited the military skills of his uncle, but rather to the physical inferiority of the average French youth. The soldiers' lack of fitness was probably less of a factor than the emperor's overconfidence in his strategic genius, but it was nonetheless true that young Frenchmen were on average less robust than their rugged counterparts on the other side of the Rhine.

In the early years of the nineteenth century, at a time when the French under Napoleon I had occupied much of Germany, Friedrich Ludwig Jahn had created an extremely nationalistic form of gymnastics. To the running, jumping, climbing, hanging, and swinging exercises that progressive German educators had developed toward the end of the eighteenth century, Jahn added a fervent patriotic motive: to unify the divided German *Volk* and to drive the hated Napoleonic invaders from sacred German soil. The Old High German name Jahn gave to this brand of gymnastics—*Turnen*—was meant to emphasis its uniqueness. By the middle of the nineteenth century, *Turnen* was the basis of physical education in German public schools as well as the raison d'être of thousands of private clubs and associations. While French schoolchildren were drilled in the Greek and Latin classics and in their own literary tradition, German children combined sedentary study with strenuous physical exercise. In an age when warfare was still waged mainly by foot soldiers, physical fitness may not have been decisive, but it certainly mattered, and German soldiers were fitter than the French. In his many books and articles, Coubertin appealed to his countrymen to mend their ways, to become as hardy as their perennial foes, to steel themselves for the task of revenge. He concluded, however, that there were better paths to physical prowess than the rather grim routines of Germanic physical education, which had become rigidified and cheerless when transferred from voluntary clubs—*Turnvereine*—to the educational system. Coubertin looked, therefore, across the channel to his nation's friendlier rival, England.

While Germans were busy with their *Turnen,* the English had apparently gone mad for sports. This was especially true of the elite public schools (which were actually private schools; they were public only in that commoners were admitted along with the sons of the nobility). At Eton, Harrow, Winchester, and elsewhere, boys were allowed to devote an extraordinary amount of their time to rowing, running, jumping, and playing ball games. But Coubertin completely misunderstood the origins of this enthusiasm for sports. In 1875, he read a French translation of *Tom Brown's School Days* (1856), a boys' book in which Thomas Hughes romanticized his memories of Rugby School. Misled by Hughes, Coubertin thought that Thomas Arnold, Rugby's headmaster from 1828 to 1842, had been an ardent advocate of sports. In his study *L'Éducation en Angleterre* (1888), the twenty-five-year-old Coubertin wrote rhapsodically of Arnold, who "could not have been English if he had not loved sport." In one of his memoirs, *Une Campagne de Vingt-et-un Ans* (1909), Coubertin described his visit to the chapel at Rugby School as if it had been a pilgrimage. If not quite a saint, Arnold became for Coubertin a kind of spiritual father figure.

In fact, the historical Arnold was far more interested in the boys' moral education than in their physical development. No matter. Coubertin, like a number of other anglophile Frenchmen, admired the rugged health of the English schoolboys. Sports seemed, moreover, to have developed not only the boys' enviable physical prowess but also their character. They glowed with a sturdy self-confidence that their teachers—most of whom were sports enthusiasts—attributed to their hours at cricket, soccer, and rugby. Although the Duke of Wellington never did remark that the Battle of Waterloo was won on the playing fields of Eton, generations of Englishmen believed in a vital connection between sports and life's more serious contests. Coubertin shared that belief. He was as sure as they were that character developed in schoolboy games manifested itself in firm British rule over "an empire upon which the sun never set."

Arnold was not the only Englishman to influence Coubertin. In 1849, Dr. W. P. Brookes had instituted Olympian Games near Much Wenlock in Shropshire. In addition to track-and-field sports, which the British called "athletics," there were cricket matches, tilting at rings while mounted on horseback, and literary and artistic competitions. There were banners in Greek and laurel crowns for the victors. The games occurred annually for some forty years. In 1890, young Coubertin visited the eighty-two-year-old Brookes, responded sympathetically to the older man's views on "the moral influence of physical culture," and discussed with him the possibility of reviving the ancient Olympic Games.

Another Englishman, John Astley Cooper, was more a rival than an inspiration or model. In 1891, Astley Cooper proposed a Pan-Britannic and Anglo-Saxon Festival to which athletes from the United States and the British Empire would be invited. Through sports they would demonstrate Anglo-Saxon superiority and tighten the bonds of Anglo-Saxon friendship. Aside from the obvious racism, nearly ubiquitous in that imperialistic age, it was a fine idea, one more or less realized in 1930 when the first British Empire Games were held at Hamilton.

Coubertin, however, was a better propagandist than Astley Cooper—and a much better organizer. *His* games became a reality a generation earlier.

A visit to the United States in 1889 familiarized Coubertin with American notions of physical education and with the national mania for intercollegiate sports. He was especially impressed by the excellent facilities that the colleges and universities had made available to their students, and in *Universités Transatlantiques* (1890) he wrote enthusiastically of what he had seen. His sojourn in North America was also an occasion for him to meet U.S. Civil Service Commissioner Theodore Roosevelt, whom he instantly recognized as a kindred spirit. Roosevelt, ever the advocate of the "strenuous life," was surprised and delighted to meet a Frenchman who was no "mollycoddle." The two men developed a friendship that lasted for decades.

This openness to English and American influences put Coubertin at odds with a number of his anglophobic countrymen. Paschal Grousset, for instance, organizer of an extremely nationalistic Ligue Nationale de l'Éducation Physique, wanted French sports with French names. When league members persisted in their lamentable desire to play *le football,* he sought vainly to rename the sport *la barrette.* Undeterred by criticisms from Grousset and other chauvinists, Coubertin produced a constant stream of publications urging the French to emulate the English (and thus to prepare themselves for revenge against the Germans). Working closely with educators at L'École Monge, l'École Alsacienne, and a number of other progressive schools, he propagandized for the athleticism that was such a prominent part of British secondary education. Initial success demonstrated just how far the reformers had to go to modify French prejudices. When the boys from the various *lycées* emerged from their classrooms and began to play soccer in the parks of Paris, the startled spectators assumed that they were boisterous English lads who spoke excellent French.

In addition to working with those few educators who shared his strange enthusiasm for *le sport anglais,* Coubertin organized or reorganized a number of sports associations, the most important of which (in these pre-Olympic years) was the Union des Sociétés Françaises de Sports Athlétiques (USFSA), which Coubertin and his friend Georges St.-Clair founded in 1890. Two years later, Coubertin decided that it was time to revive the most famous athletic festival of antiquity—the Olympic Games.

By the time he came to this decision, Coubertin had begun to outgrow the vindictiveness that had originally motivated his interest in sports. Modern technology—steamships, railroads, the telegraph and the telephone—had begun to transform the world into a "global village," and thoughtful men and women began to shed some of the xenophobia that has always hindered the development of international cooperation. Travel may not broaden everyone, but it seems to have extended Coubertin's horizons. At any rate, his youthful fantasy of *revanche* against the loathsome Prussians was gradually tempered by a more humane philosophy. He was still a patriotic Frenchman, and he remained one for all his long life, but he was no longer a chauvinist. He was increasingly drawn to the humanistic vision of a peaceful world. Sports were still the means, but the ends had been transformed.

"Nothing in ancient history inspired more revery in me than Olympia," wrote Coubertin, but he was certainly not the first to entertain the dream of Olympic renewal. Christian zeal had ended the ancient games, sacred to Zeus, because of their indelible pagan associations, but Christendom had never forgotten the games, and various humanistically inclined scholars had from time to time suggested they be revived—purged, of course, of all traces of paganism. Throughout the nineteenth century, there were more realistic proposals. Dr. Brookes of Shropshire was by no means the first to attempt a pre-Coubertinian revival. In addition to his Olympian Games, there were at least four other Olympic festivals in England between 1859 and 1870.

There were also stirrings on the continent. In Sweden, Gustav Schartau, a professor at the University of Lund, staged the Jeux Olympiques Scandinaves in 1834 and 1836. In Germany, in 1852, the classical scholar Ernst Curtius delivered a famous address in which he called for the archaeological excavation of the ancient Olympic site. (The work was actually inaugurated by German archaeologists in 1875.) The most serious attempt at revival of the Olympic Games occurred in Athens in 1859. A suggestion of Panagiotis Soustos inspired the philanthropist Evangelis Zappas to donate a million drachmas to renew ancient glory. These first games attracted scant attention outside Greece, but another attempt, eleven years later, was somewhat more successful. In 1875, however, the sporadically repeated event was little better than a joke. The Greek series ceased in 1889. Since all four of these celebrations were Panhellenic contests limited to Greek participants, they attracted minimal foreign attention. Indeed, even local interest waned to the point where historians are uncertain whether or not there really was a fourth celebration.

The world more or less ignored these games, but by the time they petered out, Coubertin had become a master at getting people's attention. As one of the leaders of the Union des Sociétés Françaises de Sports Athlétiques, he suggested a grand celebration on the occasion of the association's fifth anniversary. Since the USFSA was only three years old, his fussy colleagues thought that they should wait a bit before a fifth-year celebration, but Coubertin persuaded them to date the establishment of the association from the founding of the Unions des Sociétés Françaises de Courses à Pied—a track organization founded in 1887 that had merged with the USFSA in 1890. It was, he later recalled, a birthday party at which the babies had been switched.

The "party," held on November 25, 1892, was attended by a great crowd of French and foreign dignitaries to whom Coubertin announced his grand plan to revive the ancient games. "It is necessary to internationalize sports," he proclaimed; "it is necessary to organize anew the Olympic Games." The initial response was puzzlement. According to Coubertin, most of the delegates felt that the Olympics were "in the same category as the mysteries of Eleusis or the oracle of Delphi; things that were dead and could only be revived in a comic opera." In fact, one of Coubertin's auditors approached him four years later and confessed that she had thought at the time that he was referring to a theatrical production of *The Olympics,* which she had seen in San Francisco. Undeterred by the initial lack of response, Coubertin invited a number of prominent educators and public figures to an even more ambitious international congress to be held at the Sorbonne. The primary announced purpose was to discuss the problem of amateurism.

The concept of amateurism as it was then understood was an invention of the Victorian middle and upper classes. Its freely acknowledged purpose was to exclude the "lower orders" from the play of the leisure class. In its earliest formulations, the amateur rule specifically banned participation by those who performed any kind of manual labor. The rules for the Henley Regatta (1878) were typical: "No person shall be considered an amateur oarsman or sculler . . . Who is or has been by trade or employment for wages, a mechanic, artisan, or laborer." Spokesmen for amateurism attempted to justify their snobbery with the claim that the "lower orders" were incapable of acts of fair play and good sportsmanship.

This original definition of amateurism had at least the advantage of clarity. However, when exclusion on the basis of class membership seemed too blatantly undemocratic to defend, the concept of amateurism was revised so that it restricted eligibility to those who received no material benefit, directly or indirectly, from any sport. While this formulation was an improvement, it still seemed unattractively negative. It also seemed illogical. Why should a stableboy employed at a horse track be deemed ineligible as an oarsman? The amateur ideal was then restated in somewhat less illogical and in somewhat more positive terms. Through most of the twentieth century amateurism was defended with the argument that fair play and good sportsmanship are

possible only when sports are an athlete's *avocation,* never his or her
vocation. Amateur athletes were defined as those who competed for
the intrinsic pleasures of the contest, not because sports provided them
with the material basis of their existence. After all, the word "amateur"
derives from the Latin word for "love."

This version of the rule was an improvement over more negative
formulations, but the lack of logic was just as obvious. While it seemed
(and still seems) unfair to ask a bank clerk who occasionally boxed
after hours to step into the ring with an experienced prizefighter, the
rule was interpreted so that a coal miner who received a ten-shilling
payment for a single game of soccer was said to have become a professional athlete. The process was irreversible. Many of the world's greatest athletes were declared professionals for pocketing sums of money
inadequate to support them for more than an afternoon. Interpreted
this rigidly, the avocation-vocation distinction seemed madly irrational
to almost everyone except those whose power and privilege enabled
them to define reality.

The question of amateurism never obsessed Coubertin as it did some
of his contemporaries (and followers). Nevertheless, he was forced to
indulge others in their foible in order to gain their support for his
dream of Olympic renewal.

Hoping to win over American sportsmen for his project, Coubertin
returned to the United States in 1893 to attend Chicago's Columbian
Exposition as an official representative of the French Ministry of Education. After participation in this great international fair, he journeyed
as far west as San Francisco and as far south as New Orleans before
spending three weeks at Princeton University as a guest of Professor
William Milligan Sloane. His host, an expert in French history, arranged
a dinner party at New York's University Club on November 27; the
guests—American sports administrators—listened without enthusiasm
to Coubertin's proposals. It was especially unfortunate that Coubertin
failed to win the cooperation of James E. Sullivan, the crusty, self-
important secretary of the Amateur Athletic Union of the United States.
The two men were introduced by Gustavus T. Kirby, an AAU stalwart
and a man of great integrity and good will, but Sullivan and Coubertin
seem to have disliked each other from the moment they met. "No
evidence has been found," comments John Lucas, "to show that the
thirty-three-year-old Sullivan was even remotely interested in the idea
of a revived Olympic Games—a concept conceived by most sportsmen
in the United States as bizarre."

The British were somewhat more receptive. At a dinner held in
February at London's University Sports Club, Astley Cooper generously
welcomed Coubertin as "the prophet of a new era." The Prince of

Wales, known for his love of sports (and the actress Lily Langtry), promised his support for the baron's dream. Charles Herbert undertook to enlist the support of the country's Amateur Athletic Association.

As the day of the Sorbonne conference approached, Coubertin orchestrated his themes brilliantly. On the very eve of the conference, he published an essay in the *Revue de Paris* in which he eloquently urged the revival of the Olympic Games. He arranged for the seventy-eight delegates from nine countries to convene in an auditorium whose walls had recently been adorned with suitably neoclassical murals by the painter Pierre Puvis de Chavannes. The delegates were seduced by ear as well as by eye. On the opening day, June 16, they heard a performance of the ancient "Hymn to Apollo," discovered the previous year at Delphi, translated into French by Théodore Reinach, set to music by Gabriel Fauré, and sung by Jeanne Remacle. Fauré was also called upon to conduct a choral group accompanied by harps.

The discussions of amateurism began on Sunday and continued for several days. Like all of Coubertin's conferences, this one had a full program of festive entertainments, exhibitions, and displays. Catching the dazzled delegates at a propitious moment, the canny baron proposed the revival of the Olympic Games. Why not? On June 23, the obliging delegates voted unanimously to support Coubertin's plan. "If the Olympic Games have been reborn," wrote Coubertin in his *Mémoires Olympiques,* "it was perhaps during those instants when every heart beat as one." The conference delegates also empowered Coubertin to choose an international committee (eventually entitled the International Olympic Committee, or, in the preferred diplomatic language of the day, the Comité Internationale Olympique). At the grand banquet that closed the conference, a French classicist, Michel Bréal, offered a trophy to be awarded to the winner of a special race in commemoration of the Greek victory over the Persian invaders in the Battle of Marathon in 490 B.C. The distance from the site of the battle to the stadium in Athens was approximately twenty-two miles.

On June 19, Coubertin had suggested to Demetrios Bikelas, a prominent Greek man of letters then residing in Paris, that it would be appropriate if the first Olympic Games of the modern era were held at Athens. Bikelas agreed and made the formal proposal at the plenary session on June 23. The proposal was accepted with enthusiasm and Bikelas was asked to serve as the president of the first International Olympic Committee. In the opinion of David C. Young, Bikelas, whose name can also be transliterated as Vikelas, was "the most learned, the most international, the most cosmopolitan" of the IOC's seven presidents.

It was Coubertin, however, who determined the composition of the governing body. He was especially anxious that the IOC be as politically independent as possible. To achieve that goal, the members were asked to be "ambassadors *from* the committee *to* their respective countries." Coubertin added that it was the man that mattered, "not the country." Since the members were expected not only to pay their own travel expenses but also to contribute to the costs of the IOC, most of them were quite affluent. The members, who were much more likely to be enthusiasts for the turf than the track, were selected for their wealth and for their social status. The most active among the initial IOC members were Viktor Balck (Sweden), Aleksander Butkowsky (Russia), Jiri Guth-Jarkovsky (Bohemia), Ferenc Kemeny (Hungary), and William Milligan Sloane (USA). The other members were Britain's Charles Herbert, France's Ernest Callot, Dr. J. B. Zubiaur of Argentina, Leonard Cuff of New Zealand, and a rather useless group of titled noblemen whom Coubertin later disparaged as "une façade."

All in all, the first IOC was an influential group, and influence was needed. The Greeks were not enthusiastic about their unsolicited honor as hosts to the games. In a hurried trip to Athens, Bikelas appointed Stephanos Dragoumis, a member of the Zappeion Athletic Club, as head of the organizing committee, but Dragoumis proved to be incompetent and the committee accomplished little. By the fall of 1894, Dragoumis was suggesting that the games be postponed for four years and then moved to Paris. Although David Young has noted critically that "the Greeks got very little help from Coubertin," the baron did interrupt his marital preparations to rush to Athens in November. Once there, he fired off barrages of oratory. Flattery worked wonders and Dragoumis was cajoled into releasing funds donated by the Zappas family for the promotion of Greek sports. Coubertin, somewhat reassured, hastened back to Paris for his March 12 wedding. The bride, Marie Rothan, was a Protestant from Alsace.

The games, meanwhile, had become a political football booted about by liberals and conservatives as they maneuvered for control of the Greek government. The leader of the opposition, Theodoros Deligiannes, favored the games, but Prime Minister Charliaos Trikoupis complained that Greece was unable to bear the financial burden. He was unmoved by an appeal sent to him by Coubertin's English friend Dr. Brookes (of the Much Wenlock Olympian Games). Fortunately for the IOC, Trikoupis resigned in January 1895 and Deligiannes became prime minister.

Still, the road to Olympia was by no means clear. The organizing committee continued to be ineffective, and if it had not been for the active intervention of Crown Prince Constantine and his brothers, the games might never have occurred. Constantine called a meeting on January 13, at the Zappeion, and appealed to his countrymen to support "this great enterprise." Timoleon Philemon, a former mayor of Athens, was named secretary-general of the reconstituted organizing committee. A skillful fund-raiser, Philemon sailed for Egypt and persuaded George Averoff, a wealthy Greek businessman resident in Alexandria, to provide enough money to restore the ancient stadium originally constructed by Herodes Atticus during the reign of Hadrian.

In addition to the inevitable problems faced by anyone sponsoring an international event of this magnitude, there were administrative difficulties. Coubertin had to worry about ad hoc athletic rules and regulations. There were, in 1896, no really effective international federations to govern specific sports, and the nascent national federations were often at odds with one another. More important than rules and regulations in Coubertin's eyes was the symbolism of the games. He sketched plans for the opening and closing ceremonies, both of which were to emphasize the dominant theme of peaceful internationalism.

Publicity was a problem too. Very few people were interested in Coubertin's grand experiment. Butkowsky sent discouraging news from Russia: "Our press finds the question of physical training unworthy of mention." Since modern sports were scarcely known in czarist Russia, Coubertin was not particularly upset by the realization that few, if any, Russian athletes planned to make their way to Athens. British apathy was, however, a serious blow. An editorialist in London's *Spectator* ridiculed the games as an "athletic whim," and the Amateur Athletic Association was lukewarm about the project. Only six Britons made the trip to Athens, where they were joined by a vacationing tourist. The American team consisted mainly of four juniors from Princeton, who were excused from their classes thanks to the intervention of Professor Sloane, and a five-man contingent—all Harvard educated—from the Boston Athletic Club. A sixth Bostonian, James Brendan Connolly, was a member of the Suffolk Athletic Club and an undergraduate at Harvard. When the dean told Connolly that he might not be readmitted if he left Cambridge before the end of the semester, Connolly announced, "I *am* going to the Olympic Games, so I am through with Harvard right now. Good day, sir."

Coubertin was no longer bitterly hostile to the nation that had inflicted upon France the military humiliations of 1870-71; nor was he sufficiently familiar with German sports. Maximilian von Schwartzkoppen, Berlin's military attaché in Paris, suggested to him that an invitation be sent to General Viktor von Podbielski, whose Union-Klub ran a racetrack in Berlin. Coubertin did not receive an answer from Podbielski. He wrote to Walter Bensemann of the Strassbourg

Football Club, a founder of the Deutscher Fussball-Bund, but there was no answer to that letter either. Fortunately, Willibald Gebhardt, a chemist, got wind of the great event. In December 1895, less than six months before the games were to begin, he organized a German committee and began to recruit a team. It was not easy. "Our German sensibility," proclaimed the gymnasts of the Deutsche Turnerschaft, "cannot bear these French shenanigans." Gebhardt persuaded ten gymnasts to defy the Turnerschaft and join three other athletes on the German team. Coubertin was so pleased with Gebhardt's efforts that he recruited him for the IOC.

Coubertin's own countrymen were a particularly discouraging problem. Although Coubertin had been one of the founders of the USFSA, it remained aloof. "At this moment," commented a condescending spokesman for the organization, "the Olympic Games have brought together in Athens a rather second-rate group of athletes." This was not the only discouragement. Daniel Merrillon informed Coubertin that the marksmen of the Sociétés de Tir were not ready to associate "indiscriminately" with other sportsmen. French gymnasts were offended that Coubertin wanted to include contests on the rings and other equipment instead of the noncompetitive mass demonstrations of drilled agility that were—in their eyes—the real core of gymnastics. The French who did make their way to Athens included a pair of professional cyclists and a runner, Albin Lermusieux, who entered the 100-meter run and the marathon: "One day," he explained, "I run a leetle way, vairy queek. Ze next day, I run a long way, vairy slow." When Thomas Curtis asked the Frenchman why he was putting on a pair of white gloves just before the start of the 100-meter race, the answer was simple enough: "Ah-ha! Zat is because I run for ze king!" Lermusieux finished third in the sprint and is said by some historians to have completed the marathon (others claim that he abandoned the course).

As the opening day drew closer, Coubertin's excitement seemed almost palpable. He wrote in a letter on March 26: "The Athenian spring is double this year. It warms not only the clear atmosphere but the soul of the populace. It pushes up the sweet-smelling flowers between the stones of the Parthenon. . . . The sun shines, and the Olympic Games are here. The fears and ironies of the year just past have disappeared. The skeptics have been eliminated; the Olympic Games have not a single enemy." It was certainly not true that the games had not a single enemy, but Coubertin preferred always to stress the positive. Had he not been of optimistic disposition, he would long since have abandoned his dream.

The modern games were inaugurated in style, with the ritual and fanfare that Coubertin felt was essential to their social purpose. The king spoke a few words. Cannon were fired. Doves were released. When the contests were over, flags were raised for the victors. But many of the most familiar symbols—like the Olympic rings and the motto *Citius, Altius, Fortius*—were still to come.

Citizens of the host country comprised a majority of the approximately three hundred contestants, and most of the forty thousand or more spectators were Greek. For them, there was the enchanting vision of renascent Olympic glory—and the annoying fact of American partisanship. Many who wrote about these first games commented on the inexplicable noises ("Siss, boom, bah!") made by the American spectators, a number of whom were young sailors on shore leave from the cruiser *San Francisco*. The official Greek report on the games referred to the "absurd shouts" of the Americans, and Charles Maurras, a French man of letters, complained that the rooters were "like overgrown children."

The American team was clearly the strongest of those in Athens, but it was by no means the strongest possible team. Thomas Burke won the 100-meter dash in 12.0 seconds; Luther Cary had set the record of 10.75 seconds in 1891. Burke won the 400-meter race in 54.2 seconds; Edgar Bredin's record, set in 1895, was nearly six seconds faster. Although Robert Garrett had hardly even *seen* a real discus before his arrival in Athens, he won that event as well as the shot put, both with distances far shorter than the world record. Greek spectators were especially disappointed when Garrett hurled the discus 29.15 meters and defeated Panagiotis Paraskevopulos in this historically resonant event. With similarly modest performances, Ellery Clark triumphed in the high jump and the long jump, while James Connolly, Thomas P. Curtis, and William Hoyt were victors in the triple jump, the 110-meter hurdles, and the pole vault. Australia's Edwin Flack took the gold medal in both the 800-meter and the 1,500-meter races. The New South Wales Amateur Athletic Association had decided, for financial reasons, not to send a team to distant Greece, but Flack, who resided in London, paid his own way to Athens, where he shared an apartment with George Robertson, the English author of a "Pindaric" ode in classical Greek. Flack and Robertson also shared an interest in tennis. They joined forces and competed, unsuccessfully, in the doubles competition.

Competition in more than one sport was by no means uncommon in these early days. Germany's Fritz Hofmann won two gymnastics events and finished second in both the 100-meter and the 400-meter races. Flack and Robertson were not unique in their internationalism either. J. P. Boland and Fritz Traun formed an Irish-German tennis partnership that defeated a Greek pair in the finals (5-7, 6-4, 6-1).

The German gymnasts were quite successful, winning three of the six events. Their medals were some compensation for their expulsion from the Deutsche Turnerschaft, which had sought to prevent their involvement in these French-inspired games. A Hungarian, Alfred Hoyos Guttmann, shivered his way to a pair of gold medals in the swimming events, held in the chilling waters of the Aegean Sea. "I won ahead of the others with a big lead," he said of the 1,500-meter race, "but my greatest struggle was against the towering twelve-foot waves and the terribly cold water."

Greek pride was salved by victories in the shooting and cycling events and by a dramatic victory in the world's first marathon. Although a number of foreigners competed, including Flack and Lermusieux, the winner was Spiridon Louys, a Greek peasant, whose entrance into the Olympic Stadium brought Prince Constantine and Prince George down to the track to accompany him to the finish line. As pandemonium filled the stadium, Charles Maurras made a prophetic remark to Coubertin: "I see that your internationalism . . . does not kill national spirit— it strengthens it."

Nationalism was certainly in evidence. While preparing for the games in 1895, the Greeks had been less than candid about Coubertin's role as *rénovateur*. As John Lucas notes, "Coubertin's name was absent from official Olympic bulletins, tentative programs, royal edicts, organizing committee instructions, and the Greek press." When Coubertin claimed to have had a hand in the affair, one Athenian newspaper reviled him as "a thief seeking to rob Greece of her inheritance." Now that the dream was reality, nationalism was further inflamed. The victory in the marathon, with all its connotations of ancient military glory, led to a patriotic frenzy in which jubilant Greeks rewarded Louys with large sums of money, heaps of merchandise, and numerous offers of matrimony. King George was so thrilled by the success of the games that he proclaimed his hope that Greece might host them every four years.

Philemon greeted this idea with enthusiasm and attempted to replace the IOC with a wholly Greek committee. In his effort to usurp the games, Philemon had the support of Prime Minister Deligiannes and the royal family. At the king's banquet and at the prize ceremony, Coubertin was more or less shoved to the side, treated, in the words of John J. MacAloon, as just "another face in the crowd." While Young is correct in asserting that Coubertin subsequently belittled the contributions of Bikelas and sought to claim "all the credit for himself," the rudeness experienced in Athens may explain Coubertin's insistence that he deserved something better than a regal snub.

Coubertin's role may not have been acknowledged at the time, but he still controlled the International Olympic Committee, which met several times during these first games. New York, Berlin, and Stockholm were tentatively suggested as hosts for the next games (presumably by IOC members Sloane, Gebhardt, and Balck). Coubertin preferred Paris. It was agreed that the Greeks should not be allowed to monopolize the modern Olympics, but it was decided that intercalary (inserted into the calendar) games should occur, in Athens, in the middle of each Olympiad. The 1906 Games were the only ones thus celebrated, after which the intercalary games were abandoned.

In a retrospective essay published in the November 1896 issue of *Century Magazine,* Coubertin omitted any mention of rudeness or ingratitude at the first modern Olympic Games. Instead, he lavished praise on the Greek royal family and on Spiridon Louys. He declared himself optimistic about the games and their potential contributions to "harmony and good will" in sports and to "universal peace." In the years that followed, his optimism was put to the test.

2

Growing Pains and Increasing Success

An Olympic congress held at LeHavre in 1897 effectively scotched the Greek attempt to usurp the games. The unanswered question asked in 1896 arose once more: If the Olympics didn't return to Athens in 1900, where *should* they go? It is customary, today, for cities to campaign actively for a chance to host the games. They prepare elaborate presentations, wine and dine the members of the International Olympic Committee, and make extravagant promises about the unparalleled sports facilities they intend to construct and the lucrative television contracts almost ready to be signed. It was very different when Pierre de Coubertin suggested to the IOC that Paris act as the host for the next Olympics. The Union des Sociétés Françaises de Sports Athlétiques (USFSA), of which Coubertin was secretary-general, opposed his plans. The French government demonstrated a lack of enthusiasm that might have crushed a less-determined idealist. After much travail, Coubertin managed to pry from a reluctant governmental bureaucracy an agreement to sponsor the next Olympic Games—as part of the splendid Exposition Universelle already planned for the summer of 1900. The planners of the exposition were not at all eager to play host to the Olympic Games. As French officialdom prepared to broadcast the glories of *"la civilisation française,"* they did not imagine that runners and jumpers had much to contribute to their effort. Alfred Picart, who was in charge of the exposition, positively disliked sports.

One of Coubertin's friends, Vicomte Charles de La Rochefoucauld, a polo enthusiast, was named to head the national organizing committee, but he was forced to resign in April 1898 when the USFSA changed its position and decided that *it* should manage the games. Coubertin, who was also shunted aside, had the miserable task of encouraging international participation in an event over which he no longer had control. Caspar Whitney, editor of *Outing* magazine and a newly elected member of the U.S. Olympic Committee, said of his French counterparts that what they did not know about sports "would fill volumes." William Milligan Sloane called them "an organization of incompetents." He and others in the IOC were irked by the disdain communicated by the planners of the exposition and outraged by the cavalier mistreatment of Coubertin, but there was little the IOC could do to improve the sorry situation. These problems with the French government, coming after the rude treatment he had received in Athens, strengthened Coubertin's liberal conviction that *any* kind of state involvement in sports introduced "a fatal germ of impotence and mediocrity."

The athletic program, designed by Daniel Merillon, was a disaster. The competitions took place over a period of two months and were such a peripheral part of the world's fair that most visitors were quite unaware of them. Merillon renamed the contests: they were no longer the Jeux Olympiques but the Concours Internationaux d'Exercises Physiques et de Sport. One result of such arrogant meddling was that some of the athletes returning home were surprised to learn that they had just participated in the Olympic Games. When one considers that the ice skaters were officially listed as participants in the cutlery exhibition—along with the wielders of the latest in knives and forks—one begins to suspect that Merillon may have had a sense of humor. After the games were over, the IOC had to decide which events had been Olympic and which had not. The exciting contests in which teams of firemen extinguished standardized blazes failed to win IOC approval.

Very little thought was given to the spectators of the 1900 Games, and very few spectators took the trouble to discover exactly when and where the sports events were to take place. In fact, while most of the exposition was centrally sited on both sides of an axis running from Trocadero across the Seine and through the Champ de Mars, many of the sports contests took place on the periphery of Paris in the Bois de Boulogne, the city's largest park, which was constructed for lovers strolling hand in hand rather than for runners racing neck and neck. Races were held on the grass because the French did not wish to disfigure the park with a cinder track. A slightly off-course discus or javelin was all too likely to land in a tree. The swimmers and divers competed in the waters of the Seine. Pollution was a problem, even then, but at least the swimmers were permitted to propel themselves downstream rather than upstream. (Australia's Frederick Lane was swept along so quickly that his current-assisted time for 200 meters was thirteen seconds faster than the official world record.)

Accommodations for the athletes were so poor that members of the German team assumed that their French hosts had meant deliberately to insult them. They may have been correct in their suspicions. Felix Fauré, president of France, had opposed German participation. At the LeHavre congress three years earlier, Fauré had behaved so rudely to Gebhardt, who spoke English but not French, that Gebhardt left the congress and returned to Berlin in an understandable, if not a justified, huff.

When the games finally began, without an official opening ceremony, there was serious friction among the athletes. The Americans who ran in the marathon suspected that the course, which wound through the streets of Paris, had been designed to allow the hometown contestants to avail themselves of a number of shortcuts. Michel Théato won and Émile Champion was second. Steeplechase winner George W. Orton noted in *Outing* (September 1900) that the "Frenchmen finished comparatively fresh." (It has recently come to light that Théato, although he lived in Paris, had actually been born in Luxembourg.) A Swedish runner was third, followed by a Swiss runner and the three Americans. The Americans were puzzled because they had taken an early lead and were unable to recall a moment when they were overtaken. They were also at a loss to explain why the winners were the only runners not spattered with mud.

Doubts about fairness were not the only reason for dissatisfaction. Some members of the American team, which was composed mainly of students from Princeton, Yale, and a number of other universities, were devout Christians who expected to spend their Sundays in church rather than on the athletic field. They requested that their events be rescheduled to July 14. Since July 14 is Bastille Day, the most sacred of French holidays, their request was politely refused and several favored athletes, including Myer Prinstein of Syracuse University, declined to desecrate the Sabbath. They won their medals during the week, as Prinstein did in the triple jump and the long jump, or they went home without them.

Fortunately, there were also moments of harmony and memorable scenes of athletic prowess. American and British dominance of track and field was so complete that, except for the tarnished gold in the marathon and the medal won by Hungary's Rudolf Bauer in the discus, Americans and Britons garnered all twenty-four gold medals in the track-and-field events. Ray Ewry, an American, won the first three of his eight gold medals for the standing high jump, the standing broad jump, and the standing triple jump, three events that strike us now as strange (they were dropped from the program after 1912). Ewry's prowess, like that of many Olympians, was compensatory: he had suffered from polio as a child and had exercised to strengthen his legs. Alvin Kraenzlein, a German-American, one of the great athletes of his time, came in first in the 60-meter sprint, the 110-meter and 200-meter hurdles, and the long jump. In the first event he set a world record: 7 seconds. His teammate, John Tewksbury, garnered two golds (200-meter sprint, 400-meter hurdles) and two silvers (60-meter and 100-meter sprints). French pride was boosted not only by the questionable victory in the marathon but also by a near sweep of the fencing competition and a number of medals in other sports.

These were the first Olympic Games to which women were invited as competitors rather than as awed admirers of male prowess. In the summer of 1900, Margaret Abbott of Chicago was studying art and music in Paris. She laid down her brushes, picked up her golf clubs, triumphed in the tournament, and became the first American woman to bring home a gold medal. In tennis, Charlotte Cooper of Great Britain was invincible. She had been the Wimbledon champion in 1895, 1896, and 1898 (and was to win again in 1901 and 1908). She defeated Hélène Prévost of France, 6-4, 6-2. In mixed doubles, Cooper teamed with Reginald Doherty to vanquish Prévost and her Irish partner, Harold S. Mahony, by a score of 6-4, 7-5. The visible internationalism of tennis appeared briefly in track as well when Australia's Stanley Rowley joined four Britons to win the 5,000-meter relay. Rowley's medal was especially unusual because he never finished his part of the race. Since only the times of the four best runners were counted, the compassionate officials allowed Rowley, who was laboring badly, to abandon the track. Still, bright moments like this did little to counteract the IOC's feeling that these games had failed of their lofty purpose.

The unhappy experience of an Olympic celebration lost in the midst of a world's fair was repeated in 1904. Coubertin had been impressed by the bustle, enterprise, and organizational expertise of Chicago when he visited that city in 1889 and again during the Columbian Exhibition of 1893. President William Rainey Harper of the newly founded University of Chicago was eager for the games to come to the shores of Lake Michigan, and Coubertin was inclined to agree with him.

Difficulties intervened. In 1900, at a meeting held at the Parisian headquarters of the USFSA, Secretary James Sullivan of the Amateur Athletic Union of the United States had maintained that the IOC was defunct, and he then had vainly attempted to win recognition for an international track-and-field federation under his control. He was probably the source of a mysterious notice in the *New York Times* for July 28, 1900, to the effect that the University of Pennsylvania had arranged with British officials to stage the next Olympic Games in Philadelphia. He was certainly responsible for the contradictory announcement that the next Olympics would take place in 1901, under AAU auspices, in conjunction with Buffalo's Pan-American Exposition. In seeking to take charge of the Olympic movement, Sullivan the commoner dismissed Coubertin the aristocrat with lordly arrogance: "The Baron de Coubertin or his associates have no longer any power to name the place at which Olympian Games or international athletic events of any character shall be held." The IOC, refusing to disappear at the wave of Sullivan's Celtic wand, voted to celebrate the next Olympiad in Chicago.

Henry J. Furber, head of Chicago's Olympic Games Association, threw himself into planning and publicity, but he seems to have lost heart when he realized how complicated the task was. Meanwhile, the leading citizens of St. Louis, preparing a world's fair to commemorate the centennial of the Louisiana Purchase, realized that the Olympic Games might add a little luster to their celebration. They had the support of Sullivan, who seemed to have an endless supply of monkey wrenches to jam into the Olympic machinery. The Chicagoans, whose enthusiasm for the role of host had definitely waned, were easily persuaded to step aside. The IOC's only real option was to invite the athletes of the world to Missouri. The vote, on December 23, 1902, was 14-2 (with 5 abstentions). Coubertin, with considerable reluctance, entrusted to Sullivan the day-to-day management of the games. Theodore Roosevelt, to whom Coubertin offered the presidency of the games, declined to honor the Olympians with his attendance. The presidency of the United States kept him sufficiently busy.

Contemplating a transatlantic voyage followed by a thousand-mile train ride, most of the European athletes decided to stay at home. They had heard of Chicago, thanks to its tremendously successful 1893 world's fair, but St. Louis was beyond their ken. Distance discouraged the IOC members too. They met in London rather than undertake the arduous journey to what many Europeans imagined was a wilderness settlement menaced by Indians. Decades later, British journalists were still claiming that "the sole fare on the menu was buffalo meat." The fact that the games lasted from May to November was another disincentive to European participation. Many athletes wanted to participate as a team rather than as a squad of specialists in a single sport, but no team was ready to spend six months in St. Louis. In all, a mere twelve nations were represented by one or more participants. Of the 554 athletes, 432 were Americans.

To the horror of the more sophisticated members of the IOC, the theme of international reconciliation was drowned out by discords of racism. The American organizers set aside August 12 and 13 for Anthropological Days, during which a number of "savages" from Asia, Africa, and the Americas were rounded up from the sideshows at the fair and asked to demonstrate their native games and to compete among themselves in modern sports. The poor performances of the untrained Ingorots, Kaffirs, and Patagonians were naively taken as evidence in support of the racist theories of the day. Coubertin seems to have responded stoically to this distortion of his ideals: "In no place but America would one have dared place such events on a program—but to Americans everything is permissible, their youthful exuberance calling certainly for the indulgence of the ancient Greek ancestors, if, by chance, they found themselves at that time among the amused spectators." Although polite, Coubertin was clearly not amused. In fact, the Anthropological Days were a disgrace. It is difficult to believe in the sincerity of Coubertin's postgame expressions of gratitude to Sullivan and the other organizers.

The Olympic Games that year were a great athletic success—at least from the chauvinistic point of view of the American media. With only token opposition from the Europeans, American athletes swept to easy victories in most of the contests. In the twenty-three track-and-field events the Americans scored twenty-two firsts, twenty-two seconds, and twenty thirds. Of the seventy-four medalists in track and field, Ireland's John Daly (second in the steeplechase), Germany's Paul Weinstein (third in the high jump), Canada's Étienne Desmarteau (first with the 56-pound weight), and Britain's Thomas Kiely ("combined champion") were the only winners from outside the United States. Desmarteau, a policeman from Montreal, may have been the busiest athlete in town. In addition to his mighty heave of more than 10 meters, the versatile law enforcer is said by some to have been a member of both the lacrosse and the soccer teams.

For the first and last time in Olympic history, American gymnasts swept all but five of the thirty-six medals in their twelve events. The badly outnumbered German team was left with one gold, two silvers, and two bronzes. It was hardly a surprise when the American women took all the medals in archery, the only event for women, because all the archers were American. Cuban fencers, led by Ramón Fonst, won five of the six fencing competitions, but the American athletes won all the medals in boxing, cycling, and wrestling. They won all but one of the thirty medals in rowing. These unequal encounters were obviously not what Coubertin had had in mind, and this huge harvest of practically uncontested medals should be remembered when Americans boast of the total number of medals won over the course of the modern games.

The best that one can say about the track-and-field events in 1904 was that James Lightbody set world records for 800 and 1500 meters, while Archie Hahn, Harry Hillman, Ray Ewry, and Ralph Rose did the same for their events (200-meter and 400-meter races, standing long jump, light shot). George Poage of the Milwaukee Athletic Club finished third in the 200-meter and the 400-meter hurdles—the first Afro-American to win an Olympic medal. (Hillman won both of these races as well as the 400-meter sprint.) There was some excitement in the marathon when Fred Lorz of New York City loped across the finish line well ahead of Thomas J. Hicks of Cambridge, Massachusetts. Unfortunately for Lorz, the officials were unable to overlook the fact that he had ridden part of the way in a truck. Hicks looked as if he *should* have hitched a ride. In a contemporary report, Charles Lucas wrote, "His eyes were dull, lusterless, the ashen color of his face and skin had deepened; his arms appeared as weights well tied down; he could scarcely lift his legs, while his knees were almost stiff." That Hicks finished at all can be attributed to several shots of brandy and more than one dose of sulphate of strychnine.

The Olympic movement seemed to be on its last legs too. The games were, as Reet and Max Howell have noted, "close to disaster." Fortunately, there were the 1906 intercalary games in Athens—which Coubertin had not wanted and which he did not attend. These games were a sop to the Greeks, to allay the bitter frustration they felt when the IOC refused to accept their plans to make Greece the permanent site of the Olympic Games. The hosts proved themselves to be more skillful organizers than they had been a decade earlier. Twenty nations sent 887 athletes to Athens—nearly twice the participation in St. Louis. The most successful of them was the versatile Swede Erik Lemming. While one might imagine that his name marked him for a swimmer, he was actually a track-and-field expert who won three gold medals with his javelin plus two bronzes in the shot put and the pentathlon. Italy's Francesco Veri cycled to victory in the 1,000-meter time trial, in the sprint, and in the 5-kilometer race. Ireland's Peter O'Connor was victorious in the high jump and the triple jump. The most successful collective effort was the Americans', even if they had to share far more of the glory than had been the case in St. Louis. AAU Secretary Sullivan was delighted with the results, and President Roosevelt sent a congratulatory telegram that puzzled the Greek hosts: what did he mean by wiring, "Uncle Sam is all right"?

These interim games have been rather an embarrassment to historians who are undecided whether or not to consider them part of Olympic history. The athletic results have not been included in the various tabulations nor counted as Olympic records. Although there have been repeated suggestions that the Olympic Games be confined to Greece to avoid political entanglements, the 1906 competitions were the last on Greek soil.

Returning to the United States after the intercalary games, Sullivan renewed his verbal war with Coubertin. He sent the baron a lengthy letter in which he accused the IOC of ineptitude, asserted that he himself had lost all interest in the bungling committee, and complained bitterly that he had not been elected to membership in it. Of Sloane, who *was* a member for the United States, he wrote, "He knows absolutely nothing about athletics." In the midst of his 2,000-word tirade, Sullivan paused to make what was for him a gesture of reconciliation: "You say you do not understand my ways and manners. Perhaps not. I don't think you have tried to understand me thoroughly; if you did I think we could become firm friends." Coubertin was not taken in by this prickly offer to kiss and make up. The correspondence between the two went on until a truce was reached, but their very different temperaments—confrontational and conciliatory—made true friendship impossible.

For Coubertin, these years were also a period of intense propagandistic activity. He was the force behind Olympic congresses held in 1905 at Brussels and in 1906 at Paris. These congresses were occasions at which the idealistic spokesmen for internationalism gave voice to their dreams for a more pacific world unified by a common commitment to amateur sport. Unfortunately, the concept of amateurism was in itself divisive. Its main goal, to exclude members of the lower classes, was at cross purposes with the tenets of modern sport, which call for equal opportunity for everyone to compete on the same terms. Coubertin, who thought that wrangles over amateurism were a waste of time, was unable to prevent them. He was, however, able to persuade the delegates to the 1906 congress that the Olympic Games were incomplete without contests in the arts. The first competitions in literature, music, and the visual arts were scheduled for 1908.

The IOC acceded at its 1904 meeting in London to Coubertin's wish that the next Olympics be celebrated in Rome, a city whose symbolic importance rivals that of Athens. The choice was meant, in Coubertin's words, "as international homage to Roman antiquity." Gebhardt had campaigned for Berlin, but the Eternal City loomed large in Coubertin's imagination: "I desired Rome only because I wanted Olympism, after its return from the excursion to utilitarian America, to don once again the sumptuous toga, woven of art and philosophy, in which I had always wanted to clothe her." The organizing committee, backed by King Victor Emmanuel III and led by Prince Prospero Colonna, had grandiose plans for automobile races at Milan, combat sports in Rome's Colosseum, and nautical events in the Bay of Naples. Unfortunately, internal dissension led to Colonna's angry resignation. Nature dealt another blow: the nation was stricken by the 1906 eruption of

Mount Vesuvius, which took some two thousand lives. The organizers, concluding that the omens were unfavorable, decided to abandon their obligation. They bowed out, the British stepped in. In Coubertin's flowery language, "the curtain descended on the Tiber's stage and rose soon after on that of the Thames."

With commendable efficiency the British went to work. They erected a 70,000-seat stadium at Shepherd's Bush. There was, once again, a concurrent world's fair, but the organizers of the Franco-British Exhibition were solidly behind the IOC and did their utmost to make the games a success. In a gesture of good will, the British hosts adopted metric measurements—except for the marathon, which started at Windsor Palace as a favor to the royal family and finished at Shepherd's Bush, exactly 26 miles, 385 yards away, which is why today's marathoners still run this oddly uneven distance. The organization of the games was greatly improved by some typical bureaucratic strategies. The hosts defined what they meant by amateur (someone who had never earned money from sports) and left it up to the national and international sports federations to be more specific. All contestants had to be certified by their national Olympic committees. However, the British Olympic Association reserved for itself the last word in cases of disputed eligibility. The number of entries per event was limited and entry deadlines were established. It was no longer possible for tourists to act on whim and add an Olympic medal to their souvenirs. New procedures were also put in place to adjudicate a protested decision.

Unfortunately, there was frequent resort to these new procedures. As sports contests, the games of the Fourth Olympiad were quite successful, but they were marred by unusually strident nationalism and an unprecedented number of disputes. The most controversial political question of the day was the fate of Ireland. Despite decades of agitation for independence or, at the very least, home rule, the mostly Roman Catholic Irish were still ruled by the mostly Protestant British. Irish athletes of Olympic calibre were few, but Irish-American athletes were many. Sensitive to Britain's denial of Irish independence, they were inclined neither to ignore an affront nor to kowtow to those whom they perceived as their oppressors. As the teams marched into the stadium on opening day, national flags fluttered, but the Stars and Stripes hung at half-mast. Was it an intentional affront? Was it an intolerable insult to the hosts that the American flag bearer did not dip Old Glory as the American team passed the royal box? Many British spectators were convinced that this indeed was a slap in the face for the king and queen. In addition, King Edward, who must have forgotten his own antics as the playboy Prince of Wales, was said to have been offended by the "barbarous cries" of the American spectators.

When competition began, the officials, all of whom were British, were accused of bias. In a 400-meter heat, they disqualified an American runner, J. C. Carpenter, whom they accused of blocking and elbowing the English runner Wyndham Halswelle. The other two Americans who qualified for the finals refused to compete without Carpenter. Halswelle ran alone and was awarded the gold medal. The most memorable scandal, however, occurred at the conclusion of the marathon. The first runner to stagger into the stadium was an Italian, Dorando Pietri. An excited correspondent for the usually staid *Times* of London described the scene: "A tired man, dazed, bewildered, hardly conscious, in red shorts and white vest, his hair white with dust, staggers on to the track." The crowds cheered, then gasped as Pietri fell to the ground. He was lifted to his feet by the officials, but he collapsed again. Behind him, closing fast, was an Irish-American runner, Johnny Hayes. To avert the impending disaster, Clerk of the Course J. M. Andrews came forward, dragged Pietri across the finish line, and proclaimed him the victor. The Italian flag was hoisted. American officials protested and were upheld by the IOC, whereupon the British press denounced the Americans for their lack of good sportsmanship. Queen Alexandra presented Pietri with a special trophy and Arthur Conan Doyle paused from his stories of Sherlock Holmes to praise Pietri: "No Roman of prime ever has borne himself better; the great breed is not yet extinct." Theodore Roosevelt, who greeted the returning American team at Sagamore Hill, his summer home, was of another mind. Shaking hands with Hayes and referring to the disputed marathon, the president exulted: "This is fine, fine, and I am so glad that a New York boy won it." The president bubbled on enthusiastically, "By George, I am so glad to see all you boys!"

The *Times* (London) was less exuberant, concluding that the "perfect harmony which every one wished for has been marred by certain regrettable disputes and protests," but the editors took comfort in the illusion that the athletes and officials departed London with their friendships unimpaired. This was too optimistic a note. If the AAU secretary was typical, international amity had suffered a considerable setback. Sullivan was outspokenly bitter about the British treatment of Americans in general and of Irish-Americans in particular. Coubertin, on the other hand, sympathized with the British: "I just could not understand Sullivan's attitude here," wrote the baron about his old antagonist. "He shared his team's frenzy and did nothing to try to calm them down." The Irish-American firebrand was not, however, the only disgruntled American. Gustavus Kirby, a fair-minded man of remarkable good will, was also distressed by what he perceived to be biased officiating. The IOC must have recognized some merit in the American complaints because the committee decided shortly after the London Games that the officials for 1912 should be as international as the athletes.

Although the American team won fifteen of the twenty-seven track-and-field contests (and set all three of the world records), partisans of the home team had plenty to cheer about. Eight victories in track and field was a respectable outcome, and British athletes took all the gold medals in boxing, rowing, sailing, and men's and women's tennis. They limited the French to a lone victory in the six cycling events and won the competitions in polo, water polo, hockey, and soccer. If they succumbed to the Australians in rugby by a lopsided score of 32-3, there was at least the satisfaction of losing to a team with a large infusion of Scottish rather than Irish blood. In assembling teams, there continued to be an admirable fluidity about nationality. C. R. Cudmore, an Australian, rowed for Britain because he was an Oxford student and a member of the Magdalen Boat Club. H. E. Kerr and H. St. Aubyn-Murray competed for Australia although they were from New Zealand.

Women's golf and tennis had been dropped from the Olympic program after 1900, but tennis was reinstated in 1908 and archery (which had been added in 1904) was continued. The figure skaters competed for the first time—in competitions for men, for women, and for couples. In these sports the British won four of the five gold medals, but Germany's Anna Huebler teamed with Dr. Heinrich Burger to outskate two brother-sister couples from Great Britain.

As always, there were banquets and speeches. Coubertin used the occasion of a ball at Grafton Galleries and a dinner at the Holburn Restaurant to quote the words of an American prelate: "The importance of the Olympiads lies not so much in winning as in taking part." They became what the Germans call *geflügelte Wörter* (winged words). The slogan has been intoned by acolytes of Olympism and mocked by those who believe that only victory matters.

There were also important administrative decisions reached during the 1908 Games. Enthusiasts for swimming and diving formed the Fédération Internationale de Natation Amateur (FINA) and promptly advocated the addition of women's aquatic events for the 1912 Games. Coubertin's reluctant assent was probably obtained by a concession; the IOC accepted his proposal for a modern pentathlon (riding, running, shooting, fencing, and swimming). With the election of the Japanese inventor of judo, Jigoro Kano, the IOC had its first Asian member. The committee had grown to forty-three members from thirty-one countries. Their thoughts turned to the games of the Fifth Olympiad.

"Of all the countries in the world," asserted Coubertin in May 1909, "Sweden is at the moment best qualified to host a great Olympic Games." Coubertin was right. Boxing had to be dropped temporarily from the program because the sport was prohibited in Sweden, but that was a small price to pay. The games were, as John Lucas has noted, "the best organized and most pacific international games since the original Athens celebration." Looking back on these games, Avery Brundage—IOC president from 1952 to 1972—recalled the Swedes' organizational mastery: "I was a young engineer just from the university. The efficiency and almost mathematical precision with which the events were handled and the formal correctness of the arrangements made a great impression on me." Perhaps it is symbolic of this "almost mathematical precision" that the footraces were now timed electronically. The new device was a portent of accelerated technological innovation.

Coubertin was ecstatic about the splendidly constructed stadium, "a model of its type," and about the way the Swedish organizing committee orchestrated events. He was also delighted with the inauguration of an arts competition in architecture, sculpture, painting, literature, and music—a pet project that had finally been endorsed by the IOC when it met in Paris in May 1906 for a Conférence Consultative des Arts, des Lettres, et du Sport. At Stockholm, Coubertin's pleasure was intensified by the fact that his "Ode au Sport," entered as a composition by "G. Hohrod and M. Eschbach," won the prize for literature. (Since Coubertin had already used the pseudonym Georges Hohrod for a novella published in 1899, his identity might have been known to the judges.)

There was perfect weather for the opening ceremony on July 6. Sullivan, still a power in the Amateur Athletic Union of the United States and in the American Olympic Committee, was uncharacteristically good-natured in his account of the day: "Everything that went to make the inaugural was glorious, and a bright, warm sun shone on the arena, making the flags of all nations ruffling in the breeze resemble an enormous multi-colored bow."

The spectators seem not to have minded the intrusion of Christianity into the neopagan atmosphere of Olympism. There was a sermon in Swedish by the Reverend Oskar Aefehldt, the royal pastor, and a prayer in English by the Reverend R. S. de Courcy Laffan. The spectators were then requested to join in Martin Luther's great hymn, "Ein feste Burg ist unser Gott" (A Mighty Fortress Is Our God). Crown Prince Gustav Adolph spoke briefly and then his father declared the games of the Fifth Olympiad officially open. A fanfare of trumpets followed, and then there was a display of Swedish gymnastics.

The American team that embarked for Stockholm was even better prepared than the one that had competed in London and aroused the ire of the more casually trained British. During the ten-day Atlantic crossing, the team worked out on a special 100-yard cork track and in a canvas swimming pool, in the middle of which swimmers were suspended from the waist by a rope. Young Avery Brundage, en route to his first Olympic Games, noticed that exercise and sea breeze overstimulated some already hearty appetites: "Exposure to the unlimited menus on shipboard was fatal to some and several hopes of Olympic victory foundered at the bounteous dinner table." When the *Finland* docked at Antwerp, the athletes had a chance to stretch their limbs at the Beershot Athletic Club. Two days later, they sailed through the "alluring archipelago" to Stockholm. Since there was no Olympic village, the team lived on shipboard. Cramped space, rowdy teammates, and short summer nights made it hard to sleep.

The IOC, coming slowly to a tardy acceptance of women's sports, had decided to include women as swimmers and divers. This meant an increase in the number of female athletes from 36 in 1908 to 57 in 1912 (compared to 2,447 men). There had been quarrels over this inclusion in the United States and in Australia. Since Sullivan adamantly opposed women's sports, no American women swam or dove in Stockholm. In Australia, ironically, the opposition came from Rose Scott, an ardent feminist who feared that the presence of shapely young women in swimsuits might attract more voyeurs than sports spectators. Scott's argument—"We don't want to return to the primitive state of the blacks"—revealed the racism that was nearly ubiquitous at the time. Her protests, however, were in vain. Sarah "Fanny" Durack and Wilhelmina Wylie went to the games and returned to Australia with the gold and the silver medals for the 100-meter freestyle. Durack's time of 1:22.2 was a world record. British women won the 4 × 100–meter relay and Sweden's Greta Johansson outscored her countrywoman, Lisa Regnell, in the diving competition. Contemporary observers thought that most (but not all) of the spectators were impressed by the women's performances as well as by their looks. Everett C. Brown, one of Sullivan's AAU colleagues, was pleased by the new events: "I personally saw the [women's swimming and diving] competitions at Stockholm and if there was any criticism, it might have been brought about by foul minds."

The inclusion of women was one sign of gradual democratization. The irrelevance of skin color was emphasized by the racial composition of the American team, which included an Afro-American (Howard Porter Drew), a Hawaiian (Duke Kahanamoku), and two American Indians (Lewis Tewanima and Jim Thorpe). Kahanamoku was first in the 100-meter freestyle swim and Tewanima second in the 10,000-meter run. Drew was among the favorites in the 100-meter and 200-meter races, but he injured himself and failed to win a medal. His disappointment must have been painful, but his ordeal was brief compared with the long-drawn-out tragedy of Jim Thorpe.

"You, sir," said King Gustav to Thorpe, "are the greatest athlete in the world." Thorpe's response may be apocryphal ("Thanks, King"), but his performance was legendary. He won both the pentathlon and the decathlon. In neither was his victory in doubt. In the pentathlon he outperformed his rivals in four of the five events. His glory, however, was short-lived. At the same time that the IOC settled on Stockholm as the site of the 1912 Games, it heard a report on amateurism by Comte Albert de Bertier de Sauvigny. The members responded to the report by appointing America's Sloane, Britain's Theodore A. Cook, and Hungary's Jules de Mussa to a committee to study the problem. The rules, which had been lax, were tightened. Not long after the 1912 Games, Thorpe's amateur status was retroactively challenged under the new rules. After he admitted that he had been paid to play summer professional baseball while still a student at the Carlisle (Pennsylvania) Indian School, the IOC stripped him of his medals. Since the IOC subsequently acted to punish other athletes whose amateurism was questionable, it seems unlikely that they were significantly motivated by racism in this instance. Thorpe's punishment indicated that prejudice about social class, not racism, was then and long remained a stumbling block on the road to Olympism.

There were, of course, moments of political tension at the Stockholm Games. The Finns were not happy with Russian domination of their country and they persuaded the IOC to let them march under their own flag, a privilege not granted to the Irish. When the Finns entered the stadium, they were given a tremendous ovation by their fellow Scandinavians. The Russians were annoyed, but the Russians were relative latecomers to the world of modern sports and their annoyance was not taken seriously. Their 169-man team won one silver and three bronze medals (in wrestling, shooting, and sailing). The much smaller Finnish team was eminently more successful and their flag went up remarkably often. Hannes Kolehmainen finished the 5,000-meter race one-tenth of a second ahead of France's Jean Bouin (in world-record time: 14:36.6) and went on to win gold medals in the 10,000-meter race and the 8,000-meter cross-country run; he also won a silver medal for the team's performance in the latter race. Three Finns and three Swedes divided first-place honors in wrestling. In all, the athletes from Scandinavia were the victors in thirty-seven events. Fencing was the only sport in which they did not do well.

The British, who were disappointed with the relatively weak performances of their team, condemned the specialization that had become an inescapable aspect of modern sports. *The Spectator* claimed in its July 20 issue that specialization "has gone too far in America. ... For many months, sometimes even for years, Americans subject themselves to a professional trainer who takes possession of their lives." The British press was not immune from racism when it complained of the Negroes and Indians who had competed for the United States. In response to the cascade of complaints from London, the Irish-American humorist Peter Finley Dunne had an ethnically aware and class-conscious answer: said Dooley to Hennessy, "These boys that you see hoppin' around th' thrack ar-re the rile represintive Americans. They are our ambassadurs, not the lords ye see makin' a ginuflixion befure th' king."

Nonetheless, there is every reason to think that most of the athletes, officials, and spectators were pleased to have had a part in celebrating the games of the Fifth Olympiad. In this atmosphere of good will and mutual admiration, track-and-field enthusiasts, led by a Swedish businessman-engineer, Sigfrid Edstrøm, organized the International Amateur Athletic Federation, which quickly became the most important of the many international sports federations cooperating with the IOC. The normally truculent Sullivan was in such a mellow mood by the time he returned to the United States that he dedicated his report on the games to none other than Pierre de Coubertin. Everyone looked forward to the next celebration, scheduled for Berlin in 1916.

3

The Games Reach Maturity

By the summer of 1914, there were millions screaming, "On to Berlin!" The cry was clearly not a summons to compete in the games of the Sixth Olympiad. The call for international harmony and good will was drowned out by the roar of cannon and the moans of dying men. The International Olympic Committee was not wholly free of bellicose passion. A British member, Theodore Cook, demanded the expulsion of the German members. When his motion was defeated, he resigned from the committee. Coubertin himself was still enough of a patriot to suffer with his countrymen as German troops fought their way almost to the outskirts of Paris, but he felt that the dream of Olympism had to be preserved for a better day. Since there was no enormous bureaucratic organization to be relocated, it was a fairly simple matter for the troubled baron to move Olympic headquarters, that is, his own residence, to neutral Switzerland. To Lausanne he went, on April 10, 1915, and Lausanne remains the administrative heart of the Olympic movement. The chateau that housed the Coubertins was called Mon Repos, but there was little rest for the baron, who produced a prodigious number of historical and pedagogical volumes when not directly concerned with Olympic affairs.

The psychological wounds opened by war were slow to heal. The fighting stopped on November 11, 1918; the "lost provinces" of Alsace and Lorraine were returned to France; it was the Germans' turn to feel resentful and to nourish fantasies of revenge. Since the German invasion of neutral Belgium had been the *causus belli* that brought Great Britain into the war, the IOC decided that it was symbolically important to stage the first postwar games in Antwerp. Should the defeated Germans, whose armies had ravaged Belgium, be invited to compete? Olympic ideals dictated an affirmative answer, but a majority of the members of the IOC were citizens of nations who had fought against the Germans and the Austrians. Why, they asked, should the IOC be more forgiving than the League of Nations, which barred German and Austrian membership?

The IOC found a threadbare solution to its problem. In the retrospective words of IOC Chancellor Otto Mayer: "The problem of German participation was discussed. Solemnly to proclaim any kind of ostracism in the wake of the conflict which had just drenched Europe in blood would have been a violation of the Olympic constitution as it then was. The solution was quite simple. There was, for each Olympiad, an Organizing Committee which, according to the formula employed since 1896, sent out the invitations." In short, the Belgian organizers were not instructed by the IOC to *exclude* representatives of the defeated powers, they were simply encouraged not to invite them. The same legerdemain enabled the French not to invite their former foes to the games of the Eighth Olympiad, celebrated in Paris in 1924. It was not until 1928 that the Germans appeared again at the Olympic Games; and it was not until 1931 that French and German teams met on the soccer field.

Nationalism posed other problems less easy to evade. In the aftermath of war, the Poles, the Czechs, and many other suppressed nationalities achieved their dream of independent statehood. Most of the quickly established national Olympic committees were duly recognized, but not that of the Hungarians, who had fought on the losing side in World War I. The other losers, the Turks, were preoccupied by a civil war and the struggle to expel an invading army from Greece. And then there were the Irish and the Armenians. Their claims were rejected because they were not yet fully independent.

The IOC also wrestled with the perennial question of which sports to include in the Olympic program. Coubertin thought walking contests "grotesque," but he wished to introduce equestrian fencers. Walking survived; *escrime à cheval* failed to win favor. There were also signs that many of the members were disposed to ignore Coubertin's hostility toward increased female participation. The baron insisted that such participation would be *"impratique, inintéressante, inesthétique et incorrecte,"* but France's Comte Justinien de Clary put forth a Darwinistic argument for "strong women who produce a strong race." Clary shocked his more conservative colleagues with the thought that there were sports in which women might well compete against men. (In fact, he used the verb *lutter* rather than the milder *contester*.) Although Clary later backed away from this bold endorsement, his words were a straw in the wind.

On one other point Coubertin had his way: he successfully resisted plans to publish the minutes of committee deliberations. Instead, the

IOC launched a *Bulletin du CIO,* which Coubertin edited. His penchant for administrative privacy has made the historian's task much harder than it might have been.

The IOC's decision to revive the games had been made in April 1919, which allowed the national Olympic committees only a year for preparations. The brevity of the lead time and the shortages caused by the war were serious obstacles, even for nations spared the worst ravages of battle, but ingenuity and the spirit of self-sacrifice prevailed in most cases. Gustavus Kirby, who took over the postwar leadership of the American Olympic Committee, persuaded Secretary of War Newton Baker to lobby for a special congressional act to authorize the transport of civilians in a military vessel. Baker was partially successful: a boat was provided, but it was not exactly a flagship. The team sailed to Antwerp on a scarcely seaworthy tub, the *Princess Matioka.* It was a wretched two-week crossing during which the team shared its crowded quarters with innumerable rats and was so close to mutiny by the end of the voyage that Frederick Rubien, an official of the American Olympic Committee, feared "Bolshevik" influence.

It was a relief to disembark in Antwerp, but the facilities there were far from ideal. The stadium was unfinished. The track was poorly built and heavy rains made it worse. The Belgian public took little notice of the games. "All this is quite nice," remarked King Albert when he attended the games, "but it certainly lacks people." When a capacity crowd of 40,000 turned out for the soccer final between Belgium and Czechoslovakia, they witnessed a fiasco. Angered by some questionable calls by the referee, the Czechs walked off the field and were disqualified. There was also fiscal distress. Alfred Verdyck, the chief organizer, admitted that poor attendance (except for soccer) contributed to a loss of over 600 million francs.

Athletes complained about the inadequate accommodations and poor facilities, but good sports were ready to acknowledge that hastily organized games were better than none at all. Mindful of the destruction wrought by war, the athletes must have been moved by the symbolism of the opening ceremony. The Antwerp Games were the first at which athletes took the Olympic oath beneath the newly designed Olympic flag with its five interlocking rings.

Charles Paddock ("the world's fastest human") won the 100-meter race as expected and ran the first lap for the successful 400-meter relay team, but the happy days of American track-and-field domination were apparently over. The British won five gold medals in these events to the Americans' nine; the Finns, who were the sensation of the games, won eight. Hannes Kolehmainen, who had returned from Stockholm with three gold medals, set an Olympic record in the marathon. The games were especially memorable for the first appearance of Paavo Nurmi. The "flying Finn" was victorious over 10,000 meters in both the flat and the cross-country races (and he earned a third gold medal in the cross-country relay). It was Nurmi's reclusive manner as much as anything else that impressed the spectators—he said little, he trained with a stopwatch in his hand, he became a symbol of mechanical (some said joyless) perfection.

Less well known in 1920 was Phillip Noel-Baker, an English runner who had competed in 1912. At Antwerp, he captained the British team and won a silver medal in the 1,500-meter race. He went on to become the foremost British symbol of the idealist-athlete. A life-long pacifist, Noel-Baker was an active worker for the League of Nations and then for the United Nations. In words that Coubertin would have endorsed, he asserted, "In the nuclear age, sport is man's best hope." In 1959 he was awarded the Nobel Peace Prize.

In the absence of the Hungarian team, French and Italian fencers had the field more or less to themselves. The excellent American rugby team surprised the cocky Frenchmen and upset them by a score of 8-0. An eight-oared crew from the United States scored another upset when it edged an Oxford-Cambridge eight by eight-tenths of a second.

Of the sixty-four women at the games, the star was France's Suzanne Lenglen. Unquestionably the finest as well as the most eccentric female tennis player of the era, she defeated Dorothy Holman by a score of 6-3, 6-0 and teamed with Max Decugis to win the mixed doubles against Kitty McKane and Max Woosnam (6-4, 6-2). James Sullivan's death had removed the last obstacle to American women's participation in the swimming and diving contests. Ethelda Bleibtrey set world records over 100 and 300 meters and helped to set a third in the 400-meter relay.

The most dedicated athletes in Antwerp may have been the fifteen Japanese who journeyed halfway around the world to Belgium, gave their all physically and economically, and then successfully appealed to the Mitsui and Mitsubishi companies to bring them home. Although no corporation volunteered to provide the tickets, scores of American athletes returned to New York by commercial ocean liner rather than endure a second voyage on the decrepit *Princess Matioka*.

At the nineteenth session of the IOC, held concurrently with an Olympic congress in Lausanne in 1921, Coubertin announced his intention to retire as president of the committee and asked, as a favor, that the 1924 Games be celebrated in Paris, his *ville natale*. The majority thought this appropriate, but the enraged Italian delegates, who had wanted to bring the games to Rome, stormed out of the congress. At this 1921 session the IOC decided to establish an executive board, the first members of which were Baron Godefroy de Blonay (Switzer-land), Jiri Guth-Jarkovsky (Bohemia), Comte Henri de Baillet-Latour (Belgium), Sigfrid Edstrøm (Sweden), and Comte Melchior de Polignac (France). At this occasion, a French cleric, Père Henri Didon, suggested the now-familiar Olympic motto, *Citius, Altius, Fortius* (Faster, Higher, Stronger).

Sharp disagreements divided the committee when it turned to the question of winter sports. Ice-skating had been included in the 1908 Games and ice hockey in those of 1920. But should there be special winter games apart from the summer festival? As early as the IOC's Budapest session of 1911, the Swedes and Norwegians had suggested separate winter games and the Americans had opposed them, arguing that not all nations had the climatic conditions for skiing and skating. Now, in 1921, the British and the French wanted the innovation. After all, they had invented winter sports (as *sports*) and they saw no reason why an antiquarian homage to the Greeks should prevent full recognition of skiing and skating. The opposition, led now by the Scandinavians and supported by Coubertin, returned to the argument that winter sports were restricted by the facts of geography to a small group of nations. How could they hope to bring together "the youth of the world" as the summer events were doing? Nevertheless, the innovators won the debate and the First Winter Games were celebrated at Chamonix, France, in January and February 1924. The tradition was established, which lasted until 1992, that the winter games precede the summer games by a few months.

When the IOC met in Rome in the spring of 1923, for its twenty-first session, one of the chief topics of debate was the question of IOC-sponsored regional games. In Paris a year earlier, there had been talk of Latin American Games, which General Charles Sherrill, an American member, supported with the proviso that they be controlled by Roman Catholics. (It was not until 1951 that the Pan-American Games were begun.) The committee next turned its attention to Africa. French and Italian colonial officials were invited to discuss the advisability of such games and share their expertise. It was decided that the IOC should encourage Jeux Africains for non-Europeans, beginning in Algiers in 1925. (These games were subsequently postponed to 1927 and then to 1929. They did not materialize until after World War II.)

The First Winter Games were successful but fairly uneventful. To no one's surprise the Norwegians won eleven of the twelve medals for skiing (with Finland's Tapano Niku taking the bronze for the 18-kilometer race), and the Finns were first in four of the five speed-skating contests (with Charles Jewtraw of the United States first over 500 meters).

Remembering his troubles in 1900, when the French authorities had very nearly ruined the games, Coubertin worked hard to secure his government's cooperation in planning the games of the Eighth Olympiad. When he showed the prospective program to President Raymond Poincaré, the president noticed that he was scheduled for several highly visible appearances. "Is this definite?" asked Poincaré. "Absolutely," answered Coubertin. The president then agreed with the baron that the republic should do its utmost to make the games a great success.

Meanwhile, even without baronial flattery, French men of letters became fervent supporters of the games. Never before or after have so many distinguished novelists and poets written so movingly about sports as a metaphor for *la condition humaine*. Minor writers like Michel Berger and major ones like Henry de Montherlant published sports-centered novels and filled the pages of newspapers and magazines with essays in praise of the athletic life.

These 1924 Summer Games were an even greater triumph for Finland than those of 1920 had been. Paavo Nurmi set Olympic records for the 1,500-meter and 5,000-meter races; he won the 10,000-meter cross-country race; and he was part of Finland's winning teams in the 3,000-meter relay and the 10,000-meter cross-country relay. Nurmi, whom sportswriter Grantland Rice called a "superman," quite overshadowed another great runner, his countryman Ville Ritola, who won the 10,000-meter race in world-record time and set an Olympic record in the 3,000-meter steeplechase. Ritola was second to Nurmi in the 5,000-meter and the 10,000-meter cross-country races, and he was also part of the victorious 3,000-meter relay team. The Finns, it seemed, were everywhere. Albin Stenross won the marathon, Jonni Myyra the javelin, and Vilho Niitymaa the discus. In wrestling, the Finns took four gold, seven silver, and five bronze medals. All told, they harvested thirteen gold, thirteen silver, and eight bronze medals. In medals per capita of population, the tiny nation was incomparably superior to Great Britain and the United States. James B. Connolly, the triple-jump winner in 1896 and the author of a maudlin novel entitled *The Olympic Victory* (1908), paid the Finns the ultimate tribute: he likened them to the Irish.

A spate of publications, well described by John Lucas, attempted to explain Finland's astonishing sports superiority:

Fascinating claims were made for native foods; raw, dried fish, rye bread "hard as biscuit," and sour milk. . . . Another theory forwarded by the half-educated was that the Finns, distinctly different kinds of people from the neighboring Swedes, were direct descendants of a physically tough "wild Mongol strain." The remote harshness of the land and the relative poverty of the people . . . were proposed as reasons for Finland's superiority over softer, technocratic societies. Truth and fiction were intermingled in descriptions (by non-Finns) of the *sauna* baths. Some said it was an ice bath followed by a rolling in the snow that made them tough; others were sure that the peculiar heat of the sauna, accompanied by thrashing oneself with soft twigs and then the icy bath, couldn't help but breed tough men.

The Finns excelled as distance runners, but the British did better in the sprints (without anyone explaining their swiftness by references to roast beef, Yorkshire pudding, or indoor plumbing). Harold Abrahams won the 100-meter sprint and a great deal of retrospective fame when the 1924 Games were re-created in the somewhat fictionalized, beautifully sentimentalized feature film *Chariots of Fire* (1981). Another runner whose exploits were reenacted (and somewhat falsified) for the film was Scotland's Eric Liddell, winner of the 400-meter race.

The only athlete whose immediate fame rivaled Nurmi's and Ritola's was America's Johnny Weismuller, who swam 100 meters in Olympic-record and 400 meters in world-record times. He earned a third gold medal in the 4 × 200–meter freestyle. His Hawaiian teammate, Duke Kahanamoku, placed second in the 100-meter freestyle—quite an amazing achievement, coming as it did twelve years after his victory at Stockholm. In the world-record time of 20:6.6, Australia's Andrew Murray Charlton defeated his archrival, Sweden's Arne Borg, in the 1,500-meter race, but Charlton lost to Weismuller and Borg over 400 meters. The French did poorly on the track and field and in the pool, but they scored victories in fencing and cycling—their traditional strengths—and in shooting, wrestling, and tennis.

At the Olympic congress in Lausanne in 1921, the IOC had taken a stand against the publication of point tables, which they rightly saw as an invitation to chauvinism, but it was impossible to prevent the outbreaks of nationalism at the games. When the American rugby team unexpectedly defeated the French in a rough game, by a score of 17-3, the losers gamely congratulated the victors, but fights broke out among the spectators. Tempers also flared when one of the British boxers, Harry Mallin, was bitten by his French opponent, who was then declared the winner. When the entire British team threatened to leave, the judges reconsidered their decision and transferred their favor from the biter to the bitten. During the final bout of the middleweight division, which pitted Mallin against another British fighter, John Elliott, the French spectators rioted. Animosity toward the French and jealousy of the American "professionals" reached the point where British officials were about to withdraw their entire Olympic team from competition, but the athletes hurriedly signed a petition that persuaded the officials to reconsider.

When France's Lucien Gaudin claimed a touch against the Italian fencer Bino Bini in the foils competition, the latter denied the claim; when the jury awarded the match to Gaudin, the Italian team marched out singing the Fascist anthem. (Benito Mussolini's 1922 "march on Rome" had established a Fascist dictatorship.) The Italian fencers won the team title in sabers, but there were loud accusations of unfairness, and Oreste Puliti was disqualified for life after he challenged one of the accusers to a real duel. On July 22, the *Times* of London called for the discontinuation of the Olympic Games because they "exacerbate international bitternesses instead of soothing them," but the *New York Post* concluded that the various unpleasant incidents had been "insignificant outbursts of momentary duration." Sportswriter Grantland Rice thought the games had contributed to "mutual understanding."

Between the games in Paris and those in Amsterdam four years later, the bureaucratic tendency to regularize and standardize accelerated. The executive board of the IOC began holding meetings with representatives of the national Olympic committees and the international sports federations. The IOC organized an important Olympic congress which took place in Prague in May 1925. The "amateur question" continued to torment the delegates, and there were bitter disputes over compensation to athletes for "broken time" (i.e., time away from the job for competition). Comte de Clary was for such compensation; Sweden's Edstrøm thought it would "open wide the flood-gates." The advocates of compensation lost, but athletes were allowed reimbursement for expenses for up to fifteen days. Government-funded training was explicitly condemned. There was considerable friction between the IOC and the international soccer federation because the Fédération Internationale de Football Association broke ranks and allowed for compensation for time away from work.

Coubertin was weary of these endless debates on "the meaning of amateurism," but there was nothing he could do to halt them. The unsatisfactory amateur rule received a new unsatisfactory formulation: "An amateur is one who devotes himself to sport for sport's sake without deriving from it, directly or indirectly, the means of existence. A professional is one who derives the means of existence entirely or partly from sport." This was an improvement over previous wording, but the class bias of the rule was still obvious to most athletes. At the 1925 Olympic Congress, Olaf Ditlev-Simonsen suggested that the question of eligibility be left entirely to the international federations. It was half a century before the IOC understood the wisdom of his suggestion.

One of the most important events of the congress was the election of Coubertin's successor. In the first round, which included thirteen absentee ballots, Belgium's Comte Henri de Baillet-Latour received seventeen votes of a possible forty; in the second round, he received nineteen of a total of twenty-seven and was elected to an eight-year term, beginning September 1. Born on March 1, 1876, the count was thirteen years younger than Coubertin. He had been elected to the IOC in 1903 and he had organized the well-run Olympic congress that took place in Brussels in 1905. A wealthy man, he owned racehorses and was president of the elite Jockey-Club de Bruxelles. His conception of the Olympic movement scarcely differed from Coubertin's.

While the IOC evolved in a familiar pattern, organizational challenges sprang up around it. In the late nineteenth-century, European socialists had begun to organize their own sports federations. In 1920, their representatives met at Lucerne in Switzerland and founded an international organization. Five years later, this organization celebrated the First Workers' Olympics at Frankfurt. This four-day athletic extravaganza, which began on July 24, involved one hundred thousand workers as athletes, as participants in parades, pageants, and massed gymnastic demonstrations, and as spectators. There was music by Mozart and Wagner, and there were political speeches. In short, the Arbeiter-Olympiade was a socialist version of the baron's dream of sports used to further a social ideal. The Workers' Olympics were so successful that they were repeated in 1929, 1933, and 1937.

In the long run, the socialist challenge had less impact on the Olympic Games than did the feminist drive for a wider inclusion of women's sports in the Olympic program. Although women have always been involved in sports, they have seldom been as actively involved as men have. In the nineteenth century, the theory of "separate spheres," which called for middle-class men to attend to public affairs while respectable women concerned themselves with the home, severely limited the female athlete. When Phokian Clias published the first modern book on women's sports and exercises, *Kalisthenie* (1829), his emphasis was on graceful movement rather than strenuous competition. The "feminine" emphasis persisted for more than a century. Hysterical fears of "Amazons" with "masculine" development was one bugaboo that haunted the nineteenth and early twentieth centuries. A related fear was that strenuous sports competition was certain to destroy a girl's health and make her forever unfit to become a mother. In short, the criteria for middle-class women's physical activity were hygienic and aesthetic rather than athletic. (One has to emphasize the importance of social class: upper-class women were active in archery, in field sports, and, later in the century, in golf and tennis; lower-class women engaged in bicycle races and were sometimes active as boxers or wrestlers.)

Coubertin, sharing fully the prejudices of his age on this matter, continued to oppose the participation of female athletes in the Olympic Games. He had no objections to women's sports per se, but he felt strongly that such competitions should occur without spectators (whose motives he distrusted). There were no women at the first modern games in Athens, in 1896; a handful of female golfers and tennis players were allowed to share the stage in 1900; female swimmers and divers competed in 1912 and in the first postwar games. Since everyone agreed that track-and-field competitions were the core of the Olympic Games, the inclusion of women as runners, jumpers, and throwers was fiercely resisted. Female fencers were also barred despite the fact that they were quite common in the aristocratic milieu inhabited by most IOC members. The IOC resolved in 1924, upon a motion from France's Comte de Clary, that "as far as the participation of women in the Olympic Games is concerned, the status quo ought to be maintained."

Events, however, had already begun to overtake the committee. In 1921, a number of European women competed in the international Jeux Féminins sponsored by the sportsmen of the tiny Mediterranean principality of Monaco. These games, which included basketball as well as track-and-field events, were repeated in 1922, with great success. That year, a redoubtable Frenchwoman named Alice Milliat decided that women should take matters into their own hands. An active member of one of France's upper-class sports clubs, Fémina Sport, Milliat led in the formation of the Fédération Sportive Féminine Internationale (October 31, 1921). Less than a year later, on August 20, 1922, the FSFI sponsored international track-and-field championships for women at the Stade Pershing in Paris. Twenty thousand enthusiastic spectators cheered as the female athletes from Great Britain, led by sprinter-jumper Mary Lines, won five of the eleven events. The American team, which came in second, had been sent by the Amateur Athletic Union despite the frantic protests of the female physical educators who controlled women's collegiate sports in the United States. The educators, adamantly opposed to all but intramural competition, fought for years to prevent Olympic participation by American women.

Sigfrid Edstrøm, founder-president of the powerful International Amateur Athletic Federation (1912) and an influential member of the IOC's executive board, was unhappy about the Women's Olympics, but there was little he could do to prevent them. The IAAF voted in 1924 to sanction women's track-and-field events but not to advocate their inclusion in the Olympic Games. Pressure from the FSFI, which planned a second celebration of the Women's Olympics for 1926, increased. Reading the writing on the wall ("*Jeux Féminins!*"), Edstrøm met with Milliat, who proved a stubborn negotiator. The IAAF offered to leave the FSFI in control of women's sports if the events were contested under the rules and regulations of the IAAF (modified when necessary to suit women's needs). In return, Milliat agreed to drop the tendentious word "Olympic" in reference to FSFI-sponsored events. On April 5, 1926, the IOC accepted the recommendation of the IAAF and voted to "permit the admission of women to a restricted number of athletic events at the Games." Gymnastics as well as track and field were voted in on an experimental basis, but the former was limited to team competition and the latter to a mere five events (as opposed to the thirteen contested by the FSFI in Göteburg, Sweden, in 1926). The British women were so incensed at the limitation to five track-and-field events that their amateur athletic association boycotted the 1928 Olympic Games.

Although new world records were set in all five women's track-and-field events (according to some authorities), the experiment was considered to be only a partial success. The 800-meter race, the longest, was said by many to have been a disaster because some of the runners collapsed and the winner, Germany's Lina Radke, seemed exhausted as she crossed the finish line in 2:16.8. Such exertion was deemed unfeminine if not physically and psychologically dangerous. The *New York Times* painted a macabre verbal picture in which the cinder track was strewn with wretched damsels in agonized distress. The Canadian press, delighting in Ethel Catherwood's gold medal for the high jump and the first-place finish of the women's 4 × 100–meter relay team, was considerably more positive. Whether the concern expressed over the 800-meter race was sincere or merely a pretext is impossible to say, but the event was removed from the program, not to return until 1960.

In the men's events of 1928, Paavo Nurmi triumphed again over 10,000 meters but came in second to his countryman Ville Ritola in the 5,000 meters. He was also runner-up in the 3,000-meter steeplechase, which was won by another Finn, Toivo Loukola. In three Olympics, Nurmi had entered ten races and won seven of them. Athletes from Great Britain and its dominions and colonies did almost as well as the Finns. Mohammed El Ouafi, competing for France, became the first North African marathon champion. American track-and-field athletes were hindered by poor scheduling on the part of their national Olympic committee: the Olympic trials were held at Harvard only three weeks before the games began. Ray Barbuti, victor in the 400-meter race, and Elizabeth Robinson, winner over 100 meters, were the only Americans to win gold medals in individual races.

American swimmers fared better, and Johnny Weismuller continued to be supreme. He lowered his own Olympic record in the 100-meter crawl to 58.6 seconds and won again in the 200-meter relay. In the 1,500-meter freestyle, the results of 1924 were reversed: this time Arne Borg defeated Andrew Charlton and Clarence "Buster" Crabbe of the United States. Japan's Mikio Oda, a triple-jumper, became the first Asian athlete to return from the games with a gold medal. Kinuye Hitomi, also of Japan, won a silver medal in the women's 800-meter race. In all, thirty-three of the forty-six teams took home at least one medal.

Except for the inevitable disputes over the boxing matches, most of which were won by the Italians and the Argentinians, there was relatively little rancor in 1928. Predictably, however, the British press complained about "broken-time" payments to continental athletes and about athletic scholarships for American collegians of much brawn and little brain. The *Daily Express* remarked haughtily, "The British nation, profoundly interested in sports, is intensely uninterested in the Olympic Games." Meanwhile, an extremely interested General Douglas MacArthur reported to President Calvin Coolidge, on behalf of the American Olympic Committee, that sports are a talisman of national vitality. With his usual rhetorical overkill, MacArthur wrote, "If I were required to indicate today that element of American life which is most characteristic of our nationality, my finger would unerringly point to our athletic escutcheon." The general's ardor for sports was so great that he had the following words carved on the stone portals of West Point's gymnasium:

> Upon the fields of friendly strife
> Are sown the seeds
> That, upon other fields, on other days
> Will bear the fruits of victory.

The winter games at St. Moritz were largely an exhibition of Scandinavian skills. The United States won the bobsled race and the Canadian team outshot its opponents for a gold medal in ice hockey, but the Swedes, Norwegians, and Finns won almost everything else. The most publicized performer was probably young Sonja Henie, who swirled and glided her way to the first of three gold medals in figure skating. While the Norwegian skater eventually dazzled millions as an ice show performer and then as a film star, her post-Olympic professional career made her a bête noir for all those determined to defend the amateur ideal at all costs.

At the IOC's twenty-first session in Rome, in 1923, William May Garland of Los Angeles, elected the previous year as a member from the United States, presented such an effective case for his hometown as the host for the 1932 Games that the members accepted the bid by acclamation. Garland, chairman of the Community Development Association, worked closely with Harry Chandler, owner of the *Los Angeles Times,* and with other members of the city's financial elite. Garland also held important posts as president of the Chamber of Commerce and of the Board of Education. Crucial to the success of the city's Olympic bid was the prospect of a nearly completed 75,000-seat stadium (owned by the Community Development Association).

The prospect of West Coast Olympics did not please the mostly East Coast administrators in charge of the American Olympic Association. Avery Brundage, recalling the easterners' displeasure in his unpublished Olympic autobiography, was ironic: "They had considerable doubt that these inexperienced provincials (anyplace west of the Alleghenies was still considered Indian country) were competent to handle a sport event of this magnitude." As president of the AOA, it was Brundage's task to make peace, which he did. It was unnecessary for the IOC to intervene.

Leaving Garland and the Community Development Association in charge of physical arrangements, the IOC turned its attention—once again—to the question of female participation. During the summer of 1929, President Baillet-Latour argued before the executive board for limiting women to gymnastics, swimming, tennis, and figure skating, all suitably "feminine" sports, but the decision was postponed until after the important Olympic congress scheduled for the following year. The subsequent victory of the "feminists" at the IOC's twenty-ninth session in Barcelona, in 1931, was prepared for by the impressive demonstrations of the women athletes who performed for the delegates in Berlin in 1930. A vivid account of these performances was written by the American delegate Gustavus Kirby:

> I personally saw groups of young girls in the scantiest kind of clothing trotting around the fields or running tracks, engaging in 100 metre runs, taking part in the broad jump, and hopping about in all kinds of athletic and gymnastic movements; and to my direct statement as to whether or not such character of exercise was not bad for them, the answer invariably was that on the contrary, it was good for them.

Another American delegate to the congress, Avery Brundage, was similarly impressed. Although he has often been unfairly characterized as hostile to women's sports, Brundage returned from Berlin ready to defend them: "Anyone who observed the exhibitions put on by girl athletes in connection with the Olympic Congress in Berlin would be a strong advocate for sports of all kinds for girls under proper supervision. They are really doing some wonderful things in the athletic line in Germany today. We could well take a few pointers from them."

Just how impressed the delegates were became clear when the International Amateur Athletic Federation met during the congress to consider its stand on women's participation in the 1932 Olympics. Baillet-Latour proposed that women's track and field be eliminated from the Los Angeles Games and Kirby promptly moved that if Baillet-Latour's proposal passed, a special congress be summoned to consider the elimination of *men's* track and field! The IAAF then voted to continue its endorsement of women's inclusion. When the entire Olympic congress finally voted, track and field was endorsed by a vote of 17-1-1. The female fencers, who had competed for the first time in 1924, were in some danger of exclusion, but their participation was approved by a vote of 19-8. (The decisions made in Berlin were reaffirmed a year later in Barcelona.)

Inevitably, the "amateur question" was also discussed. The definition accepted in Prague passed muster in Berlin. The stand on "broken time" was so ambiguous that IOC Chancellor Otto Mayer later admitted that he found it impossible to understand.

The second summer games held in the United States were a vast improvement over the near-fiasco of St. Louis in 1904. The organizing committee planned an Olympic village in which the male athletes of the entire world were to mix and mingle. (The women were to stay at the Chapman Park Hotel, which offered them comforts unavailable in the men's austere quarters). Another innovation was the victory platform upon which the medal winners were to stand while their national flags were raised and their national anthems were played.

There was considerable doubt in the early months of 1932 if there would be any athletes to inhabit the Olympic village and to mount the victory platform. Six months before the games were scheduled to begin, not a single national Olympic committee had responded to the invitations sent out from Los Angeles. The distance from Europe and from South America was a problem, especially for budgets depleted by the worldwide depression. President Herbert Hoover refused to attend the games, reportedly exclaiming, "It's a crazy thing, and it takes some gall to expect me to be a part of it." There was little demand for tickets and some sponsors asked to be released from their financial obligations. The gloom lessened when the organizers began to receive acceptances from abroad and when the public suddenly began to demand tickets. In a four-day period just before the opening ceremony, some 35,000 tickets were sold. The mood lifted further when a constellation of Hollywood stars—Douglas Fairbanks, Mary Pickford, Charlie Chaplin, Clara Bow, Marlene Dietrich—volunteered to provide additional entertainment for the spectators. As it turned out, there were 105,000 people at the opening ceremony.

The sunny prospects were clouded over once again, this time by a crisis within the IAAF. Immediately before the games it was alleged that Paavo Nurmi had accepted monetary compensation, which made him ineligible to compete as an amateur. Was the IAAF executive board ready to disqualify the world's most famous runner? It was. Brundage and his German friend Karl Ritter von Halt agreed with Sweden's Edstrøm and Bo Eklund that Nurmi had become a professional and was therefore ineligible to compete. The charges brought against Nurmi were probably true. One anonymous official recalled that Nurmi had "the lowest heart beat and the highest asking price of any athlete in the world." Nonetheless, the Finnish delegation was furious. They threatened to withdraw from the games, but the IOC stood behind the IAAF and Nurmi's name was stricken from the program. Like Jim Thorpe, another great athlete tripped up by the amateur rule, Nurmi watched from the stands (along with Gary Cooper, Bing Crosby, Cary Grant, the Marx brothers, and thousands of less-celebrated Californians). There may have been an effort to mollify the aggrieved Finns, for when Lauri Lehtinen twice committed a technical foul against England's Ralph Hill in the 5,000-meter race, the judges declined to disqualify Lehtinen.

Ironically, in light of the effort to prevent women's participation, the most remarkable performer at the games was Mildred "Babe" Didrikson. Limited by the rules to only three events, she won the 80-meter hurdles and the javelin, both with new world records, and came in second in the high jump. Had justice been done to all the athletes, she would probably have been judged second in the hurdles (after Evelyn Hall) and first in the high jump (ahead of Jean Shiley). There was, however, no doubt about her supremacy in the javelin; her world-record throw landed nineteen centimeters beyond the best performance of her German rivals. Poland's Stanislava Walaciewicz broke the American women's monopoly on first-place finishes when she won the 100-meter sprint in world-record time (11.9 seconds). Almost as remarkable were the performances of the Afro-American runners: Eddie Tolan set one world record and two Olympic records in the 100 meters and the 200 meters, while his teammate Ralph Metcalfe came in second in the first race and third in the second. Britain's R. M. N. Tisdall, winner of the 400-meter race, was all the more remarkable because he was truly an amateur in the strictest sense of the term: to train for the games he gave up his job, which paid 150 pounds a month, and moved into "a converted railway carriage in an orchard in Sussex where I lived with my wife on 20 shillings a week."

The Japanese, meanwhile, had discovered that Tisdall's quaintly individualistic approach to world-class sports was less effective than a

national program of pre-Olympic preparedness. Dick Schaap's summary
is a good one:

> The Japanese men suddenly emerged as the best swimmers in the world.
> Four different Japanese won individual events, and three of them broke
> Olympic records; their 800-meter relay quartet cracked the Olympic
> mark by an amazing thirty-eight seconds. Even more amazing was the
> youthfulness of the flying fish from Japan: Kusuo Kitamura, who won
> the strenuous 1,500-meter free style, was only fourteen; Masaji Kiyo-
> kawa, the 100-meter backstroke champion, was sixteen; and Yasuji Mi-
> yazaki, the 100-meter free style champion, was seventeen.

In every one of the men's races, three Japanese reached the finals, and
the Japanese won eleven of the sixteen medals. Overcoming traditional
prejudices about the domestic role of Japanese women, Hideoko Mae-
hata earned a silver medal in the 200-meter breaststroke, a race she
won four years later in Berlin. Japanese track-and-field athletes were
less successful, but one of them, gamely finishing the 10,000-meter race
a lap behind the other runners, was warmly applauded by the appre-
ciative spectators. It was an instance of good sportsmanship that Brundage recalled decades later at a time when sports fans seemed increasingly ready to vilify any athlete who disappointed their expectations.
While most observers seemed genuinely impressed by the exploits of
the Japanese athletes, there were disturbing rumors that oxygen was
administered to them to compensate for the inevitable oxygen deficit
during the races.

The Indian field hockey team trounced the Americans by a score
of 24-1 and carried off a gold medal. The Argentines Juan Zabala and
Santiago Lovell were the winners in the marathon and in heavyweight
boxing. It was clear from the achievements of these Asian and Latin
American athletes that the Olympics were no longer the bailiwick of
the Europeans and the North Americans who had invented them. Little
by little, Coubertin's ideal of universality (on Western terms) was approached.

Grantland Rice, never one for understatement, assured his readers
that the games had been the "greatest sporting pageant in world history." They were undeniably a rare pecuniary success. When the athletes departed and the books were closed, the Community Development Association had done well enough financially to donate
$213,877.19 to the city and the county. Garland and the other civic
leaders of the CDA could take pride in the fact that their city had
become—if only for a few weeks—the sports capital as well as the
cinema capital of the world.

4

The Most Controversial Olympics

At the Olympic congress held in Berlin in 1930, the German organizers had worked hard to demonstrate to the International Olympic Committee that Berlin would be the ideal venue for the 1936 Games. As Theodor Lewald, one of Germany's three IOC members, said in what was for him unusually vivid language, "Here [at the Congress] we detonated our bombs." The effort succeeded. At its twenty-ninth session in Barcelona in April 1931, the IOC had been unable to select the site for the 1936 Games, but a subsequent mail ballot produced forty-three votes for Berlin and only sixteen for Barcelona. The choice of Berlin ratified the full reintegration of Germany within the world of international sports. When the IOC's decision was announced on May 13, 1931, Heinrich Brüning was Germany's chancellor and a shaky centrist coalition was in power. When the games were actually held, the National Socialists were in power and Adolf Hitler was chancellor. In fact, Hitler's rule began only six days after the creation, on January 24, 1933, of the Organisationskomitee. This state of affairs was certainly not what the IOC had expected when Berlin was chosen as the site of the games.

Quite apart from any general concern they might have had about Nazism, there was reason for committee members to be worried. Although Hitler thought that German boys should learn to box, in order to steel themselves for the rigors of their role as natural rulers, neither he nor his cohorts were advocates of modern sports. Sports were almost unmentioned in *Mein Kampf* and in the pages of the party's newspaper, *Der völkische Beobachter*. The problem in Nazi eyes was that modern sports had developed in England rather than in Germany and they were, at least in principle, universalistic rather than particularistic. Among the most important characteristics of modern sports—in theory if not in practice—is equality: neither race nor religion nor ideology should be a factor in the determination of athletic excellence. Such a notion was, of course, anathema to Nazis dedicated to a primitive belief in the racial supremacy of the "Aryan" people. A Nazi spokesman, Bruno Malitz, condemned modern sports because they were international, "infested" with "Frenchmen, Belgians, Pollacks, and Jew-Niggers" who had been allowed "to start on the tracks, to play on the soccer fields, and to swim in the pools." On August 19, 1932, *Der völkische Beobachter* demanded that the Olympic Games be restricted to white athletes.

The Nazi conception of modern sports was only a little more demented than the attitudes of some of the traditional *Turner*. While the British and the Americans were inventing games like soccer, rugby, basketball, and volleyball, games that quickly spread throughout the world, most *Turner* remained devoted to gymnastics as their nation's sole authentic form of physical exercise. These believers in German gymnastics condemned competition, which is an inherent aspect of sports, and they were appalled by the specialization, rationalization, and quantification that are characteristic of modern sports. The Deutsche Turnerschaft, the largest and most important gymnastics organization, had shunned the first Olympics and had been quite ambivalent about participation in subsequent games. The Nazis were ideologically close to the Deutsche Turnerschaft, whose last leader, Edmund Neuendorff, invited Hitler in 1933 to be the guest of honor at a grand *Turnfest* in Stuttgart. Hitler accepted the invitation and was received by Neuendorff with hysterical declarations of fealty. Massed displays of Teutonic vigor and parades to martial music seemed much more in tune with Nazi ideology than an international sports festival open to Afro-Americans, to Asians, and to Jews. The IOC and the organizing committee braced themselves for Hitler's announcement that he wanted another authentic *Turnfest* in 1936—not some international celebration of human solidarity.

Among the most worried were the president and the secretary of the Organisationskomitee, Theodor Lewald and Carl Diem. The former was the son of a Berlin lawyer and civil servant. A member of the IOC since 1924, Lewald had also served as president of the German National Olympic Committee (and as chairman of the Deutscher Reichsausschuss für Leibesübungen, the closest German equivalent to the Amateur Athletic Union). Although Lewald seemed to typify the austere Prussian tradition of public service, he had good reason to be anxious about his personal safety as well as about the future of the Olympic Games. His father had converted from Judaism to Christianity and *Der völkische Beobachter* had already begun screaming for his dismissal. Diem, the secretary of the organizing committee, was a self-

made man with a career in sports journalism and in sports administration. At the age of thirty he was captain of the German team that
competed in Stockholm. Despite his lack of formal education, he eventually developed into a remarkable scholar, still known for his comprehensive history of sports (published in 1960) and for many mono-
graphs in sports history. In 1920, with support from Lewald, he
founded the Deutsche Hochschule für Leibesübungen (German Sports
University). Although Diem was sufficiently the child of his times to
have been an ardent nationalist throughout the twenties, he was definitely a believer in modern sports and he was able to acknowledge
the achievements of athletes from foreign nations. For the German
tradition of *Turnen* he had less sympathy. Although Diem was not
stigmatized by Jewish forebears, his wife was. It was also held against
him that the Deutsche Hochschule für Leibesübungen had several Jews
on its faculty. For these sins, Diem was denounced in the Nazi press
as a "white Jew."

Given their endangered personal positions and the shrill hostility of
many Nazis to sports in general and the Olympics in particular, neither
Lewald nor Diem was optimistic about the 1936 Games and both were
apprehensive when they were summoned, on March 16, 1933, to meet
with Hitler at the chancellory. To their astonishment and relief, Hitler
did not order an immediate cessation of preparations but instead gave
the two men his tentative approval. He had not suddenly changed his
mind and become a convert to Olympism; rather, his propaganda minister, Josef Goebbels, had realized that the games were a splendid
opportunity to demonstrate German vitality and organizational expertise. Lewald was forced to resign from his post with the Deutscher
Reichsausschuss für Leibesübungen and Diem had to give up his position at the Deutsche Hochschule für Leibesübungen; however, pressure from Comte Henri de Baillet-Latour and the IOC prevented the
Nazis from expelling Lewald and Diem from the organizing committee.
Thus, Lewald, Diem, and Hitler became uneasy collaborators. On October 5, 1933, Hitler toured the site of the games, inspected the progress of the construction, and became positively lyrical about the prospects for the grandest Olympics ever. Five days later, at the chancellory,
he promised the startled Lewald the full financial support of his regime,
a sum later set at 20,000,000 Reichsmarks. Lewald and Diem were
stunned by their unexpected good fortune.

Hitler's willingness to act as host allayed one set of anxieties and
aroused another. The IOC was quite naturally worried by the glaringly
obvious contradiction between the Olympic Charter and the racist
principles of the new regime. In April and May 1933, the *New York
Times* questioned the appropriateness of Berlin as a venue: was the

Nazi regime ready to accept the terms of the Olympic Charter? American Jews were especially skeptical, and their fears were only partly quieted when General Charles Sherrill, one of the three American members of the IOC, wrote to the American Jewish Congress, "Rest assured that I will stoutly maintain the American principle that all citizens are equal under all laws." As Sherrill and twenty-eight other members of the IOC assembled in Vienna on June 7, 1933, the discrepancy between Nazi doctrine and the Olympic rulebook was a central issue. Baillet-Latour, elected to a second eight-year term as president (by a vote of 48-1), joined Sherrill and William May Garland as the two Americans questioned the three German IOC members—Lewald, Karl Ritter von Halt, and Adolf Friedrich von Mecklenburg—about Jewish participation. The crux of the matter was not the acceptance of Jewish athletes on foreign teams but rather the right of German Jews to try out for *their* national team. Although von Halt, a Nazi party member, resisted the idea, the IOC insisted upon a written guarantee from Berlin to the effect that German Jews did, indeed, have this right. Once a written guarantee was in hand, Baillet-Latour declared that he considered "the assurances given by the German members to be satisfactory." Sherrill later told the *New York Times* that he was surprised that his German colleagues had obtained this unambiguous written commitment: "I don't know how they did it, but they did it."

Unfortunately, the reliability of Nazi guarantees, written or oral, was immediately called into question by reports of widespread discrimination against Jewish athletes. They were allowed, for the moment, to use public sports facilities, but they were expelled from the private clubs that were the main institutional form of German sports. Avery Brundage, the most influential American sports administrator of the times, was sufficiently worried to confide in a letter to Gustavus Kirby that the "very foundation of the modern Olympic revival will be undermined if individual countries are allowed to restrict participation by reason of class, creed or race." Kirby was far more upset than Brundage by the threat to Olympic principles. For the convention of the American Olympic Committee on November 22, 1933, he prepared a resolution that threatened an American boycott unless German Jews were allowed in fact as well as in theory to "train, prepare for and participate in the Olympic Games of 1936." Brundage expressed reservations about the confrontational tone of the resolution, but Kirby was ready for a confrontation: "Undoubtedly it is generally wiser to 'let sleeping dogs lie,' but unfortunately these dogs are not sleeping, they are growling and snarling and snipping and all but biting." The

American Olympic Association passed a slightly modified version of Kirby's strong resolution.

Reichssportführer Hans von Tschammer und Osten tried to meet American concerns by issuing a statement that Jews were not barred from sports clubs by any *official* decree, but Brundage was not reassured by this kind of double-talk. He wrote to Baillet-Latour: "The German authorities have displayed a singular lack of astuteness in all of their publicity. On this subject, every news dispatch that has come from Germany seems to indicate that the Hitlerites do not intend to live up to the pledges given to the IOC at Vienna." Brundage kept his worries private because he did not wish to cause trouble for his German friends Lewald, Diem, and von Halt. However, Kirby refused to remain quiet in the face of newspaper reports of discrimination against Jewish athletes. He was among the Madison Square Garden speakers at an anti-Nazi rally held by the American Jewish Committee.

When the IOC convened in Athens on May 15, 1934, Britain's Lord Aberdare, who earlier had been ready to accept Nazi assurances at face value, now expressed concern about reports from Germany. He asked his German colleagues point blank if their government's pledges were trustworthy. Garland asked the same uncomfortable question and Lewald and von Halt responded: "It goes without saying that the Pledges given by Germany in Vienna in 1933 to admit to the German Olympic team German Sportsmen of Non-Aryan [i.e., Jewish] origin, provided they have the necessary capability, will be strictly observed and facilities for preparation will be given to all sportsmen." The IOC was satisfied; the American Olympic Association was not. When the latter met in June, it postponed acceptance of the official invitation to the games until an on-the-spot inspection by Brundage, who was then president of the AOA. The German consul in Chicago (Brundage's hometown) breathed a sigh of relief because he assumed, quite rightly, that Brundage's loyalty to his German friends and his fanatical commitment to the survival of the Olympic Games all but guaranteed a positive report. IOC members Garland and Sherrill both urged Brundage to dismiss what they considered to be exaggerated reports of discrimination against Jewish athletes.

A letter from Sweden's Sigfrid Edstrøm, whom Brundage knew well because both men were leaders in the International Amateur Athletic Federation, gave Brundage some additional unsound advice:

> As regards the persecution of the Jews in Germany I am not at all in favor of said action, but I fully understand that an alteration had to take place. As it was in Germany, a great part of the German nation was led by the Jews and not by the Germans themselves. Even in the USA the day may come when you will have to stop the activities of the

Jews. They are intelligent and unscrupulous. Many of my friends are
Jews so you must not think that I am against them, but they must be
kept within certain limits.

With Edstrøm's letter in his pocket, metaphorically if not physically,
Brundage set off for his "impartial" investigation of German conditions.
En route to Germany, Brundage traveled to Stockholm to attend a
meeting of the IAAF and to confer with Edstrøm. Since Diem, von
Halt, and Justus W. Meyerhof, a Jewish member of the Berliner Sport-
Club, were also present, Brundage queried the three of them about
the German situation. Had German Jews been expelled from clubs
and denied the right to use public facilities? Their account was reas-
suring. Things were not as bad as they had been painted. True sportsmen were not about to turn their backs on men and women with
whom they had worked and played for decades. Diem made notes of
the discussion for his journals:

> We showed Brundage documents indicating that the Jews are able to
> participate freely in sports and to train for the Olympic team. Meyerhof
> told us that he had offered to resign from the Berliner Sport-Club but
> that the resignation had not been accepted. I was seldom as proud of
> my club as at that moment. Brundage was visibly impressed. He plans
> to speak with leaders of Jewish sports when he visits Berlin.

The on-the-spot investigation began on September 13, when Brundage arrived in East Prussia. Since Brundage did not speak German
well, he was forced to rely on interpreters. (It was an additional drawback that he was never allowed to talk alone with representatives of
the Jewish sports clubs. Nazi officials monitored his conversations.) He
met Reichssportführer von Tschammer und Osten and "liked him very
much." Von Halt, Brundage's oldest German friend, told him that
there was no discrimination and that Jewish athletes were quite likely
to make the team. Brundage believed what he was predisposed to
believe. He returned to the United States and urged the American
Olympic Association to accept the invitation to Berlin.

Brundage's assurances persuaded even the skeptical Kirby. On September 26, the day after Brundage's return from Europe, the eighteen-
member AOA voted unanimously to send a team to the 1936 Olympic
Games. Any hopes that this decision might terminate the controversy
vanished as the *New York Times* reported, on September 27, that the
Anti-Defamation League was calling for a boycott. U.S. Representative
Emmanuel Celler of New York began congressional hearings and
charged that Brundage "prejudged the situation before he sailed from
America. The Reich Sports Commissars have snared and deluded him."
In December, the annual convention of the Amateur Athletic Union

voted to postpone acceptance of the German invitation. For Brundage, who was accustomed to a more acquiescent AAU, the vote was tantamount to a declaration of no confidence. Passions flamed; lines hardened.

By mid-1935, an intensive boycott campaign was in full swing in the United States, in Canada, in Great Britain, and in France. Everyone realized that the American campaign was the most important and that the embattled Brundage was the key figure. His position had always been that sports and politics should be strictly separated: "The AOC must not be involved in political, racial, religious or sociological [sic] controversies." All that could reasonably be asked of the Nazi regime, from his perspective, was that it accept Olympic rules, which the highest officials had agreed to do.

What was good enough for Brundage was also good enough for Pierre de Coubertin, whom the German organizing committee had assiduously courted. Although Coubertin in retirement was scrupulous about attending neither the IOC sessions nor the Olympic Games, he did agree, after a visit to Lausanne by Diem and Lewald, to spend some time in Berlin, where, on August 4, 1935, he recorded a radio message in which he declared his confidence in the arrangements for the games. He was delighted when, at a reception in his honor at Berlin's Pergamon Museum, the musicians played the same "Hymn to Apollo" that he had ordered performed for the delegates to the 1894 Sorbonne conference. He was presumably pleased, a few months later, when the Nazi regime nominated him for the Nobel Peace Prize (which went instead to the anti-Nazi martyr Carl von Ossietzky).

While Diem and Lewald were persuading Coubertin that these Olympic Games would be an authentic embodiment of his dream, Brundage was busy explaining why a boycott would be a travesty for Olympism. In a sixteen-page pamphlet entitled "Fair Play for American Athletes," he asked if the American athlete was to be made "a martyr to a cause not his own," and he repeated his arguments about the separation of sports from politics and religion. American athletes should not become needlessly involved in what he misleadingly referred to as "the present Jew-Nazi altercation." The entire problem, in Brundage's eyes, was that opponents of the Nazi regime were not satisfied with Olympic rules; that they really wanted a boycott to undermine Nazism; that they meant to use the games as a political weapon. Since Jews and Communists were calling for a boycott, Brundage reasoned—illogically—that all the boycotters were Jews or Communists.

Brundage's relations with Charles Ornstein, a Jewish member of the American Olympic Committee, deteriorated into petty hostility, and his friendship with Judge Jeremiah T. Mahoney, his successor as pres-

ident of the AAU, turned to outright enmity. Mahoney, once a law
partner of New York's senator Robert Wagner, had served for more
than a decade on the New York Supreme Court. Brundage, becoming
paranoid in his defense of the games, characterized Mahoney's opposition as politically motivated, explaining that Mahoney, a Roman
Catholic, had mayoral ambitions in New York and was seeking to woo
Jewish voters. Brundage refused to see that Roman Catholics had excellent reasons to fear Hitler, who had made no secret of his neopa-
ganism or his hatred for the church into which he had been born.

The Catholic War Veterans and the Catholic journal *Commonweal*
were in favor of a boycott (as was the Protestant publication *Christian
Century* and a number of respected Protestant spokesmen such as
Harry Emerson Fosdick and Reinhold Niebuhr). The boycott movement included not only Jews like Congressman Celler but also a number of politically prominent Catholics such as James Curley and Al
Smith. Three nationally known journalists, Arthur Brisbane, West-
brook Pegler, and Heywood Broun, also climbed aboard what began
to look like an unstoppable bandwagon. A Gallup poll taken in March
1935 showed 43 percent of the American population in favor of a
boycott.

Because black athletes were such a strong component of the American track-and-field team, Afro-American reactions to the boycott campaign were especially important. The *Amsterdam News* supported a
boycott, but the *Pittsburgh Courier-Journal* and most other black
newspapers were outspoken about their desire not to deny these men
and women the chance of a lifetime. The athletes were clearly anxious
to go. Sprinter Ralph Metcalfe told the *Chicago Defender* that he and
other blacks had been treated well during a 1933 tour of Germany
and he was ready to return. Regrettably, there was another side to the
controversy. Historian David K. Wiggins, who has studied Afro-American responses to the boycott, indicates that some blacks were actually
anti-Semitic: "They frequently stereotyped Jews and blamed them for
everything from economic exploitation to murder." While anti-Semitism did not make Afro-Americans especially sympathetic to the Nazis'
racist ideology, it did leave them less indignant than they might have
been about the discriminatory treatment suffered by Germany's Jewish
athletes.

Brundage refused to take notice of the obvious. He continued ob-
stinately to see the opposition as nothing but a conspiracy of Jews and
Communists. Having been assured by his German friends that their
government accepted the Olympic rules, believing as he did that the
games were the most important international institution of the century,
a force for peace and reconciliation among peoples, he simply failed

to understand that there were men and women of good will who did not agree with him. He was unable to imagine honest opposition and instead attributed what opposition he encountered to ethnic prejudice or political ideology. Once he had made up his own mind, he suspected his opponents were guilty of the most despicable motives and an almost satanic insincerity. Refusing to look at the evidence, he simply repeated his nonsensical demands that Jews and Communists "keep their hands off American sport." Brundage's hysteria reached the point where the exasperated Kirby privately accused him of anti-Semitism.

Throughout this controversy, Brundage had the strong support of Dietrich Wortmann, president of New York's German-American Athletic Club. In his appeal for funds to support the American team, the German-born wrestler, who had won a bronze medal in the 1904 Games, referred to the athletes as "apostles of truth and justice for the promotion of friendship between our two countries." Although some have interpreted Wortmann's impulsive rhetoric as a defense of the Nazi regime, Wendy Gray and Robert Knight Barney conclude that his "efforts toward Olympic participation were for the sake of American athletes, the games, and the Olympic spirit."

In response to Brundage's unfounded assertions of Nazi innocence, Judge Mahoney published a pamphlet entitled "Germany Has Violated the Olympic Code" (1935). Writing in the form of an open letter to Lewald, Mahoney cited specific cases such as the expulsion of Jews from sports clubs and from public facilities, the ban on competition between Jews and other Germans, the exclusion of world-class high-jumper Gretel Bergmann from the Olympic team. Every one of Mahoney's allegations has been verified by subsequent scholarship.

Mahoney had the facts, Brundage had the votes. Strongly seconded by Ornstein, Mahoney offered a boycott resolution at the annual meeting of the Amateur Athletic Union. The vote was close, but the motion to investigate further before accepting the invitation failed by 58¼ to 55¾. The AAU agreed to support sending a team to the winter games at Garmisch-Partenkirchen and to the summer games in Berlin. Immediately before the crucial vote, the delegates to the convention were informed that Brundage had a secret arrangement with Baillet-Latour and Edstrøm: if the AAU refused to certify the athletes, Brundage's word would be sufficient to do so! In other words, the vote was a mockery. After the AAU's decision, the National Collegiate Athletic Association gave its approval, which had never really been in doubt.

Brundage's baseless allegations about a boycott movement limited to Jews and Communists (and Mahoney) might have been true for the Canadian opposition to the games. Bruce Kidd has written of the Canadian situation that "the campaign leadership never really broadened beyond the ranks of the Communist Party." While P. J. Mulqueen and other officials of the Canadian Olympic Committee indicated their satisfaction with the assurances they had received from the IOC, Eva Dawes, one of the stars of the Canadian track-and-field team, clashed with officialdom. Already barred from AAU meets because she had competed in the Soviet Union, Dawes and five other Canadian athletes went to Barcelona in the summer of 1936 to participate in a Communist-sponsored Olimpiada. In fact, this Olimpiada never took place because it was interrupted by the outbreak of the Spanish Civil War (1936-39).

European opponents of Nazi sports policy also mounted a boycott campaign. Louis Rimet, head of the French sports federation as well as of the Fédération Internationale de Football Association, was among the influential spokesmen pleading for strong action. He was joined by the French presidents of the Fédération Internationale de Natation Amateur (swimming) and the Ligue Internationale de Hockey sur Glace (ice hockey) and by Bernard Lévy, head of the prestigious Racing-Club de France. Late in 1935, a socialist deputy asked the Chambre des Deputés to terminate the government's program for training Olympic athletes. The motion lost by a vote of 410-151. Early in 1936, however, Léon Blum led the socialists and their allies to victory in national elections. Blum's Popular Front government tried to satisfy both quarreling camps by appropriating 1.1 million francs for the Olympic Games and 600,000 francs for the Olimpiada in Barcelona. The compromise failed to calm the storm. The Communist newspaper *L'Humanité* was unhappy that government funds were sending 189 male and 11 female athletes to Berlin; at the other end of the political spectrum, the conservative newspaper *Le Figaro* expressed its disgust at the government's support for the 1,300 athletes, officials, and conference delegates preparing for the Olimpiada. The Barcelona-bound French contingent was, in fact, far larger than all the others put together. (The second largest, the Swiss, had only 150 members.)

Although only twelve American athletes sailed to Spain for the Olimpiada, many others participated that summer in a World Labor Athletic Carnival that was staged on New York's Randall's Island with AAU sponsorship arranged by Mahoney and Ornstein. Wortmann complained about the use of the AAU's name for this obviously political event, but AAU Secretary Daniel J. Ferris defended the dissenters' right to claim the sponsorship.

While Brundage was winning his victory in the United States, his American opponents had carried the battle elsewhere. The third American member of the IOC (in addition to Sherrill and Garland) was Ernest Lee Jahncke, a staunch Republican who had served as President Herbert Hoover's assistant secretary of the navy. On November 27, the *New York Times* printed his appeal to Baillet-Latour:

> ... the Nazis have consistently and persistently violated their pledges. Of this they have been convicted out of their own mouths and by the testimony of impartial and experienced American and English newspaper correspondents. ... It is plainly your duty to hold the Nazi sports authorities accountable for the violation of their pledges. ... Let me beseech you to seize your opportunity to take your rightful place in the history of the Olympics alongside of de Coubertin instead of Hitler.

Baillet-Latour, who had previously promised Brundage that he was ready to come to the United States to combat the "Jewish" boycott campaign, was furious. He had recently visited Hitler and was assured by the *Führer* that the charges against Germany were false. Baillet-Latour told Jahncke that the president's duty was to execute the will of the IOC, which was steadfastly committed to the games. The count saw Jahncke as a traitor who for inexplicably spiteful reasons accepted neither the word of Hitler nor the personal assurances of honorable men like Diem, von Halt, and Brundage. Taking umbrage, Baillet-Latour asked Jahncke to resign from the IOC. Jahncke refused: "I shall not resign solely because of my opposition to the Berlin Games."

Sherrill, meanwhile, began to back away from his previous position. While still claiming to be a friend of the Jews, he warned them that continued agitation might increase popular anti-Semitism. He had what must have been a very difficult interview with Hitler on August 24. When he mentioned to the *Führer* that two years earlier members of his government had pledged that *all* Germans would have the right to try out for the team, Hitler vehemently informed him that the German team would not include Jews. Either Hitler had not been informed of this pledge when it was given or he conveniently forgot it when it was mentioned by Sherrill. After reporting to Baillet-Latour, Sherrill had another conversation with Hitler, this one over dinner. He was now assured that the pledge would be honored. As a result of these two meetings, Sherrill was, in the words of Stephen R. Wenn, "mesmerized by Hitler's accomplishments and character." Muting his criticisms of Hitler's Germany and expressing a good deal of enthusiasm for Mussolini's Italy, Sherrill wrote to Baillet-Latour to ask sarcastically why Mahoney didn't worry about the plight of Negro athletes who suffered from discrimination not only in the South but even at the hands of the New York Athletic Club, of which both Sherrill and Mahoney were members.

The 1936 Winter Games, which began on February 6, are usually forgotten by historians of the Nazi Olympics (but not by Richard

Mandell, who discusses them in his book of that title). Wet snow dampened spirits at the opening ceremony, and there were nasty moments when boorish Bavarians and overzealous troops made foreign visitors feel less than welcome. Fair play and good sportsmanship also suffered a setback when the British ice hockey team, strengthened by Canadian professionals, swept to victory. (Ironically, it was Canada they defeated in the final match.) On the other hand, there were fantastic performances, like that of Norway's Ivar Ballangrud, who won three gold and one silver medal in the four speed-skating events. Sonja Henie, about to begin her career as a film star, edged Britain's Cecilia Colledge to win the figure skater's title for the third time in a row.

Shortly after these winter games, on March 7, Hitler sent his army into the Rhineland, an area demilitarized under the terms of the Versailles treaty. He assumed that this defiant violation of the treaty would not jeopardize the summer games, and he was right.

Had there been no political controversy, it would still have been difficult in the midst of the Great Depression for the national Olympic committees to raise money for their teams. The prolonged controversy over American participation made the financial picture of the American Olympic Association especially grim. Before the team sailed on the SS *Manhattan,* the American Olympic Committee was thanking its supporters for contributions as small as ten cents.

Difficulties dogged the team even on shipboard, but they were nonpolitical. Eleanor Holm Jarrett was a veteran swimmer who had already competed in two Olympics. As a fifteen-year-old, she had tied for fifth place in the 100-meter backstroke at Amsterdam. Four years later at Los Angeles, she won the event in world-record time. Now a married woman of twenty-two, she asked for and was denied permission to join, at her own expense, the passengers in first-class accommodations. She made the best of a bad situation by drinking, dancing, and staying up all night. After having been placed on probation, she was found drunk by the chaperone of the women's team. That Jarrett smoked, gambled, and missed meals added to the officials' horror. The American Olympic Committee decided to expel her from the team, and Brundage refused to alter the decision even after he was handed a petition signed by 220 coaches and athletes. Since Jarrett was a beautiful woman as well as a great athlete, the press reacted gleefully and newspapers published erotic photographs of the persecuted "water nymph." Brundage was pilloried as a mean old man. Jarrett quickly obtained press credentials and attended the games as a journalist. She found the Nazis were not at all as they had been portrayed by their detractors. "[Hermann] Göring was fun," she reported. "He had a good personality. . . . And so did the little one with the club foot [Josef Goebbels]."

Brundage had more important worries than what to do about Eleanor Jarrett. Counting on the repeated guarantees of his German friends and carried along by his belief in Olympism, he had risked his authority on behalf of the games. If the Nazis failed to keep their promises, what then? Later, in countless letters and speeches, he claimed that the Nazis *had* kept their word, that they had followed Olympic rules, that German Jews had been free to try out for the team, that these had been the grandest and most successful of Olympics. He was wrong about at least the first three claims. It is true that the Nazis invited two athletes of mixed ancestry to join the team—Rudi Ball, an ice hockey player, and Hélène Mayer, a fencer. Mayer, who lived in the United States, had won an Olympic gold medal in 1928 and was the American champion from 1933 to 1935. She was an ironic choice. She did not consider herself a Jew and, as George Eisen comments, she was a statuesque blonde who looked "like an advertisement for German womanhood." Dark-haired Gretel Bergmann, however, was denied a place on the team despite the fact that she was Germany's best high-jumper. On July 16, less than a month before the games were to begin, Reichssportführer von Tschammer und Osten informed her that her performance had been inadequate. Her jump of 1.6 meters was, in fact, 4 centimeters higher than that of her closest rival. To von Tschammer und Osten's fallacious statement was added the absurd argument that Bergmann was not a member of an official sports club. How could she have been when Jews were banned from membership? Other Jews who might have won places on the team were intimidated or lacked facilities to train and failed to achieve their potential. Gretel Bergmann, for example, was summoned to Germany from London and was then told that her performance was inadequate.

In all, twenty-one German Jews from the Makkabi and Schild organizations were "nominated" as candidates for the team and invited to a training camp; none was selected. Frederick W. Rubien, secretary of the American Olympic Committee, defended their exclusion with the assertion that they were simply not good enough to make the German team. George Messersmith, the American consul in Berlin, was less gullible than Rubien. He noted as early as 1933 that Jewish athletes were the victims of severe discrimination. In November 1935, six months before the games were to begin, Messersmith reported that Lewald had confessed to him, in tears, that he—Lewald—had lied when he assured Brundage and the American Olympic Committee that there was no discrimination against Jewish athletes.

One must give Baillet-Latour some credit for doing his best to hold the Nazis to their promises. Although he had written to Brundage that he was not personally fond of Jews, he did attempt to force the Nazis to admit qualified Jewish athletes to the German team and he did occasionally force Hitler to modify his policies. When Baillet-Latour heard, shortly before the beginning of the winter games, that the streets and roads of Garmisch-Partenkirchen were placarded with anti-Semitic signs, he demanded that the placards be removed—and they were.

If the 1936 Summer Games were not the triumph of Olympism that Brundage and Baillet-Latour insisted they were, were they, on the contrary, a propaganda coup for the Nazis? The question is not easily answered. Hitler had told Diem and Lewald that he wanted to impress the world with the magnificence of the games, and the world was impressed. The facilities were monumental. The magnificent Deutsches Stadion that was originally planned for the 1916 Games was expanded to accommodate 110,000 spectators. At the open-air Olympic pool, 18,000 spectators were able to follow the swimming and diving events. The pageantry, which can still be vicariously experienced in Leni Riefenstahl's documentary film *Olympia*, was truly extraordinary. Among Diem's inspired innovations was an enormous iron bell inscribed with the words *"Ich rufe die Jugend der Welt"* (I summon the youth of the world). It was also Diem's idea that a torch be lit at Olympia and carried by a relay of thousands of runners from there to the stadium in Berlin, where it was used to ignite the Olympic flame. Spiridon Louys, the Greek peasant who had won the first marathon in 1896, was invited to Berlin, where he presented Hitler with an olive branch. (In retrospect, the symbolism becomes a tragic irony. Other victors from 1896, like gymnast Alfred Flatow and his cousin Gustav, were murdered in the course of Hitler's monstrous "final solution of the Jewish problem.")

The most impressive of Diem's many artistic contributions was *Olympische Jugend* (Olympic Youth), a series of dances choreographed by Mary Wigman, Harald Kreuzberg, Dorothee Günther, and Maja Lex to music composed by Carl Orff and Werner Egk. The performers of *Olympische Jugend* included a chorus of a thousand and thousands of male and female dancers. The fourth part of this paean to youthful idealism was prophetically entitled "Heldenkampf und Todesklage" (Heroes' Struggle and Lament for the Dead). Mary Wigman called this section "a festive homage to death." The call to heroic sacrifice, much criticized by revisionist historians like Thomas Alkemeyer and Helmut König, was followed by the choral movement of Beethoven's Ninth Symphony, which Coubertin had long wanted to introduce into Olympic ritual. *Olympische Jugend*, which had its premiere the night before the games began, concluded with a *Lichtdom* (cathedral of light) created by a multitude of searchlights whose beams converged high above the stadium.

For these games, the IOC wanted to use the music performed in Los Angeles, but Lewald had Richard Strauss set to music a poem by Robert Lubahn. The text was altered to make it more rather than less nationalistic. Similarly, Georg Kolbe and Arno Breker, the sculptors whose work adorned the main stadium and the other structures, were ordered to produce statues with suitably "Aryan" physiques. They dutifully avoided the modernist styles that the Nazis had condemned as "degenerate art." Whatever art historians think of the result (most are sarcastic), the spectators seem to have been impressed by all the marble muscles.

Visiting dignitaries were invited by Hitler to the Berlin opera and by Wilhelm Frick to a concert held in the Pergamon Museum, which exhibited, then as now, a stunning collection of Hellenistic art and architecture from the ancient city of Pergamon (near the present Turkish town of Bergama), and Goebbels entertained 2,000 guests at a magnificent country estate recently confiscated from a Jewish family. Small wonder that thousands of visitors left Berlin with a sense of aesthetic fulfillment and a vague impression that National Socialism wasn't as dreadful as they had thought. The swastika was much in evidence, but Hitler's role was minimized. Baillet-Latour told him that his duty as host was to utter a single sentence, which Baillet-Latour had typed up for him: "I declare the games of the Eleventh Olympiad of the modern era to be open." Intentionally or not, Hitler's response to Baillet-Latour's instructions was comic. The dictator who was accustomed to delivering four-hour harangues replied to Baillet-Latour, "Count, I'll take the trouble to learn it by heart."

The athletes were impressed not only by the magnificent sports facilities but also by the Olympic village, where every effort was made to secure their comfort. (The second half of Riefenstahl's film begins with a pastoral sequence set in the village.) There were over one hundred buildings to house the athletes, and their national cuisines were served in thirty-eight separate dining halls. While in the village, runners were able to train on a 400-meter track, while swimmers and oarsmen utilized a specially constructed artificial lake. There was no way for the athletes to have anticipated that Captain Wolfgang Fürstner, who had been in charge of the village, was later to be driven to suicide by Nazi persecution.

The strongest evidence for Brundage's claim that the 1936 Summer Olympics were not a propaganda triumph is the fact that Jesse Owens was unquestionably the star of the games. Setting a world record of 10.3 seconds for 100 meters and an Olympic record of 20.7 seconds for 200 meters, he went on to jump an astonishing 8.06 meters and to help set still another world record in the 400-meter relay. In photographs published in the German press during and after the games, Owens appears in a favorable light. On August 7, *The Spectator* (London) commented, "The German spectators, like all others, have fallen under the spell of the American Negro Jesse Owens, who is already the hero of these Games." He was described in the text of one popular publication as the *Wunderathlet* of the games. In Riefenstahl's documentary film, he appears as if he really were an Olympian, a god of sports. A French journalist reviewed the film in an article aptly entitled *"Les Dieux du stade"* (The Gods of the Stadium). In *Olympia* the camera follows Owens as it does no other athlete. When Goebbels, whose propaganda office secretly financed the film, protested that there were too many positive shots of the black American athlete, Riefenstahl appealed to Hitler, who intervened to prevent the cuts ordered by Goebbels. Ironically, no photographs of Owens (or of any of the other black athletes) appeared in the Atlanta *Constitution,* the most liberal of southern U.S. newspapers.

Owens did figure in a story whose fog of error historians cannot dispel. Hitler, we are told, refused to shake hands with Owens. In fact, when the games began, Hitler personally congratulated a number of athletes, including the first German victors Hans Woelcke (shot put), Gerhard Stock (javelin), and Tilly Fleischer (javelin), all of whom he invited to his private box. Two Afro-Americans, Cornelius Johnson and David Albritten, were first and second in the high jump, but Hitler left the stadium before the event was concluded. The following day, Baillet-Latour, accompanied by the German IOC member von Halt, cautioned Hitler and told him to invite *all* the victors to his box or none of them. Hitler decided to save his felicitations for a postgame celebration limited to the German athletes. If anyone was insulted, it was Johnson, not Owens. The latter told the *New York Times* (August 25), "There was absolutely no discrimination at all," but the story of the snub was (and is) too good to sacrifice at the altar of historical truth.

This unexpected display of apparently unbiased treatment was actually part of a concentrated effort at shaping a favorable image of the new regime. The Ministry of Propaganda ordered on August 3 that "the racial point of view should not in any form be a part of the discussion of the athletic results. Special care should be exercised not to offend Negro athletes." When the editors of the rabidly racist *Der Angriff* were unable to restrain themselves from a much-publicized sneer at America's "black auxiliaries," they were reprimanded by the ministry. There was, in the words of Hans Joachim Teichler, a "temporary suspension of a core part of National Socialist ideology."

Notions of "Aryan" superiority began to seem quite ludicrous when Kitei Son of Korea won the marathon and the Japanese swimmers did almost as well as they had in 1932. (The Japanese swimming and diving team, which included athletes from conquered Korea, garnered four gold, two silver, and five bronze medals.) The most annoying outcome for the Nazi hosts was probably the women's high jump. Having kept Bergmann from the German team, they watched Ibolya Czak, a Hungarian Jew, win that event with a leap of 1.6 meters—exactly the height that Bergmann had cleared shortly before the games. Was it an annoyance or a pleasure for Hitler and Goebbels when Hélène Mayer, the "half-Jew" fencer, won a silver medal and raised her arm in the Nazi salute?

Ironically, in light of the expressed American concern for the fate of Jewish athletes, the most serious allegations of anti-Semitism to emerge from the actual competitions (as opposed to the pre-Olympic selection process) concerned the American team. Marty Glickman and Sam Stoller, the only Jews on the American track-and-field squad, were cut from the relay team although Glickman's times were faster than those of Foy Draper, who ran (with Owens, Metcalfe, and Frank Wykoff). The reason for the cut was probably not anti-Semitism. The American coaches, Lawson Robertson and Dean Cromwell, chose Draper because he was a student at the University of Southern California, where Cromwell coached.

All in all, the United States did well enough in track and field and in diving for American journalists gleefully to claim that the United States had "won" the 1936 Olympics. There was certainly reason to be proud not only of the black athletes but also of Glenn Morris, who won the decathlon, and Helen Stephens, whose time in the 100-meter race (11.5 seconds) was faster than Thomas Burke's had been at the first modern Olympics. It is said that even Hitler was impressed by her "virile beauty." It was easy for the Americans to overlook the aquatic achievements of the Japanese men and Holland's champion swimmer, Hendrika Mastenbroek (three gold medals and one silver). How many readers, sitting over breakfast and scanning the local paper, realized that the Egyptians were superb in weight lifting, the Swedes and Hungarians in wrestling, the Italians in fencing, the French in cycling, and the Germans in just about everything? In fact, the Germans won thirty-three events, came in second in twenty-six, and finished third in another thirty. *The Spectator* for August 21 contained that journal's quadrennial vintage of sour grapes: "When to win the Olympic Games becomes an object of British, as it has German, policy, we shall really have reached the stage of senility, the true decadence."

If most of the world's sports fans were but dimly aware of German athletic superiority, it was not the fault of the government-controlled media. In addition to pre-Olympic newsletters and other publications, there was television transmission to twenty-five TV halls and shortwave radio broadcasts that reached some forty countries. Commentators from twenty-two countries sent the message. Finally, in 1938, Riefenstahl's *Olympia* was released with English and French as well as German narration. The Nazi propaganda apparatus made much of the mostly favorable press coverage of the games and exploited to the utmost the aged, infirm Coubertin's remarks (his last public pronouncement) that these "grandiose" games, organized with "Hitlerian strength and discipline," had "magnificently served the Olympic ideal."

Propaganda coup or not, the games were undoubtedly an important step on Brundage's path to Olympic leadership. On the first day of its thirty-fifth session, the International Olympic Committee officially expelled its lone dissenter, Jahncke, by a vote of 49-0, with Garland abstaining. (Jahncke was also ousted, along with Ornstein, from the American Olympic Association.) In Jahncke's place they elected Brundage, the man who had fought successfully to block a boycott of the games. The IOC minutes state explicitly that he was elected to fill Jahncke's seat, not that of the recently deceased Sherrill. This petty vindictiveness continued when the American Olympic Committee published its official report on the games. There were photographs of the American IOC members, including Sherrill but excluding Jahncke. Reporting to the AOC, President Brundage dismissed the boycott movement as "radical propaganda." A. C. Gilbert, chef de mission, also condemned the "active boycott by Jews and Communists" that "aroused the resentment of the athletic leaders, the sportsmen and [the] patriotic citizens of America." In Brundage's eyes, the games had been a great success. "Fulfilling the visions of its founder, Baron Pierre de Coubertin, once again this great quadrennial celebration has demonstrated that it is the most effective influence toward international peace and harmony yet devised." Until his death at the age of eighty-seven, Brundage continued to lament the "viciousness" of the boycott campaign and to maintain, despite the evidence, that it was motivated entirely by disapproval "of the German government at that time, although the German government had nothing to do with the organization or content of the Games."

Government involvement was also denied by Riefenstahl, who has always insisted that her documentary film was privately financed when in fact it was paid for by funds made available to her by Goebbels (who was, however, not entirely pleased with the final product). The film, which was awarded first prize at the Venetian Biennale, had its official premiere on April 20, 1938, the birthday of Riefenstahl's admiring friend Adolf Hitler. The release of *Olympia* was accompanied by the publication of *Schönheit im Olympischen Kampf,* a book of stunning photographs taken mostly from still footage from the film. Although there was not enough Nazi propaganda for *Olympia* fully to satisfy Goebbels, there was apparently too much for the film to be distributed in the United States. Brundage attributed Riefenstahl's difficulties in this country to Jewish influence within the film industry, which was certainly an important factor, while other observers pointed to moments of nudity in the hauntingly beautiful opening scenes of the film. The American Olympic Association arranged for private screenings, and Brundage was eventually able, in 1948, to secure an Olympic Diploma for Riefenstahl (whom Kirby impishly referred to as Brundage's "beautiful affinity"). It is the nearly unanimous opinion of film historians that *Olympia* is one of the most impressive documentaries ever made, but the debate over its political significance continues. Whether or not Riefenstahl was a Nazi propagandist as well as a great artist is a question we can answer for ourselves now that the book has been republished (in 1988) and copies of the original film are widely available on college campuses.

Pierre de Coubertin, founder of the modern Olympic Games. *Avery Brundage Collection, University of Illinois at Urbana-Champaign.*

Athens, 1896. Spiridon Louys (Greece) wins the marathon. *Corbis Images.*

Stockholm, 1912. Jim Thorpe (USA) in the long jump. *International Olympic Committee.*

Amsterdam, 1928. Ville Ritola (Finland), Paavo Nurmi (Finland), and Edvin
Wide (Sweden) in the 10,000 meters. *Ronald Smith Collection.*

Coubertin's successors: Comte Henri de Baillet-Latour (Belgium), Avery Brundage (USA), and Sigfrid Edstrøm (Sweden). *Avery Brundage Collection, University of Illinois at Urbana-Champaign.*

Los Angeles, 1932. Mildred "Babe" Didrikson (USA) in the javelin throw. *Ronald Smith Collection.*

Los Angeles, 1932. Eleanor Holm (USA), swimmer. *Author's collection.*

Berlin, 1936. Jesse Owens (USA) at the start of the 200 meters. *Author's collection.*

London, 1948. Emil Zatopek (Czechoslovakia) winning the 10,000 meters. *International Olympic Committee.*

5

Destruction and Recovery

After the intense controversy over the Nazi Olympics, one might have expected the International Olympic Committee to be wary about political ramifications when choosing the site of subsequent Olympics. But the members seemed oblivious to any possible problem. At its meeting in Berlin, the IOC chose Tokyo to host the games in 1940, despite the fact that the Japanese had aroused widespread international concern when they seized Manchuria in 1931. The vote was 36-27. That the Japanese offered to subsidize visiting teams was doubtless an inducement to the majority. There is no evidence that the minority who voted against Tokyo was motivated by any concern about Japan's aggressive foreign policy. Japan's subsequent invasion of China, in 1937, made little difference to the IOC. In the eyes of the committee, the peaceful diffusion of Olympism to Asian shores was far more important than the ruthless expansion of the Japanese empire. A. C. Gilbert, a former Olympic athlete (1908) and a member of the American Olympic Association, felt differently. He wrote to Avery Brundage and urged that the games be postponed. Brundage's reply was characteristic of his thinking: he acknowledged that "it is difficult to keep the public clear on the point that politics have no part in the Olympic movement," but he nonetheless insisted that the games should occur exactly as scheduled. The IOC also ignored protests from China's IOC member, C. T. Wang.

Pressure mounted, however, and on February 11, 1938, delegates to the Empire Games Federation, meeting in Sydney, Australia, voted to boycott the 1940 Olympics if Japan were still at war. Two months later, during the IOC's Cairo session, the Amateur Athletic Association of Great Britain passed a similar resolution. Brundage responded with an irritable dismissal: "Why do the athletes meddle with politics—have they no foreign office?" When William J. Bingham of Harvard University resigned in protest from the American Olympic Association, reporters asked Brundage to comment on Bingham's resignation. He gave them his invariable answer: "The work of the committee will go on just the same." The potentially explosive controversy was defused in July 1938 when the Japanese themselves decided that the games were a costly distraction from the more important business of military conquest. The government renounced the games and the Japanese members of the IOC—Prince Tesato Tokugawa and Count Michimasa Soyeshima—had to acquiesce. "There is nothing to do," explained the latter to his colleagues, "but to say we can't help it." He then resigned from the IOC.

The committee was not caught wholly unprepared, as contingency plans had already been made to transfer the games to Finland. In a confidential meeting that had taken place on April 18 during the Cairo session, IOC member Ernst Krogius had offered Helsinki as a substitute site and the committee was now happy to accept the offer. Led by Krogius and J. W. Rangell, the Finns went quickly to work. The organizing committee was formed on August 18. Norway's Thomas Fearnley offered Oslo as a site for the winter games, which had been scheduled for Sapporo, but when the IOC met in London in June 1939, the nod went to Garmisch-Partenkirchen. The unanimous vote to return to Germany was proof positive that the IOC had no qualms whatsoever about the Nazi Olympics of 1936.

Those who were determined to stage the games, come what may, were soon faced with another obstacle. On September 1, 1939, less than a year before the games of the Twelfth Olympiad were to be celebrated, Germany invaded Poland. While Brundage admitted that World War II was "the suicide of a culture," he nonetheless clung to the illusion that the games might be saved. Sigfrid Edström reported that he, Karl Ritter von Halt, and Italy's Count Alberto Bonacossa were all "keen on having the games." As late as September 4, three days after Hitler's invasion of Poland, the Finns reported optimistically that they were ready to go forward with "undiminished energy." The definitive end to these illusory hopes came when Germany withdrew its invitation to host the winter games at Garmisch-Partenkirchen and the Soviet Union invaded Finland (on November 30).

Brundage's response to World War II was to busy himself with abortive plans for the Pan-American Games (which eventually took place in 1951). Other influential members of the IOC determined to keep their lines of communication open and to lay plans for the resumption of the games once the madness of war had passed. Since Belgium was occupied by German troops, Comte Henri de Baillet-Latour was less free than Edström and Brundage to tend the Olympic flame. In fact, Baillet-Latour's virtual captivity made him acutely aware of very real threats to the future of the Olympic movement. During the winter of 1940–41, Diem, von Halt, and Reichssportführer Hans von Tschammer und Osten visited Baillet-Latour and explained to him that Hitler had grandiose plans for a new order in postwar sports. Pierre de Coubertin's dream was to be transformed, literally, into the Nazi Olympics. Conferring with his favorite architect, Albert Speer, Hitler dreamed of a *"deutsches Stadion"* in Nürnberg where the Olympic Games would have their home—"for all time." This stadium, which was supposed to seat 450,000 spectators, was never built.

Baillet-Latour, politically helpless in any event, died of a stroke on January 6, 1942, his end doubtless hastened by the trauma of war. At this point, Diem appeared at the headquarters in Lausanne and attempted to seize control of the Olympic movement. But he was foiled by Madame Lydia Zanchi, who had been the IOC secretary since 1927. "I hid the most important documents in the cellar," she told John Lucas in 1960, "and convinced the community that Diem was a spy. I alerted Mr. Edstrøm of Sweden." Edstrøm, as IOC vice-president, took over the leadership of the menaced committee and left to Diem the publication of the *Olympische Rundschau.*

A cosmopolitan industrial engineer with an American wife, Edstrøm was gruff, opinionated, and effective. He had been the chief organizer of the 1912 Olympics in Stockholm and had used the occasion to found the International Amateur Athletic Federation. He was elected to the IOC in 1920, the same year that he took the lead in founding Sweden's National Olympic Committee. Thanks to Sweden's wartime neutrality, Edstrøm was much more able than Baillet-Latour to play the role of Olympic trustee. He was also, by temperament, an activist. In November 1944, even before the war was over, Edstrøm managed to cross the Atlantic to New York, where Brundage met him. Since Edstrøm was then seventy-four years old, he was worried about continuity within the IOC if anything should happen to him. He suggested in a circular letter to the other members that Brundage become second vice-president (and his potential successor). The majority agreed.

Edstrøm, Brundage, and Britain's Lord Aberdare were the only members able to attend the executive board's first postwar meeting in London (August 21-24, 1945). Aberdare had survived the dark days of the battle of Britain, but he had lost his optimism. Did they really want to resume the games as if the horrors of World War II had never occurred? Edstrøm and Brundage persuaded him that the games were more necessary than ever. A mail ballot of the membership resulted in the choice of London as the site of the first postwar games. The winter games went to St. Moritz in Switzerland.

At the first postwar session of the entire IOC, in Lausanne in the fall of 1946, Acting President Edstrøm was elected president by acclamation and Brundage moved up to the position of first vice-president, apparently without opposition. Acknowledging the Chicagoan's passionate concern for amateurism, his colleagues put him on a committee to study the question (along with R. W. Seeldrayers of Belgium, Bo Eklund of Sweden, and Gaston Mullegg of Switzerland). A dispute with the Fédération Internationale de Ski that had dragged on for a decade was finally resolved when the IOC agreed to accept as amateurs all ski instructors who had stopped teaching by October 1, 1947. The FIS, in turn, promised not to send professionals to the Olympic Games. The affair was "happily liquidated" (at least until 1951, when the FIS demanded the right to "deprofessionalize" ski instructors ninety days before the games).

The Lausanne session had to deal with the perennial question of the Olympic program, which many members felt, even then, had expanded to an absurd degree. Coubertin had originally eschewed choice and rather naively announced that the IOC was "not competent to judge that one sport is preferable to another." The Olympic Games were to include "all sports," but a moment's thought should have brought the realization that a program including all sports would be a practical impossibility. From 1894 to the present day, the IOC has had to choose among sports and denominate those that are Olympic and those that are not. The debates of 1946 were especially irksome because a decade had passed since the previous games and the advocates of the excluded sports were now ravenous for a share of the Olympic feast. The IOC considered and then rejected the petitions for archery, baseball, gliding, handball, polo, roller-skating, table tennis, and volleyball. (Of these sports, volleyball was accepted in 1964, archery and team handball in 1972. The attempt to balance the desire for universality against the fears of programmatic "gigantism" has continued to occupy the IOC. Tedious as these disputes are to the happy throng whose favorite sport has already ascended the slopes of Olympus, the minutes of the IOC sessions will continue to record them. The day is yet to come when the devotees of frisbee and hang gliding make their case.)

Not all questions were resolved in an aura of sweetness and light. Although the members of the committee liked to think of themselves as delegates *from* the IOC *to* their respective homelands, that is, as men above and beyond the limitations of nationalism, it was impossible to forget that their respective homelands had been at war. For delegates whose countries had been ravaged by German and Italian conquest and occupation, the presence on the committee of former Nazis and

Fascists was an intolerable outrage. Von Halt, for instance, had been a member of the Nazi party and had occupied an influential position as head of the Deutsche Bank. Upon the death of von Tschammer und Osten, von Halt had become Nazi Germany's second (and last) *Reichssportführer*. P. W. Scharroo of Holland and Albert Mayer of Switzerland were among those who pointed out that von Halt had also been a storm trooper; indeed, he was a *Sturm-Abteilung-Gruppen-führer*. The other German member, Adolf Friedrich zu Mecklenburg, was less blackly tarred by the Nazi brush, but he had been president of the Auslands-Presse-Klub (Foreign Press Club) and had worked closely with Propaganda Minister Josef Goebbels. All three of the Italian members—Count Alberto Bonacossa, Count Paolo Thaon di Revel, and General Giorgio Vaccaro—had been members of Italy's Fascisti. Comte Melchior de Polignac of France spoke up for his accused colleagues, but he himself was rather under a cloud. Suspected of treason, he had been imprisoned for six months by French authorities in Occupied Germany. Britain's Marquess of Exeter, a very influential IOC member, made an issue of Polignac's politics. Eventually, Edstrøm grew exasperated with these accusations, declaring: "All I ask for is justice!"

The controversy smoldered until the Vienna session in May 1951, when Scharroo and his Belgian colleague R. W. Seeldrayers demanded a vote on whether or not Mecklenburg and von Halt had the right to represent the newly established Federal Republic of Germany. Was it not appropriate that a new Germany be represented by new men untainted by fascism? Brundage replied by defending von Halt as a "perfect gentleman," which was scarcely the issue, and Edstrøm refused to put the matter to a vote despite protests from a number of members including Prince Axel of Denmark, General Pahud de Mortanges of Holland, Baron de Trannoy of Belgium, Olaf Ditlev-Simonsen of Norway, and Jerzy Loth of Poland, all of whose homelands had been occupied by German forces during World War II. Tempers flared until Edstrøm played his trump card: he informed the committee that Mecklenburg and von Halt were actually present in Vienna, waiting to join their colleagues. Even as Seeldrayers protested this patently unfair attempt to confront the committee with a fait accompli, Edstrøm stopped the debate with the peremptory announcement, "These are old friends whom we receive today."

The determination to forgive and forget extended to the national Olympic committee formed by the newly established Federal Republic of Germany. This committee, of which von Halt became the president, included many men—like Carl Diem, Peco Bauwens, and Guido von Mengden—who had collaborated with the Nazi regime. However, the

German National Olympic Committee was accepted without any embarrassing questions about its members' political pasts. After all, they were "old friends." (In fairness, it must be acknowledged that Diem had never joined the National Socialist party and that his postwar opinions were far less chauvinistic than his prewar views—which had been extreme.)

In another aspect of this question, the IOC carried to absurdity its stubborn and politically insensitive defense of its prerogatives. Although the committee had docilely acquiesced in 1938 when the Nazi regime ordered Lewald to resign from the committee and replaced him with General Walter von Reichenau (who was then killed in the war), the members now inconsistently refused to accede to the request of Italy's national Olympic committee that it be allowed to replace the notorious General Vaccaro, whose commitment to fascism had become a postwar embarrassment. This particular problem solved itself when Vaccaro ceased to attend IOC sessions and was eventually judged to have resigned, but the committee's policies were clear: public disagreement, like that voiced by Ernest Lee Jahncke, was intolerable, but a commitment to fascism was no bar to IOC membership. In dealing with this issue, the International Olympic Committee failed morally.

Although Japan's IOC members were less repugnant than General Vaccaro, there was some postwar resentment against Japan as well. The Japanese question arose when Brundage nominated Royotaro Azuma to be the third Japanese member. The Marquess of Exeter opposed the move and suggested that election of a third member might be construed as approval of Japanese aggression during World War II. Once again, Edstrøm used his authority to urge inclusion of members representing the defeated powers. He invited Azuma to come to Copenhagen for the forty-fifth session of the IOC (in 1950), and he managed to secure a recommendation for Azuma from none other than General Douglas MacArthur, commander of the U.S. Army of Occupation. The controversy was resolved when M. Nagai resigned for reasons of health and Azuma replaced him as Japan's second member.

Turning from bitter squabbles over war guilt, the committee renewed its prewar campaign to promote Olympism by sponsoring regional games. Whether these games enhanced or diminished the cause of international good will is debatable. The most immediately troublesome of them was the Jeux Mediterranées proposed by Egypt's Mohammed Taher Pacha in 1948. When Taher Pacha brought the matter before his IOC colleagues, he assured them that "every country bordering on the Mediterranean would be included in the games." By the time the first of the celebrations took place, in Alexandria in 1951, there was a new configuration in Middle Eastern politics. The state of Israel was in place, ringed by hostile Arab neighbors who had attempted to destroy the unwelcome newcomer and who bitterly resented its continued existence. The Israelis had formed a national Olympic committee and had requested official recognition for it, but for reasons that are not entirely clear, the IOC had delayed. The first Mediterranean Games took place without Israeli participation.

Long before the second festival, in 1955, the Israeli National Olympic Committee had been recognized. The 1955 games were scheduled for Barcelona (despite the fact that Spain was then a fascist dictatorship ruled by the unsavory Generalissimo Francisco Franco). The Spanish hosts invited Israel to participate in the games, but they had underestimated the intensity of Arab hostility toward Israel. A boycott was threatened and the invitation was withdrawn. The Israeli Olympic Committee protested to the IOC, quite correctly, that the rules for the patronage of regional games had been violated. IOC Chancellor Otto Mayer supported the Israelis, but Brundage—who had become president of the IOC in 1952—was not ready to enforce the rules: "We can not become involved in a matter of this kind. Those who organize Regional Games are quite within their rights to include or exclude any country." He advised the executive board on February 16, 1955, that the "IOC should not become involved in the administration of events other than the Olympic Games."

Brundage's bitter memories of the boycott campaign of 1933–36 undoubtedly contributed to this uncharacteristic refusal to stand up for the principle of universalism. The Marquess of Exeter, who was nearly as influential as Brundage, agreed with him. A few months later, however, Brundage altered his views, acknowledging that the exclusion of Israel was politically motivated and a clear infraction of the terms of IOC sponsorship. "As a matter of principle," he wrote, "we had to oppose them in 1936 and we may have to support them in 1955." That Brundage was unable to distinguish between American Jews in 1936 and Israelis in 1955 was, unfortunately, typical.

IOC support for Israel's participation in the Mediterranean Games was no more effective than United Nations' support for Israel's right to coexist with her Arab neighbors. Israel was excluded from the games in Barcelona and was not likely to be welcomed at the next celebration, scheduled for Beirut in 1959. At this point, Brundage returned to his original position on Israeli participation. Forgetting that he had wanted the 1940 Olympic Games to take place despite the fact that the host nation—Japan—was at war, he now asked how the Lebanese hosts could be expected to invite an Israeli team "when there is practically a state of war between the latter country and all its neighbors." In fact, Brundage seemed ready to forget all his previous principles: "I. cannot understand why anyone wants to go where he is not wanted." In the meantime, the Marquess of Exeter, who had succeeded Edstrøm as president of the International Amateur Athletic Federation, had come around to the Israeli side. For this he was criticized by Lebanon's IOC member, Gabriel Gemayel, who observed that the Marquess had been for exclusion of *his* enemies in 1948, when German athletes were not invited to London for the first postwar Olympics.

Eventually, an absurd compromise was struck: the Third Mediterranean Games took place without the track-and-field events that had been the highpoint of the previous celebrations, but there were simultaneous Jeux Libanais that consisted—how unexpectedly!—of precisely the track-and-field events that were not supposed to be a part of these Mediterranean Games. Needless to say, Israel was not invited to these games within the games. Accepting the threadbare subterfuge, Brundage offered his sympathy to Gemayel, apologized for the IAAF's stand, and flew to Beirut for the Mediterranean Games and the Jeux Libanais.

By late 1962, Brundage had rejoined the Marquess of Exeter in the opinion that regional games must include all states in the region if they were to be sponsored by the International Olympic Committee. However, the Italian hosts of the Fourth Mediterranean Games, held in Naples, refused to invite an Israeli team, and there was no attempt to impose sanctions against the Italian National Olympic Committee. Finally, on February 7, 1963, the executive board of the IOC announced that free access to all states in the region was an absolute precondition of IOC patronage. Consequently, the IOC denied its patronage to the Fifth Mediterranean Games, which were held in Tunis in 1967, to which Israel again was not invited. The IOC, which had more or less successfully maintained the ideal of universality apropos of the Olympic Games themselves, was unable or unwilling to impose that ideal on regional games. It is difficult not to believe that anti-Semitism, or at the very least anti-Zionism, obscured the committee's vision from 1948 to 1967.

These political wrangles loom large in the historical record, and quite properly so, but the sessions of the postwar IOC were actually dominated by other questions. Many hours of tedious debate were required to settle jurisdictional questions like the one raised when the Amateur Athletic Union of the United States, which controlled ice hockey, expelled a number of professional hockey players. The ousted players formed the American Hockey Association and applied to the Ligue Internationale de Hockey sur Glace for official recognition. Turned down by the LIHG, the professionals then joined with players from Canada and Great Britain to form the rival International Ice Hockey Association (1940). Both the AAU and the AHA sent teams to compete in the 1948 Winter Olympics at St. Moritz. The IOC endorsed the AAU's entry and ordered the expulsion of the AHA's team of professionals, but the Swiss organizers backed the latter, whom they concluded were more likely than mere amateurs to draw large crowds of hockey fans.

LIHG President Fritz Kraatz was Swiss, and he was inclined to support his countrymen on the organizing committee. In fact, he threatened to cancel the entire hockey tournament if the IOC sided with the AAU and the U.S. Olympic Committee. Brundage wanted to call him on this, but Edstrøm looked at the ledgers rather than at Article 26 of the Olympic Charter. "If there is no Ice Hockey," he told Brundage, "there can be no Winter Games." Brundage brushed aside economic arguments and stuck to his guns: "This is a battle in which the future of sport and the Olympic Games are at stake." But his was a lost cause. To the disgust of the believers in amateurism, the professionals were allowed to compete "unofficially." They placed fourth and were given medals and certificates by the grateful Swiss—over the protest of the IOC. The controversy over jurisdiction dragged on for years until a compromise was reached in the early fifties.

None of this mattered much to the average sports fan. The headlines went to the Canadian team, which won the gold medal, and to Richard "Dick" Button and Gretchen Fraser, the Americans who triumphed in figure skating and in skiing.

After the internal dissension caused by the disputes over amateurism, the trustees of Olympism turned with relief to the summer games of 1948. The London Olympics raised problems more severe than the amateur-professional imbroglio in St. Moritz. Switzerland was a prosperous place, unscarred by war, and the majority of the athletes at the 1948 Winter Games had come from countries that had not been World War II battlefields. The war had, however, left most of Europe in ruins. Many European athletes were "displaced persons" who had fled their homelands; few of them had had a decent opportunity to train. The *London Evening Standard* editorialized against a revival of the games because they seemed inappropriate at a time when much of Europe was on the verge of starvation. Should the gargantuan appetites of the athletes be sated while children went to bed hungry? "A people which has had its housing program and its food import cut, and which is preparing for a winter battle of survival, may be forgiven for thinking that a full year of expensive preparation for the reception of an army of foreign athletes verges on the border of the excessive," the paper declared. Such objections were at least partly overcome when the teams brought their own food and contributed the surplus to British hospitals. Once the athletes reached London, they were housed in army barracks and other makeshift accommodations.

One result of European devastation was that the Americans dominated the games with relative ease. In men's track and field, for instance, the Americans ran off with ten gold medals (and the Swedes, who had been neutral during the war, won six). Harrison Dillard, the world's best 110-meter hurdler, failed to make the American team in that event and then surprised everyone with a first-place finish in the 100-meter sprint. He won a second gold medal as part of the 4 × 100–meter relay team. Czechoslovakia's Emil Zatopek finished second in the 5,000-meter race and then won the 10,000-meter race—the first of several victories memorable for Zatopek's look of triumphant agony. Belgium's Étienne Gailly was the first marathon runner to reach the stadium; too exhausted to do anything but stagger forward, he was overtaken by an Argentine runner, Delfo Cabrera.

American weight lifters, led by heavyweight John Davis, won four of the six weight classes (the Egyptians won the other two). Stanley Stancyzk deserves to be remembered not only for his victory in the 82.5-kilo class but also for his exemplary honesty. After the judges credited him with a world record in the snatch, he explained that his knee had grazed the floor. The lift was invalidated.

The most publicized athlete at the games may have been someone hitherto quite unknown. As an eighteen-year-old, Holland's Francina Blankers-Koen had participated in the 1936 Games and had tied for sixth in the high jump. Now, twelve years, one husband, and two children later, she earned gold medals in the 100-meter and 200-meter sprints, the 80-meter hurdles, and the 400-meter relay. She was unable to enter the long jump or the high jump, in both of which she held the world record, because Olympic rules limited the number of events in which an individual could compete. Her exploits led the *Boston Globe*'s Jerry Nason to what many then thought were some reckless predictions. "Women athletes," he wrote, "are just coming into their own. It is only a matter of time when women will be high jumping six feet, broad jumping 23 feet and running 100 yards in 10 seconds." He was right. Brundage, whose opposition to women's sports has been greatly exaggerated, raved about Blankers-Koen in his unpublished memoirs: "A new type of woman [was] appearing—lithe, supple, physically disciplined, strong, slender and efficient, like the Goddesses of ancient Greece."

On this as on every other Olympic question from 1936 to 1972, Brundage's opinions mattered. Since 1934, when he and Edstrøm became close friends, the older man had sponsored the younger one for various administrative positions. In 1944, eight years after Brundage's election to the IOC, Edstrøm nominated Brundage for second vice-president. Two years later, the Chicagoan rose to be first vice-president. Three years after that, Edstrøm told John Jewett Garland, who had inherited his father's IOC seat, that he wanted Brundage as his successor. For this goal to be reached, the European members of the IOC had to be persuaded that an American was worthy of the office once held by Pierre de Coubertin.

There was certainly no doubt about Brundage's dedication to Olympism. The child of a broken home, a victim of genteel poverty, Brundage had worked his way through the University of Illinois, taken a degree in engineering, returned to Chicago, and made a fortune in the construction business. Naively shocked at the widespread dishonesty of the industry in a city where bribery and kickbacks were often the only way to win a government contract, Brundage idealized sports as a realm in which ability counted more than political influence. He was especially drawn to track-and-field events "because they are a demonstration of individual skill and supremacy. The track athlete stands or falls on his own merits." At the university, he had been the star of the track-and-field team. Selected three years after his graduation for the 1912 Olympic squad, he competed in the decathlon and the pentathlon, both of which were won by Jim Thorpe. Back home, Brundage was a three-time winner of the national all-around championships.

Despite his losses to Thorpe, Brundage returned from Stockholm inspired by the ideals of Olympism. In his unpublished "Olympic Story," he recalled his "conversion, along with many others, to Coubertin's religion." He became active in the Amateur Athletic Union and quickly rose to positions of leadership in the AAU and then in the American Olympic Association. By the mid-1930s, he was unquestionably the most important sports administrator in the United States. His speeches were full of repetitive references to amateurism, fair play, and good sportsmanship. For him as for Coubertin, Olympism became a secular religion. No wonder, then, that he had fought ferociously against the apostates who wanted to boycott the 1936 Games.

As we have seen, that battle earned Brundage his seat on the International Olympic Committee. His subsequent commitment of time and energy (and money) to Olympic affairs won him the respect of his colleagues. As early as 1949, Edstrøm let it be known that the Chicagoan was his personal choice to succeed him. When Edstrøm's term as president ended in 1952, Brundage was the official choice of the executive board. To achieve his ambition, however, Brundage had to overcome a combination of snobbery and anti-Americanism. Prince

Axel of Denmark campaigned vigorously for the Marquess of Exeter. The Englishman had the support of the members from the Soviet bloc as well as those from the British Commonwealth, but Brundage was strongly backed by the Latin Americans, whom he had nominated for the IOC and with whom he had collaborated in founding the Pan-American Games, and he was also popular with members from Western Europe. Although the election was by secret ballot, Garland concluded that the two men were tied after sixteen rounds. After twenty-five rounds, the final tally was 30-17-2 in Brundage's favor. Armand Massard of France was then elected vice-president, not as an affront to the Marquess but rather in an effort to avoid offense to the IOC's many French speakers. The twenty years of the Brundage Era would be characterized by a constant struggle to defend Olympic ideals against politics (i.e., governmental interference) and professionalism (i.e., cash payments to athletes).

6

In the Shadow of the Cold War

Unaware of squabbles within the International Olympic Committee, unbothered by the exclusion of German and Japanese athletes, most sports fans seem to have been delighted by the postwar resumption of the games. Americans were certainly gratified by American domination of track and field and of most other events. Although few fans or sportswriters showed much interest in them, the problems that still faced the IOC after the successful London Games were immense.

A disproportionate amount of time had always been devoted to the "amateur question." Brundage's rise to the vice-presidency and then to the presidency guaranteed that the IOC would continue to embroil itself in frustrating controversies over eligibility. The ice hockey quarrel at St. Moritz was one of many. At its forty-fourth session in Rome in the spring of 1949, the IOC was confronted with the awful truth that a Swedish cavalryman named Gehnall Persson, a sergeant, had been made a lieutenant by royal decree so that he could ride the equestrian events as an officer. (By Alice-in-Wonderland definition, officers who spent their lives in the saddle were amateurs but an ordinary soldier was a professional.) After the London Games, the temporary lieutenant had been demoted to his previous rank. The IOC asked that this scandal be dealt with by the equestrian federation, and in due time that federation informed the committee that the entire Swedish team was disqualified. In 1952 the Fédération Internationale des Sports Equestres revised its rules to allow enlisted cavalrymen to ride as amateurs. Sergeant Persson, unpromoted, won a gold medal.

There were more momentous questions than the sergeant's rank to be settled. The postwar world was very different from the one destroyed by the dictators. Germany and Korea were both divided into mutually hostile fragments. The Soviet Union, which had always spurned the "bourgeois" Olympic Games, had extended its control into the very heart of Europe. China was convulsed by a civil war that was soon to end with that nation's division into a Communist state on the mainland and a non-Communist state on the island of Taiwan. In addition, the worldwide process of decolonization was about to begin. While it was obvious that the IOC had little if any influence on the course of world politics, it was equally obvious that the IOC had to deal with the political consequences of World War II and the cold war that followed.

The easiest question for the International Olympic Committee to answer was that raised by the Soviet Union's extension of its power throughout Eastern Europe. Poland, Czechoslovakia, Hungary, Yugoslavia, Romania, and Bulgaria had all participated in prewar Olympics. They all had recognized national Olympic committees, many of whose members had served before the war. There was no disposition in the IOC, which then included several representatives from these Eastern European nations, to rock the boat. This much is clear from a letter IOC President Sigfrid Edström sent to IOC Vice-President Avery Brundage on September 3, 1947: "There are three Olympic Committees at present asking for recognition, Poland, Hungary and Yugoslavia. . . . The political influence in said countries is now communistic as a communistic minority has the political power in each country supported by Russia, but politics must not mix in with sports, therefore we cannot turn them down because the political influence in their country is communistic." Amenable to recognition of these national committees and the admission to the games of athletes from the satellite nations of Eastern Europe, Edström drew the line at electing Communists to the IOC. "The greatest trouble," he wrote, "will be to find men that we can have present in the IOC. I do not feel inclined to go so far as to admit communists there."

Recognition of a Soviet National Olympic Committee was a more complicated process because the Soviet Union, unlike Poland, Hungary, and so on, had never had such a committee. Although czarist Russia had participated in the games, the Soviet Union had withdrawn from them and had sponsored a rival organization, the Red Sport International, which had held international games for members of workers' sports organizations. However, during and immediately after World War II there were signs that the Soviet Union was ready to break out of its self-imposed isolation and to rejoin the world of "bourgeois" sports. After all, Stalin had cooperated with the United States and Great Britain to defeat the Axis powers, and he had committed the Soviet Union to membership in the United Nations. It was not hard to guess that participation in the Olympic Games was also on his agenda.

Despite the fact that Edstrøm, Brundage, the Marquess of Exeter, and all the other influential members of the IOC were vehemently anti-Communist, their public commitment to the universalistic ideal of Olympism was stronger than their private hostility toward communism. On March 27, 1944, Brundage wrote to Britain's Lord Aberdare, "I agree with you that the IOC should be represented in Russia which should also be a member of the International Sport Federations." To Frederick W. Rubien of the United States Amateur Sports Federation (formerly the American Olympic Association), Brundage wrote, "If the Russians would agree to live up to the rules and regulations of the Federations and the International Olympic Committee there is no reason why they should not be members."

Since track-and-field sports have always formed the core of the Olympic Games, Edstrøm took the initiative and invited the Russians to join the International Amateur Athletic Federation. He wrote to Aleksei Romanov in September 1945 and again in November but did not receive an answer. In a letter to Brundage, Edstrøm gave vent to his frustration: "I have time upon time sent invitations to Mr. Romanoff, but he does not answer. Perhaps he does not care, but probably he does not know that one should answer a letter."

Then, immediately before the start of the European track-and-field championships at Oslo in August 1946, the Russians arrived without notice. When Brundage deplaned in Oslo, the Norwegians rushed up to him with the news: "The Russians are here. What shall we do?" IAAF regulations clearly ruled out their participation because the Soviet Union was not yet a member of the IAAF, but Brundage—normally a fanatic about the rules—decided to set aside the technicalities and to welcome the thirty-five Russian athletes. Afterward, Edstrøm made it clear to the Soviets that this had been an exceptional good-will gesture. He reminded them sternly that membership in the IAAF was a prerequisite to participation in the Olympics.

There were a number of obstacles that the Soviets themselves placed in the path of their recognition by the International Amateur Athletic Federation. They demanded first that Russian be made an official language of the IAAF, second that they be allotted a seat on the executive committee, and third that Spain, then a fascist dictatorship, be ousted from the organization. (These were similar to the demands then addressed by the Soviet Union to the United Nations.) The IAAF rejected all three demands and the Soviets meekly accepted the rebuff. Recognition followed promptly.

By the end of 1947, the Soviet Union had joined a number of other international sports federations and the question of Olympic participation was on the table. Here, too, there were obstacles. Olympic rules required that all athletes be certified as amateurs by their national Olympic committees, but, as Edstrøm confided to Brundage in a letter dated November 14, 1950, "We must face the fact that many of them [Soviet athletes] are professionals." Since *Pravda* routinely announced the cash prizes and awards given to successful Soviet athletes, it was not exactly a secret that these men and women were indeed "state amateurs." As such, they were unquestionably ineligible to compete in the Olympics. Olympic rules also stipulate that every national Olympic committee must be independent of the government, and the IOC had fought a number of battles with Latin American governments who had attempted to control their national committees. Neither Edstrøm nor Brundage had any illusions about the political independence of the Soviet National Olympic Committee.

To follow Olympic rules meant to bar the Soviet Union until such time as it mended its errant ways. On the other hand, to follow Olympic rules also meant to frustrate the Western athletes who were, as Edstrøm noted, "crazy to have the Russian athletes participate." The solution was for the IOC collectively to close its eyes and pretend that the Russian athletes were amateurs and that the national Olympic committee never gave a thought to the people in the Kremlin.

When the Soviets finally did apply for recognition by the IOC, they repeated their familiar demands for acceptance of the Russian language, for a seat on the executive board, and for the expulsion of Spain. The committee rejected all three demands and, once again, the Russians swallowed their pride and resubmitted their petition for membership. Brundage was astonished: "For the first time the Russians made no demands nor were there any reservations in the application. They simply stated that they had examined our rules and regulations and accepted them." At Vienna, in May 1951, the IOC voted to accept the Soviet Union, whose national Olympic committee had been established only a few weeks earlier. There were three abstentions but not a single negative ballot.

Flexibility remained the watchword even after the Soviets had been admitted into the IOC. The committee had always been jealous of its right to select its own members, but it was not Josef Stalin's custom to allow other parties to make decisions for him. The Soviet National Olympic Committee announced that Konstantin Andrianov was the new IOC member, and the obedient Andrianov journeyed to Vienna to take his place on the committee. Edstrøm was outraged. He ordered the Russian to leave the room, which he did. The question then arose,

Who among the members knew anyone else to elect to membership? Since the titled aristocrats and wealthy businessmen who constituted the IOC had no one to suggest, they elected Andrianov. The fact that he spoke neither French nor English, and never made any effort to learn either of these official Olympic languages, was regrettable, but the IOC bent its rules and allowed him to appear with his interpreter. In 1952, Andrianov was joined by a second Russian member, Aleksei Romanov.

On another question the IOC demonstrated a kind of pro-Soviet rigidity. As Russian armies had moved westward in 1944 and 1945, millions of people had fled their homes. Others took flight after the war to escape the regimes that Soviet power imposed on Eastern Europe. Among the displaced persons were many world-class athletes who formed the Union des Sportifs Libres de l'Est de l'Europe and appealed to the International Olympic Committee to take its own charter seriously and allow them to compete as individuals. IOC Chancellor Otto Mayer replied that it was "impossible . . . to agree to the exiled athletes' request to participate." As individuals, they fit nowhere in the structure of national Olympic committees and international sports federations comprised of national sports federations. Mayer did not stress the fact that acceptance of the emigré athletes would have angered the Soviet Union and its allies.

IOC sessions were never the same after Andrianov and Romanov took their seats. For the next forty years, until the breakup of the Warsaw Pact in 1989-90, the members from Eastern Europe took their cues from the Russian members. Armand Massard of France noted sarcastically that whenever Andrianov or Romanov made a proposal they were backed by all the other Communists, who rose, one after the other, to parrot their approval and assent. The IOC was politicized in a new sense. Politics, narrowly defined, was avoided whenever possible—for example, few members were disposed to rise and condemn Stalin's tyranny or Eisenhower's commitment to a nuclear deterrent. Still, differences between the two opposed ideologies caused recurrent friction. In a circular issued on June 24, 1953, for instance, Brundage noted that Polish boxers trained in special camps for four months at a time, and he commented that "very few people can afford a preparation like that of the Polish boxers." Were these men really amateurs? The Soviet press was impelled to attribute Brundage's questions to "the ideology of imperialism."

Political divisions within the organization ordinarily took a more subtle form. Led by the Russians, members from Eastern Europe campaigned incessantly for a democratization of the IOC itself. At the forty-ninth session at Mexico City in the spring of 1953, Andrianov was nominated for the executive board. His chances seemed good until Vladimir Stoytchev of Bulgaria made a speech asserting Andrianov's right to the seat as a representative of the "peoples' democracies." At that point, J. Ferreira Santos of Brazil took umbrage. Andrianov was defeated and the seat went to Miguel Moenck, a member from pre-revolutionary Cuba.

In 1955, Andrianov observed that some nations had three of their citizens in the IOC while scores of others had none. He asked for automatic IOC representation for every national Olympic committee and every international sports federation recognized by the IOC. He suggested that a second vice-president be elected and proposed expanding the executive board from seven to nine members to provide seats for IOC members from Communist and nonaligned countries. There was resistance to an enlargement of the executive board (which had only the year before been increased from six members to seven), but the proposal to add a second vice-president was accepted and the Marquess of Exeter was elected.

Other concessions followed. The IOC executive board had begun to meet with representatives of the national Olympic committees at the forty-seventh session in Oslo (February 1952), and it was tacitly understood that these meetings should continue and that there should be real dialogue. In 1956, a Communist was elected to the executive board (Bulgaria's Stoytchev). Little by little, the outsiders gained influence. After Stoytchev's election, Andrianov once again offered a comprehensive plan to "democratize" the entire Olympic movement. Richard Espy's summary is succinct: ". . . the Soviet committee proposed enlarging the IOC to include not only the present members but also presidents of national Olympic committees and international federations. These two organizations would be given the right to replace their own members on the IOC. . . . IOC finances would come from annual fees of national Olympic committees and international federations." Needless to say, Brundage and Exeter opposed the reorganization scheme and the majority of the entire committee voted to reject it. Andrianov did, however, eventually become one of the IOC's vice-presidents and the geographical distribution of membership did gradually change. Although European and North American members continued to dominate the organization, more and more Asian, African, and Latin American members were elected (see table 1). Over time, their voices were heard.

Even before the "Russian question" had been answered, the committee had begun to wrestle with the "Chinese question." A Chinese National Olympic Committee had been sending Chinese athletes to participate in prewar games (without much athletic success), and there

Table 1. IOC Membership

	1954	1977	1990
Africa	2	13	14
America	16	18	19
Asia	10	13	18
Europe	39	38	38
Oceania	3	3	4
TOTAL	70	85	92

were also three Chinese members of the IOC. However, when Nationalist China collapsed in 1949, none of the three IOC members accompanied Chiang Kai-shek on his flight to Taiwan. C. T. Wang lived in British-ruled Hong Kong, H. H. Kung resided in New York, and Tung Shou-yi had elected to stay in Beijing; the members of the national Olympic committee were similarly scattered. Some of the international sports federations recognized the Nationalists on Taiwan (then known as Formosa); others recognized the Communists on the mainland. The question was, Who should represent China in the International Olympic Committee and who should send which athletes to the games?

Edstrøm's position wavered. In January 1952, he thought that both national Olympic committees should be recognized; in June he ruled that neither should be. The question came to a head on the eve of the 1952 Olympics. Edstrøm summoned Tung Shou-yi to Helsinki and was annoyed that the Chinese member, who had always spoken excellent English, was now accompanied by a mysterious "interpreter." Assuming, probably correctly, that Tung's ever-present companion was a political watchdog, Edstrøm ordered both of them to leave the room. On July 17, only two days before the games were to begin, the entire committee heard arguments from both claimants to represent the "real" China. The fact that a team from the People's Republic was already en route to Finland put additional pressure on the members to square the circle. The Nationalist and Communist representatives made their cases, and both of them angered Edstrøm by their introduction of blatantly political comments.

When the Chinese were done with their polemics, the IOC was hopelessly divided. Of the fifty-one members present, twenty-two wanted to exclude both teams and twenty-nine wanted to include both. François Pietri of France moved that neither national Olympic committee be recognized but that each be allowed to send athletes to compete in the events governed by the international federation that recognized their side of the dispute. This ingenious compromise, which allowed the Nationalists and the Communists to participate in different events (and never against one another), passed with thirty-three votes. Unfortunately, the compromise pleased neither party to the dispute. The Nationalists boycotted the games because the Communists were expected to be present, and the Communists arrived, forty-one strong, ten days after the games had begun. The result was that no Chinese athletes competed in Helsinki.

The IOC returned to the problem at its fiftieth session, at Athens in May 1954. The debates were always tense and often tempestuous. When Andrianov reported on the wonders of sport in the People's Republic of China, the head of the Nationalists' Olympic committee was incensed. He charged, not implausibly, that the Communists' Olympic committee was under military control. Andrianov's rejoinder was to label the Nationalist a "political leftover." A closely divided IOC voted 23-21 to recognize both national Olympic committees. Ironically, the vote would have been a tie if the two Chinese IOC members representing the Nationalists had been present.

In November 1954, both Chinas were invited to the 1956 Olympics in Melbourne. The Communists accepted on November 20, which led the Nationalists to reject the invitation. The Nationalists then changed their minds, which in turn led the Communists to change theirs and boycott the games. When the Nationalists arrived, they saw that someone—intentionally or accidentally—had raised the flag of the People's Republic of China. They tore it down.

From this low point, the situation deteriorated even further. Through most of the late fifties, Brundage and Tung Shou-yi, the IOC member for the People's Republic, exchanged insults. When Brundage insinuated that Tung's speeches at Melbourne in 1956 and at Sofia in 1957 had been political, the latter answered that it was Brundage, not he, who had introduced politics into the discussion. By the summer of 1958, the correspondence between the two men had degenerated to the point where Tung's letters became a litany of recrimination:

> I am most indignant at your letter dated June 1. Evading the questions I raised in my letter of April 23, you continued your mean practice of reversing right and wrong, wantonly slandered and threatened the Chinese Olympic Committee . . . and myself, and shamelessly [sic] tried to justify your reactionary acts. This fully reveals that you are a faithful menial of the U.S. imperialists bent on serving their plot of creating "two Chinas."
>
> A man like you, who are staining the Olympic spirit and violating the Olympic charter, has no qualifications whatsoever to be the IOC president. . . . I feel painful . . . that the IOC is today controlled by such

an imperialist like you and consequently the Olympic spirit has been grossly trampled upon.

Tung ended the letter by announcing his resignation from the IOC. Since the Chinese Communists were then in the process of withdrawing from *all* the international sports federations in which they had been accepted as members, it is obvious that Tung's displeasure was occasioned by something more than Brundage's "shamelessly" pointed barbs. The isolation of the People's Republic became complete as Chairman Mao led the Chinese into the self-destructive social convulsions known as The Great Cultural Revolution.

The voluntary departure of the Communists answered, for a time, the question of Chinese representation, but the IOC was unable to leave well enough alone. The Russian members demanded that the Nationalists on Taiwan be expelled from the Olympic movement, and the issue was debated at the fifty-fifth session, which began in Munich on May 23, 1959. The Marquess of Exeter suggested that the Nationalists be recognized but that they simultaneously discard the claim to represent all of China. The majority, by a vote of 48-7, decided to follow this course of action. The Nationalists on Taiwan were then informed that they would no longer be recognized as the representatives for the mainland and that they had to reapply for recognition under a more appropriate rubric. When they complied and asked for recognition as the Republic of China, they were rejected.

The public reaction in the United States was explosive. Brundage, who made matters worse by denying that the decision was "political in any sense of the word," was denounced as a Communist sympathizer. The Amateur Athletic Union condemned the IOC's action and demanded that the decision be rescinded. The United States Olympic Committee (the name finally adopted by the American Olympic Association) asked that the IOC recognize the Nationalists "under their rightful name—the Republic of China Olympic Committee." President Eisenhower and United Nations Ambassador Henry Cabot Lodge deplored the IOC's actions. Senator Thomas Dodd of Connecticut subpoenaed Brundage to appear before the judiciary committee's International Security Subcommittee, but Senator Thomas Hennings of Missouri persuaded Dodd that this was an overreaction. The IOC, reasoned Hennings, hadn't really threatened the survival of the United States. Brundage melodramatically described his plight as that of a man alone "confronting 175,000,000 misinformed people."

Meeting in Paris on October 2, 1959, the IOC executive board attempted to extinguish the firestorm of discontent. The board recognized the Nationalists' Olympic committee as the "Olympic Committee of the Republic of China," but the board also insisted that the

Nationalist team had to march behind a sign reading "Formosa." Predictably, the Nationalists protested, and the U.S. State Department joined them in condemnation of what it called "a politically discriminatory act designed in effect to exclude the free Chinese athletes from participation." Brundage responded blandly that the IOC "does not deal with Governments and does not propose to become involved in political controversies." At Rome a year later, the Nationalists did march behind the demeaning sign, but as they passed the presidential box the placard-bearer flashed a sign of his own: UNDER PROTEST.

The "German question" also engendered considerable acrimony but was solved more quickly than the Chinese puzzle. At the start of the cold war, the United States, Great Britain, and France merged their zones of occupation and sponsored the creation of the Federal Republic of Germany (on September 23, 1949). West Germany was barely one day old when its national Olympic committee was formed, on September 24. On August 29, 1950, the IOC executive board decided unanimously to recommend speedy recognition by the entire committee. The first opportunity for full recognition came in May 1951, when the IOC met in Vienna.

Meanwhile, the Soviet Union was gradually transforming its zone into what eventually became the self-styled German Democratic Republic. On April 22, 1951, two weeks before the IOC session in Vienna, the East Germans formed their own national Olympic committee and asked for recognition. This request was opposed by Konrad Adenauer's government in Bonn, which considered itself the sole legitimate German government. The IOC had three options: (1) to accept East Germany as a sovereign state and to recognize its national Olympic committee as well as that of West Germany; (2) to insist that West Germany was the only German state in existence and to consider its committee the only German national Olympic committee; (3) to ask that the two hostile states form a single national Olympic committee and field a single Olympic team. Although it should have been obvious that the third choice was the most blatantly political one, Brundage was delighted when the Marquess of Exeter and several other influential IOC members suggested it.

At the Vienna session, the IOC officially recognized the West German committee and requested that it be expanded to include representatives from East Germany. Since many West Germans obdurately referred to that part of the world as "the zone of Soviet Occupation," it was obvious that achieving unity was not going to be easy. The two national Olympic committees met in Hannover on May 17, 1951, but the ideological gulf was too great to be bridged. The East Germans, with one quarter of the population of the Federal Republic, demanded half the seats on the proposed reconstituted committee. Meeting in Lausanne only five days later, with Brundage present to urge unity, the negotiators agreed in principle to form a combined German team and to defer the question of a unified committee. When Kurt Edel and the other East Germans returned home, they were castigated by their political bosses and demoted. The agreement was renounced.

Negotiations dragged on for several years, during which the East German government in Potsdam reviled the International Olympic Committee as a conspiratorial gang of imperialist thugs. There was a notable fiasco in Copenhagen early in 1952 when East Germany's delegation was supposed to meet with Edstrøm, Brundage, and the West Germans. The Communists were late in arriving in Copenhagen and, once they had checked into their hotel, they refused to walk the 300 meters that separated their hotel from the other delegation's. The West German representatives waited in vain from 10:00 A.M. to 7:30 P.M., and then departed. Edstrøm, never known for his equanimity or patience, was furious. At 7:30 he banged his cane on the table and shouted, "Finish!" Memories of Copenhagen may have influenced the IOC when the East Germans later asked for recognition of their national Olympic committee, which they reconstituted on December 6, 1953. At the IOC's Athens session in May 1954, the East German request was denied by a vote of 31-14.

Eventually, the East Germans modified their rhetoric and mollified the IOC. Their quest for Olympic recognition was made easier in September 1955 when their state was officially denominated the German Democratic Republic and integrated into the Warsaw Pact (which had been formed in 1954). Another roadblock was removed when the East Germans bowed to Brundage's imperious demands and replaced the "Lausanne repudiators" with new men of a more diplomatic temperament. During the fifty-first IOC session in Paris in 1955, Brundage asked Heinz Schoebel, the publisher who was now head of the East German National Olympic Committee, "Are you or are you not a political organization?" Schoebel gave the expected hypocritical reply and the IOC granted its recognition by a vote of 27-7. The proviso, however, was that Germans from both states had to compete as a combined team, which they did. At the next IOC session, during the winter games at Cortina d'Ampezzo, Brundage boasted, "We have obtained in the field of sports what politicians have failed to achieve so far." In fact, it was to be another thirty-four years before the politicians were able to unite East and West Germany.

The IOC was able to enforce its will from 1956 through 1964, but the erection of the Berlin Wall, on August 11, 1961, made strained relationships even more difficult. Western governments retaliated with tightened visa restrictions that hampered the ability of the East Germans to participate in scientific conferences, international sports competitions, and a number of cultural activities. When the athletes of the German Democratic Republic were refused entry into France and the United States, there was little the IOC could do. Protests from Lausanne were politely rejected by Washington, London, and Paris. Fortunately, the 1964 and 1968 games were held in countries whose governments' visa policies were relatively flexible—at least for Olympic athletes.

The physical as well as ideological separation of East and West Germany intensified Potsdam's desire for an Olympic divorce from Bonn. On October 6, 1965, the IOC granted the German Democratic Republic the right to enter a separate team at Mexico City in 1968, but both teams were to fly a flag adorned with the Olympic rings, and they would have the same uniforms and the same anthem (the choral theme from Beethoven's Ninth Symphony). At its sixty-eighth session, in Mexico City, the IOC abandoned the impossible effort and voted 44-4 to extend full, complete, and unqualified acceptance of the national Olympic committee of the German Democratic Republic, with its own team, its own flag, its own anthem. When full German unification finally came in 1990, it occurred without the assistance of the International Olympic Committee.

The 1952 Winter Games at Oslo went smoothly. The Scandinavians took all but six of the twenty-four medals for men's skiing, while Andrea Lawrence of the United States won both the slalom and the giant slalom. The Norwegians dominated the speed-skating. America's Dick Button and Britain's Jeanette Altwegg were the individual winners in figure skating; Ria and Paul Falk of West Germany won the pairs competition. Almost unnoticed at the time was an ominous report: ampoules and syringes were discovered in the Olympic village, strong evidence that some athletes were resorting to drugs. It was, however, nine years before the IOC established a drug commission (chaired by New Zealand's capable Arthur Porritt) and another fourteen years before the most troublesome drug of all—anabolic steroids—was banned.

It is easy to understand why the IOC preferred to look ahead to Helsinki. These Olympics were the first at which Western athletes competed against athletes from the Soviet Union. For that reason, if for no other, they were followed with acute attention. In the rhetoric of the Olympic Charter, the games are contests among individuals, not among nations, but there is an apparently ineradicable tendency in all of us to transform the athletes into representatives of the Self with whom we can identify as they struggle against representatives of the

Other. Despite the preachments of nineteenth-century moralists who invented the doctrine of fair play, sports contests continue to be symbolic confrontations of representatives of schools, cities, regions, ethnic groups, nations, races, and religions. Theoretically, a wrestling match between two Americans or between two Russians should be as compelling for the sports fan as one in which the American grapples with the Russian, but it is not. The Olympics took on a new political dimension in 1952, one that was destined to grow increasingly important in the decades to follow.

The athletes were well aware of this new dimension. Bob Mathias, winner of the decathlon, spoke for many when he wrote: "There were many more pressures on American athletes because of the Russians. . . . They were in a sense the real enemy. You just loved to beat 'em. You just had to beat 'em. . . . This feeling was strong down through the entire team." Although the athletes must have felt that special bond of sympathy that unites Olympians in an ascetic fellowship of shared physical prowess, their expressions of mutual respect were systematically thwarted by the paranoia of the man in the Kremlin. Josef Stalin refused to allow the Olympic torch to be carried across the territory of the Soviet Union. The Russian athletes were housed not in the Olympic village, where they might have interacted with their counterparts from the rest of the world, but rather in their own isolated quarters near the Soviet naval base at Porkkala. Dour Soviet officials accompanied the athletes wherever they went and blocked their efforts at fraternization. The officials seemed to care only for the gold medals needed to certify the superiority of "new socialist man." At the Soviet camp, a huge billboard recorded the unofficial tally of points scored until, on the last day of competition, the American team suddenly surged ahead. "The board was still up," reported the *Boston Globe*, "but the points were down."

The atmosphere of official hostility failed to mar the athletic performances. In the twenty-four track-and-field events for men, twenty-one Olympic and three world records were broken; in the women's events, high-jumper Esther Brand of South Africa was the only winner who did not simultaneously set an Olympic record. The American team seemed inspired by this new opportunity to compete against the strongest possible opponents. The men's track-and-field squad took fourteen gold medals. In the 200-meter sprint, the 110-meter hurdles, the shot put, and the decathlon, the American men came in first, second, and third. These games were also a highpoint for Jamaican athletes. From that small island came George Rhoden (gold, 400 meters), Herb McKenley (silver, 100 meters and 400 meters), and Arthur Wint (silver,

800 meters). These three joined with Leslie Laing to outrun the American quartet in the 4 × 400–meter relay.

The Soviet men won not a single gold medal in men's track and field; instead, they were forced to bask in the reflected glory of Czechoslovakia's Emil Zatopek, who set Olympic records while winning the 5,000- and 10,000-meter races and the marathon. In the last race, Zatopek demoralized the favored English runner, James Peters, by asking, at about the 15-mile point, if the pace was too slow: "Excuse me, I haven't run a Marathon before, but don't you think we ought to go a bit faster?" Zatopek later confessed that his legs were so sore from the race that he was unable to walk for a week. While Zatopek was winning his races, his wife, Dana, set an Olympic record in the javelin. Russian women garnered five of the six medals awarded for the shot put and the discus, but the stars of women's track and field were clearly the Australian runners Marjorie Jackson and Shirley Strickland, who ran the 100- and 200-meter races and the 80-meter hurdles in world-record times. The American women came in first in only one of the nine women's track-and-field events, the 4 × 100–meter relay, also run in world-record time. If there had not been a poorly executed baton pass between Marjorie Jackson and Winsome Cripps, the Australian women would probably have won that event as well.

The American men dominated the swimming events with another spate of Olympic records, while the Hungarians won four of the five events for women. Led by Patricia McCormick, the American women took five-sixths of the medals for diving. The Russians triumphed in both men's and women's gymnastics, beginning a long tradition of supremacy, while the Americans did better at weight lifting and boxing. (A young fellow named Floyd Patterson defeated Vasile Tita of Romania for the middleweight title.)

It was probably inevitable that the newspapers concentrated on the "battle of the giants" and published daily statistics on the number of unofficial points earned by the United States and the Soviet Union. But, in fact, the distribution of medals among the competing teams was probably more even than it ever had been—or ever was to be in the future.

At Rome, in 1949, the games of the Sixteenth Olympiad were awarded to Melbourne after a close contest with Buenos Aires (which had to be content with hosting the first Pan-American Games in 1951). Although Brundage was pleased at the notion of Olympism at the antipodes, he was forced, as president of the International Olympic Committee, to put considerable unwelcome pressure on the Australians to make sure that the games began on schedule. At one point, on October 10, 1951, Hugh R. Weir, an Australian IOC member, was quoted in the *New York Times* to the effect that Melbourne might have to renounce the games. Brundage flew to Australia and went on one of his rhetorical rampages. His imprecations were likened, in the Australian press, to the atomic tests then under way in the South Pacific.

The 1956 Winter Games were held at Cortina d'Ampezzo in the Italian Alps. As usual, cross-country skiing was a Scandinavian and Russian show. Finnish skiers soared farther and more elegantly than their rivals, and Austria's Anton Sailer won three gold medals on the ski slopes. The Russian skaters were the fastest, but the judges thought the Americans were the best at fancy figures. Although Austria's Kurt Oppelt and Elisabeth Schwarz were first in the pairs competition, Hayes Jenkins, Ronald Robertson, David Jenkins, Tenley Albright, and Carol Heiss very nearly swept the singles contests.

In 1956 as in many other Olympic years, the summer games were threatened by political dangers that the skiers and skaters had escaped. Two unrelated political crises rocked the world in the weeks just before the Melbourne Games. Speaking to the IOC at its fifty-third session, Brundage wistfully (and erroneously) noted of ancient times that "all warfare stopped during the period of the Games." His remarks on war and peace were topical because the games in Melbourne were jeopardized by two separate wars. After a lengthy diplomatic conflict ignited by Egypt's seizure of the Suez Canal from its mostly British and French stockholders, Prime Ministers Anthony Eden of Great Britain and Guy Mollet of France arranged for the Israeli government to launch an attack upon Egypt. This gave Eden and Mollet a pretext to invade Egypt to "protect" the canal. Predictably, the Soviet Union demanded that the invaders withdraw; less predictably, the United States sided with the Soviets against the British, the French, and the Israelis. The invasion and occupation turned into a fiasco. The invaders withdrew, but Egypt, Lebanon, and Iraq boycotted the Olympics rather than compete against athletes from Britain, France, and Israel. The Egyptians also demanded that those "guilty of cowardly aggression" be expelled from the Olympic Games, but there was no possibility that the IOC would bar the British and French from competing in Melbourne.

While Israeli tanks were moving toward Cairo, Russian tanks entered Budapest. Two days before the beginning of the Suez War, Prime Minister Imre Nagy of Hungary had proclaimed his nation's desire to renounce its alliance with the Soviet Union. If Nagy had relied upon American threats to "roll back the Iron Curtain," he was soon disillusioned. Secretary of State John Foster Dulles provided him with unlimited verbal support, which had no effect at all on the Russian tanks. Thousands of Hungarians died and thousands more fled across the border to Austria.

The IOC's reaction to the bloodshed was no surprise to anyone. "Every civilized person recoils in horror at the savage slaughter in Hungary," proclaimed Avery Brundage, "but that is no reason for destroying the nucleus of international cooperation and good will we have in the Olympic Movement. The Olympic Games are contests between individuals and not between nations." The IOC voted unanimously to censure those national Olympic committees that boycotted the games. In addition to the three Islamic nations already mentioned, whose absence was motivated by the Suez War, Spain, Switzerland, and the Netherlands decided to boycott the Olympics. "How," asked the president of the Dutch National Olympic committee, "can sports prevail over what has happened in Hungary?" Switzerland's national Olympic committee joined Egypt's in asking that athletes from belligerent nations be banned from the games, but this was too bold a pacificism for the IOC members, many of whom came from nations that had recently been, that were, or that might soon be at war.

As the summer games were about to begin, Brundage spoke on a favorite theme: Why couldn't the modern world have an "Olympic truce" of the sort that he erroneously believed had halted wars during the ancient games? In antiquity, he asserted, "there was an Olympic truce and all warfare stopped during the period of the Games, [but now] after two thousand years of civilization, we stop the Games and continue our wars." (In fact, the truce was merely a promise of safe passage for those going to and coming from Olympia.)

Despite the bloodshed in Budapest, the Hungarian team made its way to Melbourne (where scores of athletes defected rather than return to life under a Soviet-imposed dictatorship). Demoralized by the realization of their country's tragic fate, the Hungarians were unable to perform as they had four years earlier. Nonetheless, the most memorable event of the games may have been their semifinal water polo match against the Russian team. This was "representative sport" at its most obvious. The play was so rough that blood colored the water and the Russians, behind by a score of 4-0, decided to forfeit the match they were unlikely to win.

The American men continued to dominate track and field, winning fifteen of the twenty-four events. Discus thrower Al Oerter won the first of four consecutive gold medals. There were also indications of future Russian strength. Vladimir Kuts set Olympic records for 5,000 and 10,000 meters. His tactics in the latter race—sprinting, slowing down to a walk, sprinting again—befuddled the favorite, England's Gordon Pirie, who probably would have won if he had not let Kuts distract him. For Roger Bannister, the steeplechase victory of Christopher Brasher was a vindication of the amateur ethos at a time when

athletes like Kuts seemed to symbolize some kind of inhumanly mechanical, state-sponsored approach to sports. For Brasher himself, the
sacrifices necessary for Olympic-level achievement had become almost
too much to bear. His comment was chilling: "I long to be free from
the body that has imprisoned me for so long."

Despite the cheers of the mostly Australian spectators, the Australian
men were unable to win a single track-and-field event. The women,
on the other hand, did better than ever before (or since). Betty Cuthbert
won the 100-meter and 200-meter races, and Shirley Strickland repeated her 1952 victory in the 80-meter hurdles. The Australian women
also won the 4 × 100–meter relay. In the pool, they stroked their way
to three more gold medals: Lorraine Crapp, who at one point held
seven world records, won the 400-meter freestyle, and Dawn Fraser
won gold in the 100-meter and silver in the 400-meter freestyle. These
two joined Faith Leech and Sandra Morgan to take another gold in
the 4 × 100–meter relay. The male swimmers, led by Murray Rose
(400-meter and 1,500-meter freestyle) managed to outperform them
(five victories, five records).

The men's and women's gymnastics teams from the Soviet Union
repeated their 1952 victories. For the women, it was the second of
eight consecutive Olympic championships. Now that women's gymnastics have become a children's sport, characterized by acrobatic
stunts, dominated by girls in their early teens, it is interesting to recall
that the women's champion, Larissa Latynina, was strongly challenged
by thirty-five-year-old Agnes Keleti of Hungary. Keleti won gold medals
for the uneven parallel bars and the balance beam, and she tied for
first place in the floor exercise.

In the seven weight-lifting classes, the Americans managed to outlift
the Russians by five to two. Boxers from five different nations won
their classifications; they included three Russians and two Americans.
In wrestling, it was the Iranians who were most successful (although
readers of American newspapers remained ignorant of this and most
of the other events not dominated by their team).

Considering the unresolved political crises that wracked the world,
one can conclude that the games were—despite flashes of anger—remarkably ironic. The IOC's desire to create an oasis of amity in a desert
of hostility was not entirely quixotic. At the closing ceremony, the
athletes took matters into their own hands. Rather than march as
members of their national teams, they broke ranks, joined hands, embraced, sang, and danced. Together, spontaneously, they created one
of the more humane traditions in modern sports. During and after the
games, Olga Fikotova of Czechoslovakia and Harold Connolly of the
United States made their own statement. They met secretly, fell in love,

and managed, after months of complicated international negotiation, to become man and wife. He had won the hammer throw; she had won the discus. And *Amor vincit omnia.*

7

The Era of (Relative)
Good Feelings

In Paris in 1955, the International Olympic Committee voted to have the 1960 Winter Games at Squaw Valley and the summer games at Rome. The first choice eventually caused some difficulties because of conflicts of interest (the chairman of the organizing committee owned some of the land intended as a site for the games). There were also problems of escalating costs (the state of California eventually contributed nearly nine times its original commitment). When only two nations indicated that their athletes wished to compete in the bobsled races, the Squaw Valley organizers petitioned the IOC for permission to drop the event. Permission was granted despite the anguished complaints of Swiss IOC member Albert Mayer, who accused Avery Brundage of prejudice not only against bobsledders but also against Switzerland.

Mayer clashed with Brundage again when the IOC met in San Francisco just before the start of the games. He urged the committee to adopt a more realistic eligibility rule because many "amateurs" were receiving broken-time payments while others had jobs at which no work was required or were simply supported by their governments. "Let us be logical," begged Mayer, "and honest with ourselves." He urged a modification of Rule 26 to define a professional as someone for whom sports were the *main,* not simply a supplementary, source of his or her material existence. This mild reform was indignantly rejected by Brundage, who explained that violation of the rules was a reason for enforcing them, not for changing them.

It was a tempest in a teapot. Much more important was the political climate. There was no Korean War, no Suez War, and no Hungarian Revolution to cloud the skies over Squaw Valley and Rome. Since

Brundage managed to persuade the U.S. State Department to waive the humiliating fingerprint requirement for visa applicants, that issue disappeared long before the games were scheduled to begin. There were, however, minor squabbles when the State Department claimed that some of East Germany's journalists were spies, which they probably were, and when Bonn and Potsdam quarreled over the number of officials each should contribute to the combined team. (The IOC took Potsdam's side in defending the journalists and Bonn's in allotting officials.)

Otherwise, the 1960 Winter Games were almost uneventful. Walt Disney acted as impressario and dazzled the spectators with ice statues and fireworks displays. Austria's Anton Sailer and America's Tenley Albright had overshadowed the other athletes at the 1956 Winter Games in Cortina d'Ampezzo, but now it seemed almost as if the medals were distributed on the basis of some kind of quota system. The Alpine honors went to six different skiers from Austria, Germany, Switzerland, France, and Canada. The Finns, Swedes, and Norwegians won the men's cross-country events (there was none for the women). The Soviet team completely dominated men's and women's speed-skating. Americans, chastened by generally poor performances, were cheered by victories in figure skating (Hayes Jenkins and Carol Heiss) and by a rather unexpected gold medal in ice hockey. All in all, Squaw Valley was a good show and a widely seen one. Berliners had watched televised Olympics in 1936 and Londoners had done so in 1948, but these were the first games seen "live" on American television.

The amity and good will that seemed to characterize these winter games lasted through the summer. Brundage and most of his colleagues were enthusiastic about Rome as a site for the summer Olympics because they responded, like most educated men of their times, to the rich historical associations of the Eternal City. The religious associations were also important to those members of the IOC, like Brundage, who thought of the Olympic movement as a "modern religion." When Brundage rather tendentiously contrasted the games with the "medieval asceticism that considered all physical activity not only useless, but perhaps harmful to mental and spiritual development," he implied that Olympism was certainly superior to medieval Catholicism and perhaps preferable to modern Christianity as well. Pope John XXIII seemed placidly undisturbed by such provocative remarks. He entertained committee members and blessed the athletes. But the jolly pontiff was not uncritical of sports. While watching the rowing competitions at Castelgondolfo, he turned to twelve-year-old Redmond Morris and warned the lad against excessive ardor: "Remember, not only sport, read books."

When the combined German team marched into the Stadio Olimpico, President Giovanni Gronchi of Italy marveled that the IOC had been able to accomplish a miracle—the unification of bitterly divided Germany. Brundage beamed. "In sport," he boasted, "we do such things." For him, the combined German team was a powerful symbol of what the games were all about—the transcendence of differences. In a speech delivered three years later, Brundage underscored the significance of the accomplishment: "The spectacle of East and West German athletes in the same uniform marching behind the same leaders and the same flag is an inspiration under present political conditions and a great service to all the German people who wish for a united country."

These were, in the words of the German journalist Heinz Maegerlein, "the loveliest games of the modern era!" They were certainly the most widely seen. There had been no television cameras in the stadium at Melbourne because the networks had refused to pay for what they still regarded as public property. In 1960, Eurovision transmitted "live" throughout Western Europe and CBS-TV paid $660,000 for the right to fly film from Rome to New York for prime-time telecasts. The perennially impoverished IOC noted with chagrin that the enterprising Italian National Olympic Committee earned approximately $1.2 million from the sale of television rights. Much as Brundage hated the idea of commercialization, the executive board agreed to accept 5 percent of the profits.

The athletes seemed to behave as if they knew that they were now on camera. Americans and Russians forgot all about NATO and the Warsaw Pact and wished each other good luck. Winners and losers embraced in what seemed at moments like an orgy of good sportsmanship, and the officials, not the athletes, were responsible for most of the disputes that occurred. Neutral observers felt that boxers and gymnasts suffered from politically motivated bias on the part of the judges. (However, Boris Shaklin and Larissa Latynina, both of the Soviet Union, seem to have fairly earned their titles as the best gymnasts in Rome.)

As a team, the Australians were unable to match the achievements of Melbourne, but Dawn Fraser repeated her 100-meter freestyle victory in swimming and won two silver medals in the relays. In men's swimming, Australia received an undeserved medal when the judges ignored the timers' numbers and awarded first place to John Devitt rather than to the American Lance Larsen. After American protests were overruled, W. Berg Phillips, the Australian vice-president of the Fédération Internationale de Natation Amateur, gloated, "We rubbed your noses in it and we'll show you some more when we're through."

The most memorable athletic performance was probably Wilma Rudolph's. Tall, graceful, and *fast,* she sped to victory in the 100 meters (ahead of Britain's Dorothy Hyman) and the 200 meters (ahead of Germany's Juta Heine). Rudolph also anchored the 4 × 100–meter relay team, which finished ahead of the German and Polish teams. In comparison to the three gold medals in track and field won by the American women, the Russians came away with six. For the first time since the "experiment" of 1928, women competed in the 800-meter race, which was won by Ludmilla Shevtsova of the Soviet Union. (The IOC had voted 26-22 to restore the race.) As for the American men, Al Oerter won the second of his four consecutive gold medals in the discus, and Rafer Johnson finished the decathlon ahead of his close friend Yang Chuan-kwang, who trained in the United States but competed for the Republic of China.

There were some surprises, of course. Crew aficionados reacted with astonishment when Germany's team, coached by the innovative Karl Adam, won three gold medals, including one for the eight-man shell, which had set an unprecedented tempo of forty-seven strokes a minute. (The Russians and the Americans had to be satisfied with one victory each.) Ethiopia's unknown Abebe Bikila won the marathon—in bare feet. Among the least surprising results was Herb Elliott's victory in the 1,500-meter race. Elliott, who had been the clear favorite, ran a world-record time of 3:35.6. In fact, all six finalists bettered the Olympic record.

For the American team, there were a number of disappointments. David Sime and Ray Norton, favored in their races, lost to Germany's Armin Hary (100 meters) and Italy's Livio Berutti (200 meters). Norton's disappointment was intensified when his misstep in the finals of the 400-meter relay caused the disqualification of the American team. John Thomas was expected to win the high jump, but the medal went to Robert Shavlakadze of the Soviet Union. In boxing, the Italians won as many gold medals as the Americans (three each). For the moment, Francesco de Piccoli, heavyweight champion, enjoyed the limelight, but future glory was to go to a young American named Cassius Clay, the winner of the light-heavyweight division. Heinz Maegerlein thought Clay was "the greatest" of the boxers—a prophetic phrase.

Japanese fans, delighted that their male gymnasts outpointed the Russians for the team championship, looked forward to their role as hosts of the next Olympics. In 1959, at its Munich session, the IOC had chosen Tokyo by a wide margin over Detroit, Vienna, and Brussels. In Rome, just before the summer games began, the IOC unanimously elected Japan's Royotaro Azuma to the executive board. (Another seat went to Brazil's J. Ferreira Santos, who defeated Konstantin Andrianov by a vote of 38-21.) Brundage was reelected by acclamation to a second eight-year term as IOC president. Armand Massard of France and Britain's Marquess of Exeter continued as first and second vice-presidents.

As the Roman glow of good will dissipated, the committee had to confront its severest political problem: South Africa. That government's policy of apartheid, which resulted in severe discrimination against black athletes, was obviously a breach of Olympic rules. As early as 1958, Olaf Ditlev-Simonsen of Norway informed Brundage that his country was prepared to exclude the all-white South African team from the 1960 Winter Games in Oslo. Brundage replied sympathetically: "Sooner or later the subject will be on our agenda, and there can be only one answer, unless changes are made." A year later, Brundage wrote to IOC Chancellor Otto Mayer, "This . . . is another situation that we cannot evade much longer." When the executive board met with the national Olympic committees in Rome on May 19, 1959, delegates from the Soviet Union and South Africa clashed over the question of apartheid. The South African National Olympic Committee (SANOC) claimed that there was no discrimination because the national team was composed of the best athletes (who happened all to be white). Seconding this subterfuge, IOC member Reginald Honey assured his colleagues that as soon as the black athletes of South Africa were of Olympic calibre, there would be places for them on the team.

Flimsy alibis of this sort became less tenable early in 1962 when South African officials began making public declarations like that of Interior Minister Jan de Klerk: "government policy is that no mixed teams should take part in sports inside or outside the country." The internal conflict within South Africa became completely polarized later that year when Dennis Brutus and other opponents of apartheid organized the South African Non-Racial Olympic Committee (SANROC). Impelled by its own principles as well as by increasing pressure from the newly independent states of black Africa, the International Olympic Committee then voted, at its sixtieth session, which took place in Moscow that June, to suspend SANOC "if the policy of racial discrimination practiced by their government . . . does not change before our Session in Nairobi takes place in October 1963." At that session, which had to be moved to Baden-Baden when the Kenyan government barred SANOC's delegation, the IOC relented to a degree and gave SANOC until the end of the year to effect a change in official policy. There was no change and SANOC was suspended at the sixty-second session (January 1964). Since the IOC was not yet ready to recognize the nonracial committee, SANROC, South Africa was not allowed to send a team to the 1964 Games in Tokyo.

As white-ruled South Africa was slowly forced out of the games, the rest of the African continent was gradually integrated into the Olympic movement. Ali Mohammed Hassanein of Egypt was the first African to compete when he entered the sabre and foil competitions in 1912. His countrymen Ibrahim Mustafa and Said Nasser won gold medals in 1928 in Greco-Roman wrestling and in weight lifting. That year, Mohammed El Ouafi won the marathon as a member of the French team. The first black African to win a gold medal was Abebe Bikila of Ethiopia, who won the marathon in 1960 and 1964.

IOC member Angelo Bolanaki, who represented Greece but lived in Egypt, hoped to arrange for IOC-sponsored regional games at Alexandria in 1927. His colleagues welcomed the idea, but there was a series of delays and pan-African games were not inaugurated until after World War II. The first important African games were the Jeux de l'Amitié, sponsored by the French in conjunction with their former colonies. The first celebration of these games was at Tananarive, Madagascar, in 1960; the second was at Abidjan on the Ivory Coast in 1961. At the third in the series of Jeux Africains, held at Dakar in Senegal in 1963, Brundage and France's Comte Jean de Beaumont were present to symbolize IOC approval. Both men were impressed by the Jeux d'Amitié. A few months later, Brundage nominated a distinguished Nigerian jurist, Sir Adetokunbo Ademola, to become the first black African member of the International Olympic Committee.

When thirty nations competed two years later at the Jeux Africains at Brazzaville, Congo, leaders of the Olympic movement came once again to offer their moral support. Brundage was there with the Marquess of Exeter, with Italy's Giulio Onesti, and with the presidents of eight international sports federations. Brundage rejected Reginald Honey's complaint that South Africa, Rhodesia, Angola, and Mozambique had been excluded from these allegedly pan-African games. He told Honey that the first two countries had violated Olympic rules and the other two were not yet independent. (Angola and Mozambique were then Portuguese colonies.) More important to Brundage than Honey's protest was the fact that teams from Congo-Brazzaville and from Congo-Leopoldville competed despite the "strained relations" between their respective governments.

Brundage was unquestionably pleased by the progressive incorporation of the African peoples within the Olympic movement (even when he was not always happy about their demands for reform of that movement). Beaumont was another who worked assiduously to bring the newly independent African nations, many of which had been French colonies, within the gambit of Olympism. He took it as his special vocation to secure subsidies to support the development of sports in underdeveloped countries. In 1962, he joined Andrianov in proposing an International Olympic Aid Commission to provide technical and financial aid to third-world sports organizations. The commission was established, but its funds were so meager that it expired two years later. Beaumont's interest and concern remained lively and his plans were eventually realized in 1972. Thanks largely to him, and to the television largesse that made generous subsidies possible, the African presence at the Olympic Games became increasingly pronounced.

In this period, the early 1960s, the IOC still extended its patronage to regional games, but the problems caused by the Asian Games might have persuaded the committee to renounce its role as sponsor and overseer if the troubles connected with the Mediterranean Games had not already convinced the members that regional games were a political briar patch from which they had best escape as soon as escape was possible.

At a conference in New Delhi in February 1949, India's prime minister Jawaharlal Nehru had provided the impetus for an Asian Games Federation whose quadrennial Asian Games were first celebrated in Manilla in 1954. There were no major political incidents until 1963, when the games took place in Jakarta, Indonesia. At that time the Indonesian government denied visas to the Israeli and Nationalist Chinese teams, and the Indonesian National Olympic Committee failed to issue a protest. G. D. Sondhi, an Indian member of the IOC as well as of the executive board of the Asian Games Federation, was distressed at this acquiescence in government fiat. On August 28, four days after the games had begun, Sondhi persuaded the executive board to declare that these games were *not* the IOC-sponsored Asian Games but should be known as the Jakarta Games. When this declaration was publicized, a riot broke out. An angry mob attacked the Indian Embassy in Jakarta and stormed into Hotel Indonesia, where Sondhi was staying. The considerably frightened Indian managed to escape to the airport and flee the country. In reprisal for this flouting of the rules and this insulting of one of its members, the IOC suspended the Indonesian National Olympic Committee on February 7, 1963. This rebuke so angered Indonesia's dictator, Sukarno, that he was motivated to inaugurate what he grandly termed The Games of the New Emerging Forces.

The impetus for GANEFO may, in fact, have come from Beijing, where the Chinese Communists were eager to embarrass the IOC and to combat the "forces of imperialism and sports organizations manipulated by imperialist countries." Delegates from China, Cambodia, North Vietnam, Pakistan, Iraq, the United Arab Republic (i.e., Egypt and Syria), Mali, Guinea, and the Soviet Union met in Jakarta in April 1963 and nodded approval as Sukarno proclaimed, "Let us declare frankly that sport has something to do with politics." Since the People's Republic of China was not then a member of the International Amateur Athletic Federation or of the Fédération Internationale de Natation, these powerful organizations warned their members that neither track-and-field athletes nor swimmers and divers were to compete in GANEFO. Those who did would be barred from the next Olympic games. Pressure from the IAAF, from FINA, and from the IOC itself deterred most of GANEFO's forty-eight participating nations from sending their best athletes to Jakarta for the games that were celebrated in November 1963 (with all the pomp and ceremony now associated with great international sports festivals).

Early the following year, Sukarno and the IOC worked out a compromise that promised the full reintegration of Indonesia within the Olympic movement. This was not, however, the end of the affair. Indonesia and North Korea reignited the controversy in 1964 when they sent a number of disbarred athletes to compete in Tokyo. When these athletes were declared ineligible, both governments reacted by withdrawing their entire teams. It was a particularly painful sacrifice for the North Koreans because their national Olympic committee had just been recognized (after the South Koreans had spurned IOC requests for a combined Korean team on the German model). The North Korean track-and-field team was subsequently barred from the 1968 Games in Mexico City because the athletes had participated in GANEFO II in the winter of 1966.

The absence of the South African, Indonesian, and North Korean teams seems to have upset few of the thousands who journeyed to Tokyo for the 1964 Games and few of the millions who watched the satellite-relayed television images. The Olympic torch that was borne into the stadium by ceremonial runners had come by air, with stops in Istanbul, Beirut, Teheran, Lahore, New Delhi, Rangoon, Bangkok, Kuala Lampur, Manila, and Hong Kong. The IOC and the U.S. State Department were in agreement for once when they criticized NBC-TV for delaying the West Coast broadcast of the opening ceremony until 1:00 A.M.—to avoid a conflict with Johnny Carson's "Tonight Show." Having invested some $2 billion and incalculable psychic energy in the games, the Japanese were also miffed—and puzzled. There had been 3.5 million requests from sports-mad Japanese for the 60,000 tickets available for the opening ceremony. NHK, Japan's state-run television network, reported that 99 percent of Tokyo dwellers had watched at least part of the games on television. Did the Americans care so little for *supōtsu?*

By all accounts, the games were enormously successful. The track-and-field events were especially memorable. Robert Hayes of the United States became the first person to run 100 meters in just ten seconds. Peter Snell of New Zealand, who had won his first Olympic victory in the 800-meter race in Rome, came from behind to finish this event ahead of George Kerr of Jamaica and Wilson Kiprigut of Kenya, both of whom had lowered Snell's Olympic record in the semifinals. Snell set an Olympic record in winning the 1,500-meter race in 3:38.1. Americans Robert Schul and William Mills were the unexpected victors over 5,000 and 10,000 meters, races in which American runners had never before excelled. Abebe Bikila, the "metronome on legs," triumphed for the second time in the marathon. The Russian track team did rather poorly, with the men winning only the hammer throw and the high jump, and the women only the shot put and the discus (Tamara Press) and the pentathlon (Irina Press).

Collecting a chestful of medals, America's Donald Schollander was the star of men's swimming, while Australia's Dawn Fraser continued to dominate the women's races. Fraser went to Tokyo planning to break the one-minute barrier for the 100-meter freestyle, and she succeeded. Her teammate Betty Cuthbert added a gold medal in the 400-meter race to the three she had earned in Melbourne. Among the American champions were a boxer named Joseph Frazier and a basketball player named William Bradley. The queen of the gymnasts was clearly Czechoslovakia's Vera Caslavska, who wrested the combined title from Larissa Latynina (who had won in 1956 and 1960). Caslavska also won gold medals on the balance beam and in the vault.

Having invented the sport of judo, the Japanese had high hopes for a sweep of the matches in that newly introduced sport. Three victories in the lighter classes set the stage for a tremendous battle between two heavyweights—Japan's Akio Kaminaga and Holland's Anton Geesink. As John Lucas notes, the Japanese were uneasily aware that Geesink had defeated Kaminaga in an earlier encounter:

> Kaminaga, the aggressor in the early going, was unable to throw the powerful Geesink, who, in turn, made several unsuccessful moves on his opponent. In the ninth minute, Geesink caught Kaminaga with the classic judo stranglehold. There was as much drama and agony among the massed audience as on the mat as the Dutchman relentlessly held his man, winning the world title, releasing a kind of collective sorrow among the Japanese, and solidifying judo as a permanent fixture in the Olympic Games.

The pain of the loss was alleviated by the surprising victory of the Japanese women's volleyball team over a much taller Soviet squad.

The Japanese, who looked like schoolgirls, had been trained by a coach who subjected them to an almost sadistic regime of Zen-like intensity and rigor. Climbing the victors' podium, the young women beamed as if their years of intensive training had been spent in cherry-blossom viewing. It seemed, for a magical moment, as if all Japan smiled with them.

8

Organizational Strains

In the midst of these struggles, which often provided front-page stories for the international press, there were behind-the-scenes conflicts of the sort experienced by all complex international or transnational institutions. One problem was the distribution of income. In 1960, the Italian National Olympic Committee had simply kept 95 percent of the money earned from the sale of television rights. In 1964, the executive board of the International Olympic Committee decided on an ad hoc basis how the profits should be divided among the national Olympic committees (NOCs), the international federations, and the IOC. Such informality made sense when the sums involved were small, but competition among television networks became as fierce as competition in the stadium. For 1968, the American rights were sold for $4.5 million. There had to be some systematic way to deal with the IOC's new wealth.

At its sixty-fifth session in the spring of 1966, the executive board decided to divide the first million dollars of revenue equally among the international federations, the NOCs, and the IOC; the host organizing committee would receive one third of the second million, with the remainder being divided equally among the international federations, the national Olympic committees, and the IOC; with the third million, the organizing committee's share would increase to two thirds. Subsequent variations on this formula have increased the share of the organizing committee.

Money may be the root of all evil, but some conflicts at the IOC headquarters were simply a matter of personality. When Avery Brundage became president in 1952, Otto Mayer had been the IOC chancellor for six years. Mayer, a Lausanne businessman with a jewelry and watch shop, was an intelligent and energetic man. In fact, he was *too* energetic for someone as willful as Brundage. Rather than wait for instructions from the executive board or from the president, Mayer sometimes took the initiative when confronted with a problem. Brundage scolded Mayer more than once for premature or totally unauthorized statements. On his own, for instance, Mayer reassured the worried Italians that their favorite sports—soccer and cycling—were in no danger of removal from the 1960 Olympic Games. (The possibility of removal had arisen because most of the Olympic soccer players and cyclists were clearly professionals who moved back and forth between the Olympics and football leagues or the Tour de France.) Although Mayer had strong support from his brother Albert, an IOC member from Switzerland, he was nonetheless persuaded to resign in 1964.

Brundage's relationship with Albert Mayer did not improve when the young man whom Albert recommended as Otto's replacement, Eric Jonas, failed to win Brundage's confidence. The atmosphere in Lausanne deteriorated further when Jonas, who left with a sense of grievance, sued the IOC for breach of contract. Nearly as unhappy was the IOC's experience with Jakarta-born industrialist Johann Westerhoff, who became the committee's executive secretary in May 1966. Brundage felt that Westerhoff gave the job less than his full attention, and he complained to Comte Jean de Beaumont, who consulted with Mexico's influential member José de Clark Flores. Westerhoff made his exit.

At this critical moment, Brundage recognized in Monique Berlioux the talents—and the tact—he wanted in an administrative assistant. Berlioux, thirty-eight years old when she met Brundage, had been a very successful swimmer. In her fourteen years of competition she had won some forty national championships. An appendectomy three weeks before the 1948 Olympics had kept her from the French team, and a quarrel with the Fédération Nationale de Natation Amateur had led to her refusal to participate in 1952. Working as a journalist, she met Myriam Mewley, one of Otto Mayer's assistants at IOC headquarters, and through Mewley she met Brundage while on assignment to cover the 1963 Jeux Africains at Dakar. Berlioux moved to Lausanne in 1967 and was hired by Westerhoff to work on the *Bulletin du CIO*. She quickly became the IOC's director for press and public relations and then, when Westerhoff was forced out of office, the IOC director.

Berlioux's analysis of her predecessor's problems was acute. Of Westerhoff she commented: "He forgot that the president was the boss. You never forget that. Maybe that's the advantage of being a woman. You accept more. I like to stay in the shadows." Brundage was delighted with Berlioux, who soon emerged from the shadows and became very nearly indispensable. Mewley's characterization of Berlioux was incisive: "She is a career woman with great will-power, great talent, and great capacity for work. . . . She loves power. When she arrived in Lausanne, we were a small group. We had no money. She was very tough. Little by little, she got organized and built up the secretariat." Berlioux stayed on as IOC director after Brundage's retirement and continued in office under the two presidents who followed him.

Personnel problems in Lausanne were a minor irritant compared with the insistent demands that the organizational structure of the entire Olympic movement be transformed. When the IOC was created in 1894, there were no well-established international amateur sports federations and no national Olympic committees. It was the IOC that encouraged the formation of the former and midwived the latter. As late as 1900, for example, there were only seven NOCs, but over the years that number slowly increased. In retrospect, it is astonishing that the men who controlled track and field, always considered the very heart of the Olympic Games, waited until 1912 for the creation of the International Amateur Athletic Federation.

As long as Pierre de Coubertin was president of the International Olympic Committee, his influence within the Olympic movement was paramount; but even he had to share some of his power with the executive board that was created in 1921. Under Comte Henri de Baillet-Latour, Sigfrid Edstrøm, and Brundage—all strong leaders—the executive board continued to play an important role. As the Olympic movement grew in size and complexity, it experienced the organizational conflicts that are endemic to all bureaucracies. By the 1960s, it was apparent that the entire IOC had to share some of its power with the NOCs and the international sports federations. That Brundage and other institutional conservatives refused to recognize the obvious caused severe and protracted controversy within the Olympic movement.

The rebellion of the NOCs began in 1963. While still a member of Italy's committee, Giulio Onesti had urged the IOC executive board to meet annually with the NOCs. Elected to the IOC the following year, Onesti arranged for the Comite Olimpico Nazionale d'Italia (CONI) to invite representatives of the NOCs to meet among themselves just before the IOC session in Tokyo in 1964. He suggested the formation of a Co-ordinating and Study Committee. In the past, the NOCs had met frequently with the IOC executive board, but the meetings had always been so dominated by the latter that they were very unsatisfactory to the former. As the American IOC member Douglas Robey recalled, "We'd have meetings with the national Olympic committees or the international federations and [Brundage would] say, 'We'll take it under advisement.' It was a brush-off. . . . He just wouldn't listen. . . . Let them talk, and then forget it." In Robey's view,

Brundage had treated the NOCs like children. And treatment of that sort was no longer tolerable.

The Italian proposal was patently more than an attempt to clear blocked channels of communication. Onesti's statements of personal loyalty to the IOC failed to allay Brundage's suspicions, and Brundage warned Onesti from the start that "the formation of a permanent organization of NOC's is fraught with many dangers." What Brundage, and others, most feared was that such an organization was but a step toward an IOC in which every NOC was automatically entitled to one (and no more than one) representative. Such a system would guarantee majority rule by the smaller nations of the Third World. This model of representation was familiar in the United Nations General Assembly, which Brundage considered an ineffective body, and he invariably argued that a nation's representation in the Olympic movement ought to be proportional to its stage of sports development, a position that ensured for the foreseeable future the continued dominance of Europe and North America.

As it turned out, plans for an assembly of NOCs at Tokyo were premature and the foundation of the Co-ordinating and Study Committee did not take place until the beginning of October 1965. Three days before the executive board's scheduled meeting with the NOCs in Madrid, the representatives of sixty-eight national committees caucused in Rome as guests of CONI. The committee they set up was headed by the ever-present Onesti and included Hugh R. Weir (Australia), Konstantin Andrianov (USSR), Jean-Claude Ganga (Congo), Tsuneyoshi Takeda (Japan), K. S. Duncan (Great Britain), Gabriel Gemayel (Lebanon), H. Corenthin (Mali), José de Clark Flores (Mexico), R. W. Wilson (USA), and Jean Weymann (Switzerland). The majority of this group resolved that the NOCs ought to receive 25 percent of whatever television revenues flowed into IOC coffers and that the question of amateurism ought to be shifted from the IOC to the international sports federations.

Onesti continued to assure Brundage that the Co-ordinating and Study Committee posed no threat whatsoever to the International Olympic Committee. He sent texts of resolutions to Chicago and was thanked by Brundage for his "friendly personal references" and for the "sensitive phraseology" of the initial report. Indeed, Brundage confided to the Italian that he was "not very happy with our Madrid Session." The world, Brundage told Onesti, needed leadership. The clear implication was that the world needed people like the president of CONI. The president of CONI wrote back that the new NOCs of Asia and Africa were inexperienced and unhappy about their lack of representation in the IOC. He, Onesti, hoped not to alter the basic structure of the organization but rather to integrate the newer units more closely within the Olympic movement.

The exchanges of sweetness and light continued even after Onesti initiated a series of moves to bring the People's Republic of China back into the Olympic fold. Curiously, Brundage did not explode with reproaches as he had when Otto Mayer took similar liberties.

While Onesti was busy with his overture to the East, plans progressed for the second meeting of the Study and Co-ordinating Committee. When it did meet in Rome, in 1966, the committee adopted a constitution incorporating most of the features Andrianov had been advocating for years: a president, three vice-presidents, an executive committee composed of these officers, plus two representatives from each of the five continents. Another general assembly was planned just before the IOC's Teheran session in April 1967. As consultations and discussions led to a more institutionalized kind of opposition to the IOC leadership, there was less receptivity in Chicago and in Lausanne. In addition to Brundage, Duncan, Clark Flores, and Denmark's Ivar Vind agreed there was no need for the NOCs to form their own organization. Vind assured Brundage that he and the other Scandinavian members considered Onesti to be disloyal and motivated by personal ambition.

Onesti continued to protest that he wished only to aid and abet. When he invited the representatives of the NOCs to meet in Teheran prior to the official IOC session (at which they were supposed to consult with the executive board), he stressed that this preliminary meeting was to take place "with the agreement of the International Olympic Committee." Onesti's friend and collaborator Dr. Marcello Garroni was said to have been working closely with IOC Secretary-General Westerhoff. These assurances met with an angry reaction from Brundage, who denied the claim of IOC sponsorship and ordered Westerhoff to dissociate himself from Onesti and the other troublemakers. On March 29, 1967, Brundage sent out an official circular letter informing the national committees that the IOC executive board had decided that no new organization was needed. He made it clear that Onesti's plans were *not* endorsed by the IOC.

Onesti was annoyed but not deterred. Ignoring Brundage's imprecations, representatives of sixty-four NOCs convened in Teheran on April 29 and voted to establish a Permanent General Assembly (PGA) when they met in Mexico City in 1968. The effects of Brundage's opposition were visible in the changed proportion of Western to non-Western representatives. There had been twenty-seven European delegates and thirteen Americans at the Rome assembly; now there were twenty-three and seven. The number of African committees remained at fifteen, and the Asian contingent increased from eight to twelve. The shift in the organization's geographical center of gravity signaled that an ideological earthquake was not far off.

In Brundage's irate view, the official meeting of the executive board with the NOCs, which took place on May 3, was "loaded with dynamite and there could have been a serious explosion. We were on the edge of a precipice and one slip . . . and we would have been over the edge. They were like a pack of hungry lions and only by talking louder were they held at bay." The medley of images—dynamite, precipice, hungry lions—and the errors in syntax indicate that Brundage was thoroughly disconcerted. He suffered from his nightmare of an Olympic movement fallen into the hands of the smaller and more radical third-world nations. The IOC seemed about to go the disastrous way of the U.N. General Assembly. To Brundage it was insufferable that Jean-Claude Ganga, representing the Congo, was taken seriously as a spokesman for Olympic sports.

In his opening address to the IOC's Teheran session, Brundage hoped to calm the roiled waters with flattery. He praised the NOCs for their "promulgation of Olympic principles and ideals" (which, in fact, interested the NOCs far less than the acquisition of gold, silver, and bronze medals). Brundage attempted to soothe the delegates: "Since the National Olympic Committees as agents of the International Olympic Committee are the organizations that control Olympic affairs in their respective countries, the International Olympic Committee is ever concerned with their well-being and is always eager to strengthen their powers and to help them with their work." As proof of its sincerity, the IOC authorized a subcommittee, chaired by Vind, to investigate the relations between the IOC and the NOCs. Although Onesti was named to this subcommittee, he was outnumbered by Brundage supporters like Clark Flores, who lectured Onesti on the idyllic relations that had been the rule before the agitators had begun their senseless campaign.

Even as the IOC insiders worked to contain the rebellion of the national committees, the international sports federations began to articulate *their* demands. As early as 1920, the international federations, led by Henri Rousseau of the Fédération Internationale Amateur de Cyclisme, had demanded greater influence within the Olympic movement. Now the representatives of the federations had decided to follow the example of the NOCs and to meet among themselves as well as with the IOC executive board. The General Assembly of the International Federations (GAIF) was founded in 1967, barely a month after the Teheran session. Led by Australia's crusty Berge Phillips (of the Fédération Internationale de Natation Amateur) and France's Roger

Coulon (of the Fédération Internationale de Lutte Amateur), this new organization had already, in Brundage's outraged view, intruded into "matters which are not of their competence and only concern the IOC." The Olympic movement was unmistakably in an organizational crisis. The unstable situation was made almost chaotic by the fact that the GAIF and the PGA were often at odds with each other as well as with the IOC.

From Teheran the scene of the drama shifted to Grenoble, where the 1968 Winter Games were about to be celebrated. When the IOC executive board met with the international federations immediately before its sixty-seventh session, Phillips urged that the federations be given one-third of all television revenues and that an Olympic congress be convened. There had not been a congress since the one in Berlin in 1930 because Brundage's position was that such affairs were a waste of time and money. A congress was obviously also an occasion for outsiders to challenge insiders.

At the session itself, which began on February 1, Vind reported on behalf of his subcommittee on relations with the NOCs that there was difficulty in communication but no necessity for a separate organization. His point about difficulty of communication was well illustrated when Onesti rose to speak for the PGA. He delivered a major speech in which he gave a history of this new organization and an ardent defense of his own initiative. Proclaiming his loyalty to the IOC and condemning the leaders of the international sports federations for *their* subversive actions, Onesti resigned from the subcommittee on IOC-NOC relations.

Preparations now went ahead for the Third General Assembly of the NOCs. Since Brundage's second term as president was due to expire in 1968, Onesti's supporters began to ponder an electoral coup. Perhaps it was time for the dynamic and imaginative Italian to wrest the IOC presidency from the aged (but far from infirm) Brundage. A number of Italian newspapers thought so. The timing couldn't have been worse. Clearly, the International Olympic Committee could ill afford to be wracked by internal dissension just as the Olympic movement was about to split apart over the issue of South Africa's right to participate.

Each side to the dispute over the role of the NOCs gathered its forces. Drawing on the good will he had accumulated as a supporter of the Pan-American Games and of Latin American membership in the IOC, Brundage sent out a form letter in Spanish to the Hispanic national committees asking them to announce to Onesti that they saw no need for the PGA. Almost every nation of the Western Hemisphere complied, some using Brundage's form, some composing their own letters. Brundage profited in another way from his Hispanic connections. In a ploy that reminds one more of backroom maneuvers at a political convention than of Olympic fair play, the president of the Mexican Organizing Committee for the 1968 Games informed Onesti that there was no space available for a session of the PGA because the organization was not a part of the official program of events.

Brundage warned Onesti in person and by letter not to convene his organization in Mexico City. When Onesti let Brundage know how bitterly he resented this small-mindedness, Brundage reiterated his stand: "No NOC in good standing has ever been refused IOC support. All NOCs are and have been invited to submit their problems directly to the IOC at any time. . . . .There is no reason whatsoever for any permanent association of NOCs." When Andrianov cabled Brundage an appeal on Onesti's behalf, Brundage brushed him off, declaring, "I have not interfered."

Andrianov was not the only person who concluded that Brundage had been too inflexible and authoritarian in his response to the PGA. On September 7, Beaumont, acting as president of the Comité Olympique Français, rather than as an IOC member, chaired a meeting in Versailles attended by representatives of twenty-two European NOCs. Those present agreed to participate in the PGA's meeting in Mexico City and to accept Onesti's invitation for a 1969 meeting in Dubrovnik, Yugoslavia. The group also called for a new Olympic congress at some future date.

Beaumont now emerged as a possible successor to Brundage. At a press conference, he remarked that Brundage looked upon the IOC as if it were his child. He added that reelection of the eighty-one-year-old president would be "a challenge to common sense in the eyes of the world." Stories about Beaumont's candidacy appeared in *Le Monde,* in the *Times* (London), and in other papers around the world. There were new rumors of a challenge from the very active, very ambitious Giulio Onesti.

The Italian had little support, but there was no doubt that Beaumont was a forceful person and an attractive candidate for those who felt that Brundage had been president long enough. Brundage, who insulted Beaumont by calling him Onesti's "second lieutenant," failed to understand that Beaumont's dissatisfaction was the result of frustration. The Frenchman felt himself to be a loyal follower not of Onesti but of Brundage. He felt rebuffed and kept at a distance by the coldness that most of the members experienced when they tried to express their more personal emotions to the IOC president. Contrary to the usual stereotypes, it was the European aristocrats—the Marquess of Exeter and Beaumont—who were able to charm by gregarious informality. Except for a handful of close friends, Brundage was unapproachable.

There was no doubt that his authoritarian style of leadership had cost him support within the IOC. The atmosphere was poisoned by intrigue, rumor, and innuendo.

Kenya's Sir Reginald Alexander, a blunt speaker of unpleasant truths, tried to persuade Brundage to step aside: "Avery, you're eighty; you're on the top. You've been at it now for sixty years and president for twenty years and when you're on the top, there's only one way to go, and that's down. Move now, and history will record you as one of the greatest." Brundage shrugged off the advice and Alexander joined Robey in asking Ireland's Lord Killanin to stand for the presidency. Indeed, Alexander sounded out the members and felt that at least thirty were ready to vote for the Irishman. The ever-cautious Killanin preferred to bide his time, and the "dump Brundage" campaign fizzled. On October 10, 1968, Avery Brundage was reelected by a wide margin. Killanin became vice-president, defeating Beaumont by a vote of 29-27. But the losers won something too: Beaumont became a member of the executive board, and it was understood by everyone that Brundage would retire in 1972, at the age of eighty-five.

Brundage remained in office, but Onesti was now president of the PGA, which was officially founded by a meeting of seventy-eight national Olympic committees on September 30 and October 1. The organization included not only Andrianov and Ganga, as leaders of the Communist and neutral blocs, but also Duncan of Great Britain, Takeda of Japan, Weir of Australia, and even Robey of the United States. The PGA voted to meet again in Dubrovnik, immediately before the next official IOC session. It was obviously time for some sort of compromise if the conflicts among the IOC, the NOCs, and the international federations were not to destroy the Olympic movement. The IOC's response was to set up five joint commissions with six IOC and six NOC members each. The fifth commission was devoted to relations among the three parts of the Olympic structure.

As the date for the Dubrovnik session approached, tempers flared and confusion reigned. Onesti faulted Brundage for supposedly reneging on the agreement made in Warsaw to allow the NOCs to meet among themselves. Brundage was infuriated when the Yugoslav organizers of the Dubrovnik session printed and distributed a program that had been created, allegedly, "in agreement with the International Olympic Committee and the Permanent General Assembly of the National Olympic Committees." When Killanin placed some of Onesti's spokesmen on the IOC program, Clark Flores burst out, "These are not Lord Killanin's tactics, they are Mr. Onesti's." By the time the session was under way, the five Nordic committees seemed to have reached a state of despair: "Where is our Headquarters? Is it in Mexico,

Rom[e], Chicago or Lausanne? Or is it in Paris. So many good plans and suggestions have been offered, everyone has done a good job, everyone has been carrying his colours, only—too many colours have been on parade."

The PGA met on October 21-23 and busied itself with committee reports and suggestions for improved IOC-NOC relations. Brundage spoke to the NOCs on October 25 and called for a return to "the lofty ideals laid down by the Baron de Coubertin." Not even the magic name of the revered founder was enough to exorcise the demons of conflict. Andrianov and others asked for official IOC recognition of the PGA, but Brundage refused and repeated his argument that only the IOC represented all 127 national committees. At the closed meeting of the IOC executive board, Beaumont too asked that the IOC not fight the PGA, but Brundage was adamant. To Khaw Kai-Bow of the Olympic Council of Malaysia, who had written him to beg that the leaders of the IOC not behave like "tiny tin Gods—incommunicado to all and sundry," Brundage replied dismissively that there had been "a quite satisfactory dialogue between the NOC's and the IOC"—at least until dissidents like Onesti had disrupted the harmonic relationships.

In 1971, at the executive board meetings in Luxembourg, Brundage recommended that committee members should choose between the IOC and the PGA and that those who preferred the latter organization should resign from the IOC. Andrianov, Killanin, and Takeda protested. Andrianov blamed the IOC for the plain fact that many NOCs felt that the PGA was necessary, and Killanin agreed. Even Sir Adetokunbo Ademola of Nigeria, no admirer of Onesti, commented that many African NOCs felt neglected by the IOC and appreciated the attention given them by the PGA. The same point had been made two days earlier, when the IOC executive board met with the national committees, by Ademola's countryman H. E. O. Adefope.

Despite the sound conciliatory advice given by Olympic leaders such as Andrianov, Beaumont, Vind, and Killanin, and from obscure and dedicated NOC members like Khaw Kai-Bow and Adefope, Brundage was unmoved. To the three vice-presidents of the IOC he wrote, "The PGA must be buried NOW and perhaps the three vice-presidents will have the courage to report that any IOC member who [wishes] to participate in the PGA activities must first resign from the IOC."

The vice-presidents ignored Brundage's fulminations and the PGA continued to meet and to agitate for a greater role in Olympic affairs. After Brundage's retirement in 1972, Killanin formalized the "tripartite relationship" by which the IOC, the PGA, and the GAIF functioned cooperatively. The simultaneous establishment of Olympic Solidarity, an organization whose goal was to provide technical and financial assistance to the sports organizations of Asia, Africa, and Latin America, also ameliorated relations between the IOC and the NOCs, many of which were in dire need of such aid. Onesti was named to the Olympic Solidarity Commission along with Killanin and the three IOC vice-presidents. In many ways, the IOC president was an ineffective leader, but his conciliatory approach to organizational problems calmed waters that Brundage's adversarial manner had roiled. In the 1980s, Killanin's successor as IOC president, Juan Antonio Samaranch, combined strong personal leadership with the skillful use of bureaucratic machinery. Differences in perspective and conflicts of interest remained, but they never again wracked the organization to the point where it threatened to self-destruct.

9

A Time of Troubles

In the aftermath of the 1964 Games, Avery Brundage—doggedly optimistic—announced that the Japanese had been converted to Olympic principles. Unfortunately, he was unable to say as much about the white minority of South Africa. Having suspended the South African National Olympic Committee for its refusal to take a stand against apartheid, most members of the International Olympic Committee were eager for some sign of a change of heart. As soon as SANOC was in compliance with the IOC's demand, they were ready to terminate the sanctions. Frank Braun, representing SANOC, appeared before the IOC in Rome at its sixty-fifth session (April 1966) and he *seemed*, at that moment, conciliatory. Looking ahead to 1968, he promised that SANOC was prepared to send a nonracial team selected by a nonracial committee. Once back in South Africa, however, Braun sounded a different note. The *Johannesburg Star* quoted defiant speeches in which Braun praised those who did not "pander to Afro-Asians." There were other signs of stubbornness as well. When the IOC decided to send a trio of members to investigate conditions in South Africa, SANOC failed to supply promised information and the visit had to be postponed.

Intransigence in white Johannesburg and Pretoria begot resistance in black Bamako, Mali, where representatives of thirty-two African states gathered in December 1966 to form the Supreme Council for Sport in Africa. The delegates resolved "to use every means to obtain the expulsion of South African sports organizations from the Olympic Movement and from International Federations should South Africa fail to comply fully with the IOC rules." The SCSA urged its members to "subject their decision to participate in the 1968 Olympic Games to the reservation that no racialist team from South Africa takes part."

At Teheran in 1967, SANOC seemed to have become slightly more amenable to compromise. Braun announced that there would be a single team for South Africa, composed of whites and nonwhites, and that the athletes would travel together, live together, wear the same uniform, and compete under the same flag. This was what the IOC wanted to hear, but the members had come under increased pressure from black Africans whose patience had worn thin. Jean-Claude Ganga, speaking for the SCSA, urged the IOC not to take SANOC's assurances at face value. "We do not wish," said Ganga, "that the Blacks of Africa appear like costumed apes [who are] presented at a fair and then, when the fair is over, [are] sent back to their cages."

The IOC decided to postpone its final decision until after Lord Killanin, Sir Reginald Alexander, and Sir Adetokunbo Ademola had seen for themselves what steps had been taken to end apartheid in sports. During mid-September 1967, the group spent ten days in South Africa, traveling together and staying at the same hotels. (Killanin and Ademola were, however, ordered by a Cape Town police officer not to sit together on the same seaside bench.) The commission resisted Braun's desire to have a SANOC observer present whenever they interrogated opponents of apartheid. While the commission was still in South Africa, Minister of Sport Frank Waring gave a defiant interview in which he said, "We are not going to have [Olympic] trials between whites and non-whites in South Africa." The most the three negotiators were able to wrest from the government was an offer to send a mixed team assembled not on the basis of direct competition but rather by statistical comparisons.

Returning via Nairobi, where they spent three days discussing their findings, the trio prepared a 114-page report that was exactly what most members of the IOC had hoped for. Killanin, Alexander, and Ademola concluded that SANOC's proposals were "an acceptable basis for a multiracial team." Their report was issued on January 30, 1968, shortly before the IOC met at Grenoble (during the winter games). By a mail ballot, the committee voted to reinstate SANOC and to welcome a multiracial team to the summer games. Brushing aside protests from nonwhite South Africans, Brundage announced that the IOC had struck a blow against apartheid. It was not the obnoxious government of South Africa that had been invited to Mexico City but rather "a multiracial team of individuals selected by a multiracial committee."

The IOC's decision was announced on February 15. Two days later, Algeria and Ethiopia announced their intention to boycott the 1968 Games. On February 27, the thirty-two-nation Organization of African Unity called for the same action. Brundage's initial response was to appear unconcerned, but the Africans soon found support among the nations of the Caribbean, the Islamic world, and the Communist bloc. On March 6, the Soviet Union threatened to withdraw from the games. Pressure mounted and the panicky Mexican organizers begged Brundage to reconvene the IOC for a reconsideration. Hoping to save the committee from the appearance of irresolution, Brundage flew to South Africa in a quixotic effort to persuade SANOC to withdraw voluntarily. Braun retorted that he would "rather be shot in Mexico City than hanged in Johannesburg." The IOC executive board met in Lausanne on April 20 and decided to poll the entire membership. When the results were in, the members had voted 47-16 (with 8 abstentions) to withdraw the SANOC invitation. Brundage, shaken by the result, pretended that he had not suffered a defeat and that the IOC had not behaved like a political weather vane.

A little more than a month later, the U.N. Security Council condemned the white-dominated government of Rhodesia, which had declared its independence from Great Britain, and asked that Rhodesian passports not be accepted for international travel. Pedro Ramírez Vazquez, head of the Mexican organizing committee for the 1968 Games, was told by Mexico's foreign minister that athletes carrying Rhodesian passports would not be allowed to enter the country. In the eyes of the IOC, the Rhodesian situation was quite different from the South African situation because sports facilities in Rhodesia were not strictly segregated by race, as was the case in South Africa. Another important difference was that the Rhodesian National Olympic Committee had decided of its own volition to send a mixed team of fourteen white and two black athletes to Mexico City. Brundage condemned the decision of the Mexican government as "a flagrant violation of international law." Protests from the IOC were, however, useless. There was no Rhodesian team at the 1968 Games.

The late sixties were a time of troubles, but the winter games, celebrated at Grenoble, were relatively free of political overtones. The hero of the games was France's Jean-Claude Killy, who won the men's downhill, the slalom, and the giant slalom. Marielle Goitschel completed the women's slalom twenty-nine hundreths of a second ahead of Canada's Nancy Greene, and Annie Famose finished second, behind Greene, in the giant slalom. The French, it seemed, had some reason to feel that they had not fallen into athletic obscurity. The Austrians, however, were not happy. Karl Schranz had been given an opportunity to repeat a run because spectators had blocked gate 22 of the slalom course. After announcing that his time was three seconds faster than Jean-Claude Killy's, the officials reversed themselves on the grounds that Schranz had missed two gates. The gold went to Killy. In the cross-country races and the newly introduced biathlon, the Scandi-

navians, especially the Norwegians, were the stars. Italy's Eugenio
Monti piloted the two-man and the four-man bobsleds to victory.
America's Peggy Fleming and Austria's Wolfgang Schwarz were the
winners among the solo figure skaters. Ludmila Belusova and Oleg Pro-
topopov of the Soviet Union were as unbeatable a pair as they had been
four years earlier in Innsbruck.

For Brundage and the other apostles of amateurism, the most significant thing about the 1968 Winter Games was the accelerated pace
of their commercialization. "The Olympic idea died somewhere in
Grenoble," moaned a writer for *Skiing*, "because there are limits to
what the human psyche can stand in the name of belief." Citing this
article as well as other evidence, Brundage fired off a circular letter
complaining of numerous rules infractions. There was hucksterism
("We had Olympic butter, Olympic sugar, Olympic petrol") and broken
promises. The Fédération Internationale de Ski, for instance, had violated its pledge to remove advertisements from ski equipment. Athletes had been tempted for decades to accept small sums of money
for advertisements painted or sewn on their equipment or clothing,
but the opportunity to reach a global television audience made ad-
vertisers frantic. Athletes were corrupted, rules and regulations were
mocked, money flowed, hypocrisy flourished. The French National
Olympic Committee was said to have paid 300,000 francs to an Italian
ski manufacturer so that Killy could be released from his contract and
freed to endorse a rival French brand. When Killy was told by Olympic
officials not to brandish his trademark skis in front of the television
cameras, he submitted to an extravagant congratulatory hug from a
friend—who held *his* trademark gloves in front of the cameras.

Worst of all, many athletes boasted openly of their enormous under-
the-table incomes and, in effect, dared the IOC to take punitive action
against them. Brundage, who refused to attend the Grenoble Games,
fumed that "many of the Alpine skiers had the impudence to brag
about how they broke the Olympic rules." He fired off a number of
press releases, including one that shouted, "Alpine skiing does not
belong in the Olympic Games!" When he protested to Marceau Crespin
that half the French skiers failed to live up to the amateur rule, Crespin
answered, "You have been misinformed, Monsieur. No one on the
French ski team lives up to your definition." Irate, Brundage vowed a
showdown at Sapporo in 1972.

New political troubles seemed to accumulate throughout the spring
and summer of 1968. The optimism generated in Czechoslovakia by
a somewhat more liberal Communist regime turned to despair as the
tanks of the Warsaw Pact rumbled into Prague and crushed the possibility, for another twenty years, of "socialism with a human face."

Czechoslovakia's most famous athlete, Emil Zatopek, protested against the invasion and was ousted from the Communist party and from his country's national Olympic committee. Jan Staubo, IOC member from Norway, cabled Brundage and urged that the Soviet Union and the East Germany be barred from the 1968 Games in Mexico City. Brundage responded to the crisis as he always did: "If participation in sport is to be stopped every time the politicians violate the laws of humanity, there will never be any international contests." The majority of members agreed with him—and it is hard to deny that he had a point. How could a humane and peaceful world be a precondition for the games that were meant to contribute to the creation of a humane and peaceful world?

Other problems impinged upon preparations for the upcoming games. It was, in many ways, a year of intense frustration. The Tet Offensive of the Viet Cong and North Vietnamese proved that the non-Communist government in South Vietnam was barely viable despite the support of over half a million American troops. Anger against Lyndon Johnson was so intense in that election year that he dropped out of the presidential race almost before it was begun. His announcement that he was no longer a candidate for the nomination seemed to open the way for Robert Kennedy—until an assassin's bullet subverted the electoral process. Students at Columbia and other universities exploded in rage against the war, against racism, against unresponsive academic bureaucrats. Almost simultaneously, French students took to the streets and were joined by tens of thousands of French workers impatient with the endless wait for social justice. The turmoil spread to other countries, including Mexico.

Brundage and his IOC colleagues had been justifiably pleased with themselves when they chose Mexico City as the site of the 1968 Games. Following the first Olympics ever celebrated in Asia, it had seemed appropriate that a developing nation be the next host, in an effort to actualize the universalistic ideals proclaimed by the Olympic Charter. Enthusiasm faded when it became clear that Mexico, too, was in the midst of domestic turmoil. Social unrest, led by students angry at what they saw as the betrayal of the Mexican Revolution by an entrenched bureaucratic party, intensified. Less than a month before the Olympic Games were scheduled to begin, the Mexican army moved against the protesters; on October 2, a number of demonstrators were killed in the Plaza of Three Cultures. The government admitted that 35 people had been slain, but *The Guardian* estimated that 267 had been killed and over a thousand wounded. Brundage rushed to Mexico City, met with Pedro Ramírez Vazquez, the head of the organizing committee, and issued the inevitable statement: "We have conferred with the Mexican authorities and we have been assured that nothing will interfere with the peaceful entrance of the Olympic flame into the stadium . . . nor with the competitions which follow."

There was no attempt on the part of the Mexican dissidents to interfere with the games. There was, however, considerable interference in a form less public than the protests that had rocked the capital. Hucksters were as clever in Mexico City as they had been in Grenoble— and just as willing to ignore Brundage's impotent fulminations. Consider, for instance, the enterprising shoe manufacturers Horst and Armin Dassler. On October 11, according to British runner Christopher Brasher, they brazenly paid the athletes who agreed to run in Adidas and Puma shoes. Brundage was probably the only person still obsessed by the amateur rule, and even he had more important things to think about.

Once the games began, there was reason for optimism. At the opening ceremony, Brundage, who has been painted as an obdurate opponent of women's sports, was pleased by a feminist gesture. The Mexican organizers chose a young woman, Enriqueta Basilio, to carry the Olympic torch into the stadium and to climb the ninety steps that led to the Olympic flame, which she lit. This was a political statement that Brundage approved of (because he refused to classify it as a political statement).

The women's performances in Mexico City were impressive. America's Wyomia Tyus blazed to victory in the 100-meter sprint, and Madeline Manning, another black runner, came within a second of breaking the two-minute barrier for 800 meters. Poland's Irena Kirszenstein was the fastest for 200 meters, and France's Colette Besson won the 400-meter race. West Germany's Ingrid Becker won the pentathlon, and the women from Eastern Europe took all the gold medals in the field events. According to the official report of the United States Olympic Committee, "The US mermaids seemed to be a race apart." The most impressive performance in the pool was by Claudia Kolb, who won the 200-meter and the 400-meter medleys, both in Olympic-record time.

None of these stellar achievements has been as fixed in historical memory as the photograph of two black athletes, standing on the victory podium, raising black-gloved fists in the "black power" salute, ignoring "The Star-Spangled Banner." For Brundage and his colleagues, this was an inexplicable act (and one to be punished by expulsion from the games), but millions of Afro-Americans knew exactly what Tommy Smith and John Carlos wanted to express by their symbolic gesture.

The civil rights movement in the United States, which made significant gains in the early sixties, had slowed as the nation's resources were diverted to the vain effort to halt a Communist takeover of South Vietnam. That the "grunts" fighting and dying in Southeast Asia were disproportionately black intensified the anger felt by Afro-American activists. When the murder of Martin Luther King, Jr., seemed to snuff out the possibility of peaceful progress toward racial justice, many despairing blacks turned to violence. Cities burned.

Although the members of the International Olympic Committee prided themselves, with some justice, as defenders of a multiracial movement specifically opposed to racism, Harry Edwards, a black sports sociologist, had a different perception of reality. In his eyes, the Olympic Games were an occasion for mostly white officials to use black athletes to divert attention from the basic inequalities of American society. In November 1967, Edwards called for a black boycott of the Olympics as a means to call attention to all those ways in which ordinary Afro-Americans continued to suffer the indignities of second-class citizenship. The call to boycott failed despite initial support from Lee Evans, Tommy Smith, and a number of others because most Afro-American athletes felt that they had worked too long and too hard to sacrifice their chance at fame (and, in some cases, fortune). They joined the team, but their mood was sullen and resentful. In Mexico City, black athletes blocked white athletes from the tartan track and prevented their training. Tommy Smith spoke sharply to reporters: "I don't want Brundage presenting me any medals."

Not all the Afro-American athletes were angry. There were those, like the boxer George Foreman, who thought that it was an act of senseless ingratitude to protest against an institution that had proven itself less racist than most. Some black athletes who seemed as politically docile as Foreman may, however, have been intimidated by economic coercion. Christopher Brasher was told by one of the black athletes that the National Football League had telephoned prospective players and warned them not to join a boycott. There is no way to verify this plausible rumor.

In terms of publicity, Smith and Carlos were the most successful militants, but they were not the only ones to protest. On the day the U.S. Olympic Committee suspended the two athletes from the team and expelled them from the Olympic village, Lee Evans set a world record for 400 meters and mounted the podium with Larry James and Ron Freeman, the black athletes who had come in second and third. All three wore black berets. Careful to remove the berets during the playing of the national anthem, they waved them provocatively when the music stopped. Then they walked jauntily away, and escaped censure by the USOC. Brundage fumed. In fact, several years later he was still furious enough to write in his unpublished autobiography,

"Warped mentalities and cracked personalities seem to be everywhere and impossible to eliminate."

Brundage did succeed in eliminating pictures of the black-power protest from the lavishly illustrated official report published by the USOC. When the Mexican organizing committee released a film in which Smith and Carlos appear, Brundage objected, "The nasty demonstration against the United States flag by negroes . . . had nothing to do with sport. . . . [It] has no more place in the record of the games than the gunfire" at the pregame riots. Coming from a man unbothered by the prominent appearance of Adolf Hitler in Leni Riefenstahl's film *Olympia*, these were odd remarks. Indeed, one might argue that the gunfire provoked by social unrest was as important a part of Olympic history as the pigeons released to symbolize a world at peace.

Politics were, of course, only a small part of the 1968 Olympics, but they seemed to intrude again and again. It was as impossible to ignore the brandished fists and waved berets as it was to overlook the tiny American flag flourished by George Foreman as he celebrated his second-round knockout of Ionis Chepulis from the Soviet Union. The Japanese men won their third straight team title in gymnastics, but the focus of attention was on Czechoslovakia's Vera Caslavska rather than on Japan's Sawao Kato (the men's champion). Caslavska was involved in a close contest with her Russian rivals Zinaida Voronina and Natalia Kuchinskaya. Except for the East Germans, whose army had contributed importantly to the occupation of Czechoslovakia, most of the Communist athletes and spectators cheered for Caslavska. She won the hearts of the host-country audience when she chose the "Mexican Hat Dance" as the musical accompaniment for her final floor exercise. When it was over, she had four gold and two silver medals, and she had defeated Voronina and Kuchinskaya for the individual title. Larisa Petrik of the Soviet Union was fourth; Erika Zuchold and Karin Janz, both of East Germany, were fifth and sixth. It was a small consolation for the tragic dénouement of the "Prague Spring."

Not every memorable moment was imbued with obvious political significance. America's Dick Fosbury revolutionized high jumping with his totally unorthodox and completely successful "Fosbury flop." And then there was "the leap." On October 17, America's Ralph Boston set an Olympic long-jump record of 8.27 meters. The next day, his teammate Bob Beamon, an erratic jumper known for taking off on the wrong foot, shrugged away his nervous inhibitions and did everything right. Tearing down the runway as if he were running a 100-meter race, he launched himself from the very edge of the board. It may well be that the most vivid image of the entire games was of Beamon hurtling through the thin air of Mexico City to an astonishing world record of

8.90 meters, some 63 centimeters beyond the old mark. Jerry Nason of the *Boston Globe* described Beamon as "a typewriter ribbon unwinding in space." Sportswriter Dick Schaap and sports physiologist Ernst Jokl were but two of many experts who called the leap the greatest single athletic achievement of all time. It was a phenomenal performance that Beamon himself found hard to believe.

The rarefied atmosphere of Mexico City helped Beamon and others whose feats required anaerobic bursts of strength. However, athletes whose sports required endurance suffered from a lack of oxygen. In an effort at acclimatization, the American team had spent two months at Lake Tahoe, but neither they nor others who trained to overcome the oxygen deficit were able to stay with the distance runners from East Africa. World-record-holder Jim Ryun trailed Kenya's Kipchoge Keino in the 1,500-meter run and others panted vainly after Mohammed Gammondi, Naftali Temu, Mamo Wolde, Amos Bisworth, and Ben Kogo in various endurance contests.

To complain as Britain's Christopher Brasher did that Temu's time for 10,000 meters was slow was to assume that the purpose of the Olympic Games is to set records rather than to let the world's best athletes come together and compete against each other. Defending the International Olympic Committee's choice of Mexico City, Brundage commented to Daniel J. Ferris, "The Olympic Games belong to all the world, not the part of it at sea level." Brasher was especially upset that Australia's world-record distance specialist, Ronald Clarke, was able to do no better than sixth place. Brasher described him, "unconscious, an oxygen mask clamped over his nose and mouth," and added bitterly, "They call this sport." When Maurice Herriott, who had won a silver medal in the steeplechase at the 1964 Games, was carried off the field on a stretcher, Brasher "felt like throttling the whole of the International Olympic Committee." He and other angry critics seemed to forget that the imperatives of modern sports have driven athletes to maim and kill themselves at sea-level too. "These are the Olympics," said Al Oerter, competing despite a slipped disk in his neck. "You die for them." Oerter's words were tragically prophetic, but no one then took them literally.

Shortly after the closing ceremony in Mexico City, the IOC was once again bogged down in the morass of racial politics. As the committee prepared to meet in Warsaw in June 1969, South Africa was once again on the agenda. Should suspension become expulsion? IOC member Reginald Honey fumed, "The IOC is a farce today, as they do whatever they want and break their own rules every day." At the session, Honey protested that South Africa had never broken an Olympic rule. "There is no possible reason why we should be expelled, except for political reasons." His arguments were persuasive enough for the IOC to postpone a final decision until the Amsterdam session of May 1970. At that meeting, Brundage begged for "a correct solution to our thorny problems." A solution was found, correct or not, after South Africa's Frank Braun fulminated against the IOC in general and Brundage in particular. Brundage confided to the Marquess of Exeter that the South African delegation "certainly dug their own grave." The final vote for expulsion was 35-28, with 3 abstentions.

Although the walls of apartheid were breached in the 1980s, when some multiracial sports events were allowed, the IOC actually increased its pressure on the white South Africans. The Commission on Apartheid and Olympism, set up in 1988, recommended that any athlete who competed in South Africa be automatically disqualified for Olympic competition. The full committee accepted the commission's recommendation. It was not until 1991, when the South African government began to dismantle the entire system of apartheid, that the IOC declared itself ready to reinstate SANOC.

SANOC was gone, as of May 1970, but Abraham Ordia of the Organization of African Unity asked that Reginald Honey be allowed to keep his seat on the IOC, which he did. (During a reception at the Olympic congress in Baden-Baden in 1981, I noticed an elderly man propped motionless against a wall. When I asked about him, I was told that it was the ninety-year-old Honey, present physically if not mentally as "our last link with South Africa." When Honey died a year later, the link was broken.)

From these debates over apartheid there was some respite. Amateurism was the great issue at the 1972 Winter Games in Sapporo. It was the last time that Brundage was able to make an issue of the fact that most Olympic athletes were now professionals in the sense that they were materially rewarded for their prowess by government support (as in the Communist world), by athletic scholarships (in the United States), or by secret and not-so-secret payments (as in Western Europe). In Brundage's eyes, the skiers were the worst culprits because they were more brazen than the other athletes in their subversion of Olympic rules. It was, for instance, infuriatingly common to see their photographs in ski advertisements. Since it was unthinkable (except for Brundage) to eject all sinners from the games, Austria's Karl Schranz, the most brazen of them all, became the scapegoat. Disqualified for receiving payments from ski manufacturers, he resorted to the time-honored "everybody does it" defense. "The Russians," he pointed out, "are subsidized by their government and all international athletes get help from one source or another." When Schranz returned to Austria, he was given a hero's welcome. The Austrian government honored him with the Order of Merit for Sports, and Brundage was hanged in effigy.

Meanwhile, Holland's Ard Schenk won three of four speedskating races and Switzerland's Marie-Thérès Nadig starred in the Alpine events. When the games were over, the Russians, the Germans, and the Scandinavians had won 110 of the 228 medals.

From Sapporo, the focus of the Olympic movement shifted to Munich. Knowing all too well that the mention of Munich summoned up unsavory memories of Hitler's first attempt to topple the Weimar Republic and of Neville Chamberlain's misguided policies of appeasement, the German organizers of the 1972 Games were determined to change the city's image. These were to be the "cheerful games" (*heitere Spiele*), but the organizers' hopes were threatened even before the games began.

Having more or less solved the South African problem by the expulsion of SANOC, the International Olympic Committee had searched for an answer to the Rhodesian question. A special investigation by the International Amateur Athletic Federation, conducted early in 1971, found that Rhodesia had no separate clubs for whites, no special facilities, and no separate championships. For the black Africans organized in the Supreme Council for Sport in Africa, however, the issue was not sports but rather the white minority government of Ian Smith, which had proclaimed its independence from Great Britain. The IOC hoped to mollify the black Africans by stipulating that Rhodesian athletes, black and white, would have to travel with British passports (the only ones recognized by the United Nations) and would have to compete under the same colonial flag used in Tokyo in 1964.

This ruling was not good enough for Guyana, Liberia, Sierra Leone, Ghana, Tanzania, Zambia, Ethiopia, and the Sudan. By midsummer they had withdrawn from the games, and Kenya threatened to do so as well. The attempt at a compromise broke down completely when the Rhodesian team showed up in Munich in 1972 with Olympic identity cards rather than the agreed-upon British passports. The cards had been altered to include the words "British Subject," but this modification failed to placate the SCSA and its allies within the International Olympic Committee (Nigeria's H. E. O. Adefope and the Soviet Union's Konstantin Andrianov). Germany's Willi Daume, an influential IOC member as well as head of the Munich organizing committee, reported to Brundage that twenty-one African teams were prepared to boycott the games if the Rhodesians were allowed to participate. An angry Brundage characterized the threat as "naked political blackmail" and "a savage attack on basic principles." But he no longer commanded a majority of the IOC, and a motion to bar the Rhodesians passed by a vote of 36-31, with 3 abstentions.

For most of the members this was a depressing outcome, but the somber mood brightened when the games began. Daume and the rest of the organizing committee felt sure that they had done all that was possible to dispel memories of the Nazi Olympics of 1936. Drawing on the financial resources of the city, the Länder, and the federal government, as well as on the bank accounts of the world's television networks, they had raised some $750 million. The German organizers were rightly proud of the Olympic village, the futuristic stadium (which cost $45 million), and the other facilities constructed for the games. Every visual detail, down to the choice of colors and the design of the logos for different sports, had been carefully planned by Otl Aicher. A new subway system whisked athletes and spectators back and forth from downtown Munich to the site of the games. The Bavarian people seemed almost desperately anxious that everyone have the time of his or her life.

With the athletes from the East Germany competing for the first time in their own uniforms and with their own flag and anthem, the twenty-year-old East-West rivalry was more intense than ever. In track and field, the United States and the Soviet Union shared the honors. The Soviet men won the 100 meters and the 200 meters (Valery Borsov), the high jump (Juri Tarmak), the triple jump (Victor Saneev), the hammer throw (Anatoli Bondarchuk), and the decathlon (Nikolai Avilov). The American men won the 400 meters (Vincent Matthews), the 800 meters (David Wottle), the marathon (Frank Shorter), the 110-meter hurdles (Rodney Milburn), the 4 × 100–meter relay, and the long jump (Randy Williams). The Americans might have done still better if Eddie Hart and James Robinson had shown up in time to participate in their race. (They were not the last American athletes to be disqualified for appearing late or not at all. It was, unfortunately, a familiar pattern in subsequent Olympics.)

The East and the West German men each won two track-and-field events, and Finland's Lasse Viren doubled in the 5,000-meter and 10,000-meter races. Experts expected the East German women, led by sprinter Renate Stecher, to dominate track and field, and they did indeed win six of the fourteen events, but the West German women upset many predictions by winning four golds. When sixteen-year-old Ulrike Meyfarth cleared the bar at 1.92 meters and set a new world record in the high jump, she was as surprised as anyone in the stadium. The victory in the newly introduced 1,500-meter race for women went to the Soviet Union's Ludmilla Bragina.

Although women swam to nine world records, three of them set by Australia's Shane Gould, the television cameras featured Mark Spitz, who set four world records in individual events and won three more gold medals with the American relay teams. Roland Matthes of East Germany and Gunnar Larsson of Sweden set two world records each. Japan's Sawao Kato was once again the world's best gymnast, and he was once again outshone by the women. Unlike Mexico City, where Vera Caslavska's defeat of her Russian rivals had obvious political overtones, the contest now seemed to be a matter of gymnastic styles. The traditional emphasis on strength and grace brought medals to Ludmilla Tourischeva (USSR), Karin Janz (GDR), and Tamara Lazakovitch (USSR), but Roone Arledge of ABC-TV made diminutive Olga Korbut (USSR) the most famous woman in Munich. The enterprising Arledge, who in recent years had captured a lion's share of the American television audience with "Wide World of Sports" and "Monday Night Football," recognized an opportunity and seized it. Tourischeva, the reigning world champion, was the center of attention until Korbut slipped and fell from the uneven parallel bars. The youngster quickly remounted, continued her routine, dismounted, then burst into tears. Realizing instantly that he had the makings of a new heroine with attention-getting "human interest," Arledge ordered the camera to focus on her, and a new era began in which "pixies" displaced women and the sport of women's gymnastics was transformed into children's acrobatics.

Meanwhile, Eastern Europe's strong men won all but one of the nine competitions in weight lifting. Vassily Alexeev's three-lift total of 640 kilograms broke the previous Olympic record by nearly 70 kilograms. Except for two Italians and one Frenchman, athletes from the East also dominated the men's and women's fencing matches. It was no surprise that Russians, Bulgarians, Hungarians, Romanians, and Czechs defeated their opponents in fifteen of twenty wrestling matches, but American spectators were shaken by the prowess of the Communist boxers, who triumphed in all but two of the weight categories. Cuba's Teofilo Stevenson was an easy winner over the other heavyweights. Ray Seales was the only American finalist; he defeated Bulgaria's Anghel Anghelov for the gold medal.

The most disputed sports event undoubtedly was men's basketball. When the final horn sounded, the Soviet team trailed the Americans by 50-49, but then R. W. Jones, head of the International Basketball Federation, announced that there was still some time left on the clock, and he ordered the officials to continue the game. The Soviets had failed to score by the time the horn sounded a second time, but they were given an additional three seconds on the grounds that the clock had not been adjusted after the first continuation. In those three seconds, Alexander Belov made a basket and the Soviets won, 51-50. Supporting the vociferous American protest, Italy's Renate Righetto, one of the referees, signed the official scoresheet but complained that the additional time was "completely illegal and an infraction [of] the rules of a basketball game." Timekeeper H. J. Tenschert agreed with Righetto, but an international jury rejected the official American protest. The jurors from Cuba, Hungary, and Poland outvoted the non-Communist minority.

In David Wolper's brilliant collective documentary film *Visions of Eight,* one of the eight directors assembled a sad sequence on the injured, the fallen, the defeated Olympians. A clever idea, considering that disappointments are inevitable in sports—you can't have winners without losers. What no one expected, however, was that these Olympics were to be remembered for one of the world's most horrifying acts of political terror. In the predawn hours of September 5, a little after 4:00 A.M., a small group of Palestinian terrorists clambered over the fence of the Olympic village and made their way to the quarters of the Israeli team at 31 Connollystrasse. The six who had climbed the fence were joined by two Palestinians who worked in the village. Together they made their way to apartment 1 and rang the bell. When Yousef Gutfreund realized who they were, he blocked the doorway long enough for Turia Sokolovsky to escape through the window. Gutfreund and three others were captured. Moshe Weinberg and Shmuel Rodensky were seized as they returned from town (where they had gone to see *Fiddler on the Roof*). The terrorists believed Weinberg when he explained that apartment 2 was occupied by the Uruguayan team, and several of the Palestinians then moved to apartment 3. During the scuffle there, Gad Tsobani managed to break loose and escape, but five more hostages were taken back to apartment 1. David Berger and Weinberg managed to grab knives and wound two of their captors before they were killed. Meanwhile, the Israelis in apartments 2 and 5, alerted by the sound of gunfire, escaped. In apartment 4, two Israeli doctors were too frightened to flee.

It was now nearly 5:00 A.M. The police had been alerted and the siege began. The terrorists' first ultimatum demanded the release by 9:00 of 234 Palestinians held in Israel and of 2 German terrorists—Andreas Baader and Ulrike Meinhof—who were imprisoned in West Germany. To emphasize their seriousness, the terrorists threw Weinberg's mutilated body out a window.

By 7:15, Minister of the Interior Hans-Dietrich Genscher and other German officials were consulting with Brundage (who actually played a minor role on the so-called crisis staff). By 9:10, a new deadline was negotiated and the two Israeli doctors, reassured by a hand signal from one of the negotiators, escaped from apartment 4. The talks dragged on for hours. Among those who sought a peaceful solution to the deadlock was Ahmed Touny, an IOC member from Egypt, but the best he and other Arab diplomats were able to achieve was a series of postponements of the terrorists' deadline. Eventually, the Palestinians were allowed to take their hostages to Fürstenfeldbruck airfield, where they expected to be flown to an Arab destination. As they moved toward the plane, the German police opened fire. When the shooting stopped, three of the captors and all of the captives were dead. The police had underestimated the number of terrorists involved and had deployed too few sharpshooters. They had also failed to use infrared lights.

While the German authorities had struggled to find a means to free the hostages, the International Olympic Committee had wrestled with its own problem: should the games be continued or should they be suspended? Many committee members felt from the first that the executive board should be called into immediate session, but Brundage resisted the idea, which infuriated Comte Jean de Beaumont. According to Killanin, the Frenchman was "particularly upset by Brundage's seemingly insane attempt to deal with the whole situation himself." "To Brundage," sputtered Beaumont, "he is the IOC—no one else, just he!" After consulting with Willi Daume, Brundage announced at 3:15 P.M. the cancellation of the rest of that day's events. He also announced a memorial service for 10:00 A.M. the next day (September 6). Brundage had earlier told Killanin, in Kiel for the yacht races, that there was no need for the executive board to meet, but the Irishman, furious, had flown back to Munich and demanded that the board be convened. Brundage gave in.

The board, which consisted of Beaumont, Killanin, Ademola, Andrianov, Hermann van Karnebeek (Holland), Sylvio de Magalhães Padilha (Brazil), Prince Tsuneyoshi Takeda (Japan), and Juan Antonio Samaranch (Spain), convened at 7:00 P.M. on September 5 and unanimously endorsed the memorial; it also called the entire committee into session. At a stormy meeting, which the American representative Douglas F. Robey called a real "knock-down-drag-out session," many of the members agreed with Killanin that Brundage had behaved badly, but they concurred with their president that cancellation of the games would have been a surrender to terrorism. Before the meeting broke up, Daume rushed in with the news that the hostages had been rescued. He had been misled by false radio and television reports.

At the memorial service on September 6, which was boycotted by the athletes and officials from Arab nations, Germany's President Gustav Heinemann expressed his grief and sorrow. Brundage spoke last:

Every civilized person recoils in horror at the barbarous criminal intrusion of terrorists into peaceful Olympic precincts. We mourn our Israeli friends[,] victims of this brutal assault. The Olympic flag and the flags of all the world fly at half mast. Sadly, in this imperfect world, the greater and more important the Olympic Games become, the more they are open to commercial, political and now criminal pressure. The Games of the Twentieth Olympiad have been subject to two savage attacks. We lost the Rhodesian battle against naked political blackmail. We have only the strength of a great ideal. I am sure that the public will agree that we cannot allow a handful of terrorists to destroy this nucleus of international cooperation and good will we have in the Olympic Movement. The Games must go on and we must continue our effort to keep them clean, pure and honest and try to extend the sportsmanship of the athletic field into other areas.

We declare today a day of mourning and will continue all the events one day later than originally planned.

The unnecessary reference to "the Rhodesian battle against naked political blackmail" sounded a discordant note that angered Abraham Ordia and Jean-Claude Ganga, leaders of the Supreme Council for Sport in Africa. Killanin, too, deplored Brundage's "insensitivity" in this matter and eventually persuaded him to issue a statement of regret for these "misinterpreted" remarks.

The IOC's decision to continue the games was one that Red Smith and many other journalists condemned as inhumane and coldly self-interested. Smith's column in the *New York Times* for September 18 was typical of the criticism: "This time surely, some thought, they would cover the sandbox and put the blocks aside. But no. 'The Games must go on,' said Avery Brundage, high priest of the playground, and 80,000 listeners burst into applause. The occasion was yesterday's memorial service for eleven members of Israeli's Olympic delegation murdered by Palestinian terrorists. It was more like a pep rally."

The Israeli government, however, agreed with the decision to continue the games. During the crisis, Prime Minister Golda Meir had sent the Germans a message: "The Israeli government does not negotiate with terrorists." It was clear that she concurred with the IOC that cancellation of the games would have been interpreted as a victory for the terrorists. Cancellation also would have encouraged repeated acts of terror. Even Killanin, no admirer of Brundage, had some words of praise for his firmness: "The decision—to cancel [the games] or not—was a hard one to make, but I am sure that Brundage's instinct was right, and that his stubborn determination saved the Olympic Movement one last time." In his memorial statement, Brundage had expressed his belief that the public would agree with the IOC. In the long run, the public—or most of it—did.

10

The Era of the Boycott

Youssef Nagui Assad was a physical education teacher in Cairo. And a shot-putter. In 1968, at the age of twenty-three, he tried out for Egypt's Olympic team but failed to qualify—by two centimeters. In 1972, he made the team and went to Munich, but he was ordered home because his government wished to show solidarity with the Palestinian cause. In 1976, he again made the team and went to Montreal but was ordered home because his government joined the boycott to protest New Zealand's rugby ties with South Africa. In 1980, at the age of thirty-five, he made the team once more, but his government chose to boycott the games to protest the Soviet Union's invasion of Afghanistan. Small wonder that the German journalist Willi Knecht has taken Youssef Nagui Assad's disappointments as a symbol of an unhappy era of politicized sports.

Los Angeles and Moscow had coveted the 1976 Games, but Montreal got them, which was the source of some bitterness. When the International Olympic Committee decided the question in May 1970, Moscow had led on the first ballot by a vote of 28 to 25 (only 17 votes went to Los Angeles, a sign that the members may have recognized the widespread international opposition to continued American involvement in a lost war in Vietnam). On the second ballot, Montreal secured a 42-28-1 majority, and there were angry comments from TASS, the Soviet news agency, to the effect that the "capitalists" had ganged up to deny the "socialists" an opportunity to host the games. The Russians were not completely paranoid. Mayor Sam Yorty of Los Angeles declared that he was relieved that the games had been saved for "the free world." When Moscow *did* get the nod for the 1980 Games, forty U.S. congressional representatives protested.

On August 23, 1972, shortly before the start of the Munich Games, the IOC elected a new president. Feeling, as one member remarked to

John Lucas, that "twenty years of Brundage were ample," the IOC looked for someone with a less abrasive personality. Comte Jean de Beaumont was the choice of the Latin bloc, but he was too forceful for those who had been uncomfortable under Brundage's authoritarian rule. Instead, the mantle settled on the shoulders of fifty-eight-year-old Lord Killanin.

Born on July 30, 1914, Michael Morris was still a schoolboy at Eton when he inherited his title in 1937 at the death of an unmarried uncle. After a year at the Sorbonne and three at Cambridge, where he boxed and rowed, Killanin became a journalist for the sensationalist *London Daily Mail.* He specialized in gossip and political affairs. After wartime service with the British army, he moved from journalism to a variety of enterprises calling upon his talents as businessman, industrialist, author, and filmmaker. Among his publications was a biography of Geoffrey Kneller, the seventeenth-century portrait painter, and a co-authored guide book—the Shell Oil Company's *Guide to Ireland.* As head of the Olympic Council of Ireland, Killanin had maintained good relations with both Dublin and Belfast. This ability to walk a political tightrope brought him to the attention of the Marquess of Exeter, who nominated him for membership in the IOC. Elected in 1952, he became a vice-president in 1968.

Killanin was a popular committee member whose most important attributes were versatility and geniality. "One thing I can tell you," he said, "I am not Avery Brundage." His predecessor thought as little of him as he did of his predecessor: "We need a leader," remarked Brundage to Willi Daume, "and Michael isn't a leader." During the eight years of Killanin's term in office, many veteran members of the IOC who had chafed under Brundage the martinet voiced their regret that they had not chosen a more forceful and effective president. William E. Simon of the U.S. Olympic Committee was especially acerbic in his characterization of the Irishman. "Explaining something sensible to Lord Killanin," he exclaimed, "is akin to explaining something to a cauliflower. The advantage of the cauliflower is that if all else fails, you can always cover it with melted cheese and eat it." The committee was probably lucky that IOC Director Monique Berlioux remained in office through the Killanin years. Killanin described her in his autobiography, *My Olympic Years,* as "authoritarian," and he acknowledged that he had originally thought of replacing her. He professed, however, to be thankful that he had kept her on.

One of the new president's ambitions was to adjust the amateur rule to the reality of sports in the late twentieth century. "I try to deal with things as they are," he commented, "not as we'd like them to be in a more perfect world." By 1978, Rule 26 of the Olympic Charter had been modified to the point where athletes were allowed openly to earn money from endorsements if the money went to their national sports federation or their country's national Olympic committee. The receiving organization was then permitted to pay the athlete's expenses, including food, shelter, clothing, equipment, travel, medical care, and pocket money. "Broken-time" payments for time away from the athlete's regular job were also authorized—if the athlete *had* a regular job. Rule 26 continued, however, to declare "professional athletes" ineligible. This sort of cautiously pragmatic adjustment to reality proved to be an inadequate response to the political convulsions of the seventies.

The 1976 Olympic Games were in trouble long before the athletes began to arrive in Montreal. In 1970, when the city made its bid for the games, Mayor Jean Drapeau had promised austerity. "The Olympics," he said, "should not come as an astronomical enterprise. We promise that in Canada, in Montreal, we will present the Games in the true spirit of Olympism, very humble, with simplicity and dignity." In fact, Drapeau had, or soon developed, grandiose ideas about the scale of the games; at the same time he demonstrated insufficient insight into the construction business by promising "modest games" at no cost to the city's taxpayers. Everyone seemed to have forgotten that Expo '67, which Drapeau had planned, had ended up costing more than twice the original estimate of $60,000,000. The popular success of Expo '67 may have gone to Drapeau's head. He planned for the Olympic Games as if he were a Roman emperor rather than an elected official. The estimated costs of $125,000,000 were ridiculously off the mark; the games actually cost nearly $2 billion and left the city of Montreal and the province of Quebec with burdensome debts.

Drapeau's chosen Parisian architect, Roger Taillibert, designed a magnificent $350-million stadium whose spectacular retractable roof was not completed until years after the games. Drapeau rewarded Taillibert with a bonus that Nick Auf der Maur estimated at nearly $50,000,000. In the face of considerable adverse criticism, Taillibert was by no means abashed: "The West will one day have to acknowledge that sports installations, however costly they may be to build and maintain, must be included in the State's budget in the same way as the manufacture of arms."

Drapeau, whose support of Taillibert never wavered, appointed his cronies to the organizing committee, which proved unable to cope with the extortionate demands of the construction firms and labor unions working on the facilities. Workers struck, workers lollygagged, workers demanded and received overtime pay to make up for time lost in labor disputes. The judgment voiced by Reet and Max Howell seems just: "In addition to the astronomical architect's fees and structural design problems, contributory factors were inflation, strikes, fraud, corruption and inept coordination."

And then there were—not surprisingly—political problems. After the intemperate exchanges between Brundage and a number of American critics of the IOC's China policy, the Chinese controversy continued to simmer. In October 1973, shortly before the Olympic congress in Varna, Bulgaria, the executive committee of the Asian Games Federation voted to admit the People's Republic of China to the 1974 Asian Games and, simultaneously, to expel Taiwan, whose expulsion was a condition of the PRC's participation. The international sports federations, few of which recognized the PRC, condemned the decision. At Varna, the IOC warned the Asian Games Federation that it risked the loss of IOC patronage—a mild threat that was easily ignored. Realizing at this point that they had nothing much to fear from the IOC, a number of international federations decided to recognize the PRC and to oust the Republic of China. By the middle of 1975, the Communists had been accepted into nine international federations and had formed a new national Olympic committee. This committee then petitioned the IOC for recognition with the familiar condition that Taiwan be expelled from the Olympic movement. The Nationalists, although willing now to acquiesce in a "two Chinas" policy, were understandably reluctant to accept their own athletic demise. Killanin's inspired solution to the dilemma was to delay and hope for a miracle.

None came. In 1976, the ideological pot boiled over. As Geoffrey Miller has remarked, "the Olympic Games were turned into a political cauldron." When the city of Montreal had made its initial bid to host the games, the IOC had insisted that "free entry must be accorded to teams from all National Olympic Committees recognized by the International Olympic Committee." Minister Pierre Trudeau gave his government's guarantee. That was in 1969. The next year, the Canadian government altered its foreign policy, withdrawing recognition from the Nationalists on Taiwan and conferring it upon the People's Republic of China. "With more foresight," writes Miller, "the IOC might have challenged the Canadian government in 1970 when Trudeau first changed his China policy."

There were other omens. In 1975, the world's judo championships, scheduled for Barcelona, were canceled after the Spanish government refused to admit the athletes from Taiwan. More ominously, that same year boxers and cyclists from Taiwan were denied the visas they needed to participate in international meets in Montreal. The reason given by the Canadian authorities was that the athletes from the island, availing themselves of permission granted by the IOC in 1968, had described themselves as representatives of the Republic of China.

Unfortunately, the IOC took no notice of Canada's new course. Killanin was stunned, shortly before the games were to begin, to receive a letter from Mitchell Sharp, acting secretary of state for external affairs, informing the committee that the Nationalists would not be admitted into Canada as long as they called themselves representatives of the Republic of China. Beaumont favored the cancellation of the games, but Killanin was temperamentally predisposed to shy away from strong measures. He protested vainly to Trudeau and then, when the prime minister proved adamant, he appealed to the Chinese to participate on Canadian terms. The Chinese refused. Richard Espy's assessment in *The Politics of the Olympic Games* is that the IOC's position was "politically naive" and demonstrated "a serious lack of political acumen."

The absence of a team from Taiwan made it easier for the Fédération Internationale de Football Association, meeting in Montreal, to readmit the People's Republic of China to the soccer federation, from which the Chinese had angrily withdrawn in 1958. FIFA General Secretary Helmut Kaser cabled the good news of readmission on September 20. The Communists remained dissatisfied because the Nationalists on Taiwan had not simultaneously been expelled, and they replied to Kaser on October 6 that "the decision of the Montreal Congress of the FIFA is entirely illegal and in violation of Article One of the FIFA Statues which stipulate that only one Association shall be recognized in each country." Years would go by before the People's Republic was ready to rejoin sports organizations that also recognized the Chinese on Taiwan. In short, neither the Communists nor the Nationalists participated in Montreal.

Even more serious in the days just before the opening of the games was the anger of the Supreme Council for Sport in Africa. At issue were the rugby games played between teams from New Zealand and South Africa. Although IOC Vice-President Mohammed Mzali of Tunesia pointed out that twenty-six other countries also had sporting ties with South Africa, the SCSA demanded that the IOC bar the New Zealanders from the games. Since the IOC had no control whatsoever over rugby, which was not an Olympic sport, Killanin tried to persuade the black Africans not to retaliate against the IOC. He failed. The teams from Ivory Coast and Senegal were allowed by their governments to remain and compete, but twenty-eight African national Olympic committees bowed to political necessity and ordered their athletes— already in Montreal—to return home. The bitterness of the athletes' disappointment was intensified by the fact that the Soviet Union and

its allies refused to join the boycott. For most events, the absence of
the Africans made very little difference, but Kenyans and Ugandans
had won three track contests in 1972 and were expected to do at least
as well in 1976. Those familiar with the runners' world had looked
forward to a 1,500-meter duel between New Zealand's John Walker
and Tanzania's Filbert Bayi. It was not to be.

Although many commentators felt that forceful action might have
averted the African boycott, John Lucas has praised the IOC president's
studied inaction. Killanin "kept a typically low profile and allowed the
defection to happen without any intervention from the IOC. The Taiwan issue was still hot, the African withdrawal lacked credibility even
in the most liberal press, and Killanin sat smoking his pipe, at least in
the figurative sense, waiting for the Olympic pageant to begin. Probably
it was the wisest move—or lack of action—on his part." When the
Soviet Union made a stormy issue of the defection of one of its athletes,
Killanin calmed the waters. The incident passed.

Since the Olympic program had grown to include 198 events in 21
different sports, it was theoretically possible for most of the nations
represented in Montreal to lay claim to at least one gold medal. But,
in fact, three teams—those from the Soviet Union, East Germany, and
the United States—accounted for an absolute majority of the victories.
That the Soviets headed the list with 47 gold medals was no surprise;
that East Germany, with a population of sixteen million, outscored
the United States by 40-34 was cause for considerable anguish in the
hearts of American chauvinists.

The shock was greatest in women's swimming because the American
team, led by Shirley Babashoff, was considered one of the strongest
ever assembled. Babashoff, however, finished a distant fifth in the 100-
meter freestyle and second in the 200-meter, 400-meter, and 800-meter
races. Her only victory came as the anchor of the 4 × 100–meter relay
team. The games' most successful swimmer was East Germany's Kornelia Ender, who set Olympic records in the 100-meter and 200-meter
freestyle and in the 100-meter butterfly. Her fourth gold medal came
in the 4 × 100-meter medley. In all, the amazing East German women
won eleven of the thirteen races, and in five of them they also took
second place. In her disappointment, Babashoff implied that her rivals
had had recourse to anabolic steroids (artificial compounds of male
hormones)—how else could one explain their muscular development
and their unusually deep voices?

With a witty comment, the officials of the East German team
shrugged off Babashoff's implied accusation—"They came to swim, not
to sing"—but anabolic steroids have become—and probably already
were—widely used by athletes determined to win no matter what. The

International Olympic Committee took cognizance of doping in 1961 when a commission was established under the able Arthur Porritt of New Zealand. In 1962, a number of substances were banned; since then, a long list of female athletes, most of them from Eastern Europe, have been disqualified for the use of these substances. Alois Marder, the East German trainer who first realized Kornelia Ender's potential (on the basis of a blood sample), charged in 1977—after his defection to the West—that anabolic steroids had been given to swimmers as young as fourteen and fifteen years old. The end of the German Democratic Republic, in 1989-90, revealed further evidence of illicit recourse to systematic drug use. In short, Babashoff's suspicions, if not her demeanor, may have been justified.

The superiority of East German women in track and field was almost as marked—and just as suspect—as in swimming. They won nine events and finished one-two-three in the pentathlon (but with lower scores than Britain's Mary Peters, the winner in 1972). The only non-Communist winner in women's track and field was West Germany's Annegret Richter, who ran the 100 meters in 11.08 seconds. The stars of men's track and field were Cuba's Alberto Juantorena, who won the 400-meter and 800-meter races, Finland's Lasse Viren, who repeated his 1972 triumphs over 5,000 and 10,000 meters, and Bruce Jenner, whose victory in the decathlon was one of six won by the American track-and-field specialists.

Unfortunately, suspicion was aroused by Viren's achievements as well as by those of the East European women. It was rumored that he had had recourse to "blood doping." In this technique, which violates the spirit but not the letter of Olympic rules, athletes train at high altitudes to increase the number of oxygen-carrying red blood cells. A portion of the blood is then removed and preserved until just before the contest. Then the athletes receive a last-minute transfusion with their own blood to maximize their endurance. The rumor that Viren had resorted to this technique was never substantiated, but it was typical of the suspicion and distrust engendered by modern sports medicine. Were the amazing, record-shattering performances of the Soviet-bloc weight lifters in all nine weight classes made possible by anabolic steroids? The question is unanswerable, but seven weight lifters, including a number of gold-medal winners, were disqualified for having used the substance (and one was ejected from the games for using amphetamines). Olympic officials were right to fear that modern science had created a miasma of doubt. Drugs began to replace "professionalism" as the nightmare that haunts the IOC. "The Olympic ideal," lamented Killanin in his memoirs, "is to create the complete person—not an artificial one."

The specter of chemically altered bodies made concern about amateurism seem increasingly anachronistic. The IOC president's attitude was to let the international sports federations decide who was eligible and who was not (a suggestion made as early as 1925 by Norway's Olaf Ditlev-Simonsen). In the short run, this policy led inevitably to an even crazier patchwork of inconsistent rules. Some federations were almost as strict as the nineteenth-century athletic clubs had been; others were ludicrously permissive. As we have seen, the 1978 rules for track and field allowed athletes to earn huge amounts of money for their clubs, but direct payments to superstars like the American high jumper Dwight Stones brought wrathful reprisals. By 1982, the rules were revised again to permit payments into a trust fund that provided expenses during the athlete's active career—and substantial sums afterward. The IOC's condemnations of commercialism produced cynicism among those who noticed that the committee itself had grown embarrassingly rich from its share of the sale of television rights.

There had, in fact, been a quantum leap in the bidding for television rights. For Montreal, ABC won with an offer of $25 million. With such sums at stake, ABC's sports director, Roone Arledge, planned the coverage with the kind of detailed attention that coaches give to training schedules. "We figured [Nadia] Comaneci would be big for us," he told *Sports Illustrated*'s Frank Deford. "People may be discovering her for the first time, but we've been working her into Wide World [of Sports] for a year or more now. And in the second week, [Frank] Shorter is attractive enough to be big again. We'll go with that. And Bruce Jenner, of course. He could really come out of this hot. He's charismatic. I think he could be another Dorothy Hamill." East Germany's Kornelia Ender, who was considered an unattractive commercial prospect, received scant notice from ABC.

Some of the TV network's decisions were easy to understand. American athletes generally received more attention than foreigners. Track and field and swimming were extensively covered. The cameras lingered twice as long on the female as on the male gymnasts (sixty minutes for the women compared to thirty-one minutes for the men). Basketball fans had ninety minutes of their favorite sport, while most soccer fans probably missed the thirty-five seconds devoted to the world's most popular game. Needless to say, European and Japanese television networks also tailored their offerings to their audiences. An acerbic Monique Berlioux told the listeners of Radio France that the games had been without a soul, but the television viewers of the world were—as always—less demanding. All they asked was that their athletic representatives come home with gold, silver, and bronze medals.

Realizing that innovative sports coverage had enabled ABC to woo viewers from CBS and NBC, the executives of all three networks prepared to bid aggressively for the rights to telecast the 1980 Games. The executives assumed, quite correctly, that the men in the Kremlin would overcome their dislike of capitalism long enough to do business with them. In fact, the Russians were behaving as if they had never heard of Marxism-Leninism. As early as 1970, Soviet sports administrators launched a Madison Avenue–style public relations campaign in which they touted Moscow as the ideal Olympic site. In 1973, thirty-two IOC members were invited to Moscow, where the princes and pashas and CEOs were royally wined and dined. In 1974, all eighty members were guests of the Soviet Union. After the campaign to secure the games was concluded successfully, on October 23, 1974, the Soviets bargained with the American networks and eventually struck a deal with NBC for $85 million.

From the IOC's perspective, the decision to celebrate the 1980 Games in Moscow was obviously a calculated risk. As more and more time became necessary to prepare for the Olympics, the decision on a site was made earlier and earlier, which meant that there was less and less certainty about what to expect on the day the games were to begin. When the IOC chose the Soviet Union as the first Communist state to host the Olympics, East-West relations were problematical, as they had been for decades, but there was no immediate political crisis.

Still, the committee's choice was definitely not "universally welcomed," as claimed by Killanin in *My Olympic Years*. Prominent anti-Communists voiced their displeasure, among them George Meany, president of the AFL-CIO. Meany refused an honorary membership in the U.S. Olympic Committee, and on August 8, 1978, his union called for a change of venue. James Burnham, writing in the *National Review*, repeatedly denounced the approaching games as a propaganda opportunity reminiscent of the Berlin Games in 1936. In Great Britain, the Liberal party discussed a possible boycott as a way to protest the persecution of Soviet dissidents. Israel's Menachim Begin, supported by Jewish groups in the United States, condemned the choice because of the Soviet Union's restrictions on Jewish emigration to Israel.

The real drama began on December 28, 1979, when Radio Moscow reported that the Soviet Union had been asked by the government in Kabul to intervene in Afghanistan. It was a major crisis, but the foreign policy options available to President Jimmy Carter were meager. Diplomatic protests were clearly useless, and the Soviet Union was in a position to veto any measure considered by the U.N. Security Council. Economic reprisals are always costly, and the Carter administration was already in economic trouble as a result of inflated oil prices. The failure of the African boycott in 1976 had demonstrated that an Olympic boycott is an ineffectual tool to work political change, but it was attractively available and relatively inexpensive in political and economic terms. The prolonged crisis over the seizure of American hostages in Teheran was unquestionably on Carter's mind when he determined that *some* kind of action was necessary as a statement of principle (and as a way to preserve his chances for nomination to a second term in the White House). On January 4, Carter suggested the possibility of an Olympic boycott. On January 20, he made public his ultimatum: Soviet withdrawal from Afghanistan or an American boycott of the 1980 Summer Games. Between the two statements came some unexpected support from the Russian dissident Andrei Sakharov, who appeared on ABC-TV with a call for a boycott.

Ironically, the *Final Report of the President's Commission on Olympic Sports* (1977) had deplored "the actions of governments which deny an athlete the right to take part in international competition." Carter indulged in a president's time-honored right to ignore the resolutions of presidential commissions. On January 20, he wrote to Robert Kane, president of the United States Olympic Committee, "I . . . urge [you] . . . to advise the International Olympic Committee that if Soviet troops do not fully withdraw from Afghanistan within the next month, Moscow will become an unsuitable site for a festival meant to celebrate peace and good will." Kane's initial response was to protest in the name of a classically liberal separation of sport and politics: "if we started to make political judgments, it would be the end of the games." His reluctance to countenance a boycott was clearly authorized by the USOC's charter. (Article 9 reads, "No member of the USOC may deny, or threaten to deny, any amateur athlete the opportunity to compete in the Olympic Games.") When the athletes too spoke up to defend their civil rights, Carter became uncharacteristically tough: "I cannot say what other nations will not go. Ours will not go."

On January 21, a compliant House of Representatives endorsed the president's boycott proposal by a vote of 386-12. This resolution was not binding on the USOC, but two days later Kane reassured Congress of the committee's patriotism (if not about his own rhetorical skills): "I cannot imagine that when the national interests are involved that the USOC will be in any position other than [one] in accord with that of the Congress of the United States." In other words, "We surrender." The Senate fell in line on January 29 by a vote of 88-4. Then, Carter insulted the heads of state of sub-Saharan Africa when he sent Mohammad Ali to explain to them the complexities of international politics. The mission turned into a complete fiasco when Ali announced that the Africans had persuaded him that the boycott was a mistake.

Carter also dispatched a special envoy to Dublin to inform Killanin of his wishes. "I discovered," wrote the IOC president, "that Mr. [Lloyd] Cutler had not flown in from Washington to discuss, but rather to instruct." At the winter games at Lake Placid, in February, Secretary of State Cyrus Vance stunned the IOC with a speech that Killanin characterized as "outrageously political and in questionable taste." It was, indeed, a tirade filled with cold war rhetoric. The IOC president remarked in his memoirs that the speech was "greeted with absolute silence by everybody." Subsequently, all seventy-three IOC members, including the Americans, voted to reject Vance's demand that the summer games be transferred to another site or, if that was impractical, that they be canceled. Immediately after the IOC's vote, labor leader George Meany called for the USOC to withdraw from the International Olympic Committee (of which it was not a member).

The winter games were a more or less nonpolitical triumph for the Soviet and East Germans athletes, but American disappointment was mitigated by the totally unexpected victory of its ice hockey team, which defeated a far more experienced Soviet squad. These were the first games at which athletes from the People's Republic of China competed. The way had finally been cleared a year earlier, at the IOC's Nagoya session, when Killanin persuaded the PRC to return to the fold *and* to coexist with the Nationalists. A magic formula was found that identified the latter as "the Chinese Olympic Committee in Taipei." The IOC president, alas, was no Merlin. The magic failed and it was now the Nationalists' turn to boycott, which they did.

After the interlude for sports, the IOC returned to the political crisis. Having failed to persuade the committee to accept his policy, Carter concentrated his fire on the USOC. Since he had no *legal* right to command the USOC to comply with his wishes, the president resorted to threats and intimidation. Where would the USOC be if the federal government not only ended financial support for Olympic sports but also began to tax the organization on its other sources of income? What would the committee do if the president invoked the International Emergency Economic Powers Act, which allowed him to embargo trade in the event of a threat to national security? What if he simply ordered the athletes to stay away from the Soviet Union? When the committee convened in April, Vice-President Walter Mondale addressed them: "History holds its breath," he intoned, "for what is at stake here is no less than the future security of the civilized world." Abject capitulation followed. The members of the U.S. Olympic Committee may or may not have thought that civilization depended on their vote, but they surrendered by a two-to-one margin (1,604 to 797).

The lame excuse given by Kane and others was that it really had been, as Carter and Mondale claimed, a matter of national security.

Many of the athletes were embittered by the sacrifice of their dreams to political expediency. Pentathlete Jane Frederick commented: "whichever way it goes this time, I must accept the inescapable conclusion: I am a pawn." Hurdler Edwin Moses was equally angry. "These," he said, "are *our* games." Others, like high jumper Dwight Stones and discus thrower Al Oerter, proudly subordinated their athletic careers to what was portrayed as the national interest. Public opinion was clearly behind the president. A poll published on February 2 showed that 73 percent of those surveyed favored the boycott. The press, which had expressed great indignation apropos of the African boycott of 1976, was now overwhelmingly in favor of the administration's policy. Red Smith, surely one of the nation's most respected and influential sportswriters, attacked the IOC president in a column entitled "His Lordship's Tantrum."

As soon as Carter had determined to demand a boycott, he launched a drive to persuade the rest of the non-Communist world to join the United States. Aside from the Islamic nations of Asia and North Africa, who were eager to demonstrate solidarity with the Islamic people of Afghanistan, it was not a notably successful campaign. It seemed, at first, that Great Britain was ready to fall obediently into line. Prime Minister Margaret Thatcher announced her support on January 17 and the House of Commons voted by a margin of 315-147 to endorse the boycott. One week later, however, Britain's national Olympic committee lived up to its tradition of independence and defied the government by a vote of 18-5. Thatcher spitefully refused permission for military personnel to go to Moscow and a few national federations opted for a boycott, but the rest of the team made the journey. The British defection was a major defeat for Carter.

Still, the president had some successes. His message was heard clearly not only in the Islamic world but also in countries militarily and/or financially dependent upon the United States. On January 1, Prime Minister Joseph Clark of Canada spoke against the proposed boycott, but he quickly announced his conversion on January 27. When Pierre Trudeau ousted Clark from office, he too decided that it was in Canada's best interest to stay away from Moscow. On April 26, the Canadian National Olympic Committee bowed to realpolitik and voted in favor of the boycott, 137-35.

Although all four of West Germany's major political parties had campaigned in 1980 for sports free from political interference, they seemed not to have had any real convictions about *Einmischung.* Initially, the coalition government was divided on the question of a boycott. Foreign Minister Hans Dietrich Genscher was in favor; Otto Graf von Lambsdorff was opposed. "An Olympic boycott," said the latter, "is nonsense. If it comes, then everyone will be talking about the ruined games and nobody about the invasion of Afghanistan." Carter, however, put immense pressure upon the West German government, which then turned the screws on its national Olympic committee. The struggle was complicated by the fact that West Germany's Willi Daume, head of the national Olympic committee as well as an influential member of the IOC, was generally expected to be Lord Killanin's successor as IOC president (the election was scheduled for Moscow). The West German press, which had vigorously and almost unanimously opposed the idea of a boycott, performed an about-face and denounced Daume for his lack of patriotism. The leading conservative journal *Die Welt,* noted for its vehement opposition to government controls on business, was harsh in its attacks on the athletes who spoke out in the name of individual freedom. When the West German athletes appealed to the government to stand by its liberal principles, the Bundestag replied by voting for a boycott: the tally was 446-8-9. The fight within the West German National Olympic Committee was fierce, but a 59-40 majority acceded to the government's demands (May 15). The second strongest Western team would not be in Moscow.

For once, Israel and the Islamic world were on the same side of a political issue. On May 22, the Israeli National Olympic Committee—which had never been enthusiastic about sending a team to Moscow—voted to stay away. Two days later, Japan followed suit. Military dependence on the United States was unquestionably a factor in both of these decisions. The People's Republic of China, which had its own quarrel with the Kremlin, also decided to honor the boycott.

Most of the other national Olympic committees, however, chose another course. The prestigious newspaper *Le Monde* urged the French National Olympic Committee to shun the Soviets' invitation, but the committee decided, without a single dissenter, to go to Moscow (May 13). The Italians and most of the rest of Europe sided with the British and the French rather than with the West Germans. Although Australia's most widely read newspapers editorialized for the boycott, the Australian Olympic Federation voted 6-5 to send a team. Chile, ruled by the dictator Augusto Pinochet, was the only Latin American nation to boycott the games. Most of the non-Islamic African nations, remembering the ineffectiveness of *their* 1976 boycott, spurned Carter's appeals; Kenya, Liberia, and the Congo were the only African states to join the boycott. In the end, sixty-two nations boycotted; eighty-one participated. The 5,929 athletes at the 1980 Games were fewer than those at the three previous games.

NBC-TV canceled its plans to cover the games and American audiences saw almost nothing of them. Although British athletes went to Moscow, Independent Television reduced its coverage from 170 hours to 40; German and Japanese television carried even less of the 1980 Olympics. Television commentary in the West generally denigrated the Moscow Games, and there were many allegations of skullduggery on the part of Soviet officials. It is impossible, of course, to know if there was any truth in the charges of rampant discrimination.

In the opinion of Baruch Hazan, an expert on Soviet sports, "the possibility that its foreign policy or some characteristics of its political system could trigger a boycott of the . . . Olympic Games did not occur to Moscow." Confronted with the unexpected reality, the Soviet Union and its allies in Eastern Europe explained the boycott by references to American militarism, to Jimmy Carter's campaign for renomination, and to the alleged American fear of Soviet athletic prowess. The Soviet news agency, TASS, explained that the boycott violated the Olympic Charter, the Helsinki Accords, the United Nations Charter, and the Amateur Sport Act of 1978. *Sovetsky Sport* argued that the boycott was contrary to the United States Constitution. "From the outset," says Hazan, "the Soviet Union refused to accept the fact that the boycott was a reaction to the invasion of Afghanistan"—which was said to have provided a shabby pretext for Carter's predetermined anti-Soviet policy.

In their condemnations of Carter for the misuse of sports for political purposes, Russian spokesmen did not dwell on their country's threats to boycott the 1968, 1972, and 1976 games nor on the actual boycotts that had occurred. In 1975, for instance, the Soviet Union refused to compete in the championships of the Fédération Internationale de Gymnastique (FIG) because they took place in West Berlin. In 1976, the Soviet Union boycotted the world chess championships because they took place in Israel.

When it became clear that the boycott was not to be averted, the Soviet press alerted its readers to the dangers they faced as hosts to Western spectators. There was apparently more to worry about than the threat of subversive ideas. On April 16 *Pravda* warned that the CIA planned to recruit spectators as spies and that enemy agents were prepared to smuggle concealed bacterial weapons into the country. It was also said that the CIA had a stash of poisoned chewing gum and explosive toys for the spectators to distribute to unwary toddlers.

When it was all over and no child had been blown to bits by a detonating doll, Moscow minimized the impact of the boycott and the protests made at the games. The 1980 Games were proclaimed to be the most glorious ever. In the opening ceremony, sixteen teams marched behind the Olympic rings or the ensign of their national Olympic committee, but none of these banners was shown on Soviet television. Despite the claims of unprecedented success, it was obvious to almost everyone that the games were seriously diminished by the absence of the American, Canadian, German, Japanese, and Kenyan teams. Whether they were much enhanced by the red-carpet treatment given to Yasir Arafat of the Palestinian Liberation Organization is doubtful.

There were some victories at the games by Western European athletes. In track and field, Britain's Allan Wells won the 100 meters in the relatively slow time of 10.25 seconds and was nipped by Italy's Pietro Mennea in the 200 meters (20.19 seconds to 20.21 seconds). Steve Ovett beat his rival Sebastian Coe in the 800 meters and was beaten by Coe in the 1,500 meters. Another Briton, Daley Thompson, defeated two Russians to take the decathlon title. Sara Simeoni of Italy, who set an Olympic record of 1.97 meters in the high jump, was the only Westerner to triumph in women's track and field.

The field hockey tournament, long dominated by teams from India and Pakistan, was decimated by the boycott. At the last minute, the men's and women's teams from Zimbabwe were rushed to Moscow, where the women won the gold medal. When they returned to Zimbabwe, each of them was awarded an ox by the beaming minister of sport.

In all, the British, the French, and the Italians were the most successful challengers to the Eastern European athletes, but their total of five, six, and eight gold medals was minuscule compared to the harvest reaped by the Soviets and the East Germans. One Russian, the gymnast Aleksander Dityatin, won more medals—eight—than most national teams. The Soviet team won eighty golds, sixty-nine silvers, and forty-six bronzes; the German team won forty-seven golds (eleven of them in women's swimming), thirty-seven silvers, and forty-two bronzes. If the times recorded for American swimmers on August 2 had been achieved in Olympic competition, these Americans would have won ten gold, twelve silver, and five bronze medals, but the swimmers were in Irvine, California, and their rivals were in Moscow. In all, there were thirty-six new world records set at the games. Although a number of athletes surpassed their personal bests by an astonishing margin, none of the nearly 6,000 athletes failed the official drug tests. On the other hand, a single *unofficial* test conducted by the IOC's Dr. Arnold Beckett found "exogenous testosterone" (i.e., anabolic steroids) in sixteen female swimmers.

Thanks to the influx of television money, which was considerable
despite NBC's cancellation of its contract for the Moscow Games,
Killanin was able to boast that he had inherited a treasury with $2
million and bequeathed to his successor one with $45 million. It was
a small consolation. Rejecting the Russian claim that these were the
finest Olympics ever, the IOC president admitted, "The Games were
joyless." This was an overly dismal judgment; photographs from Moscow suggest that the victors of 1980 were as ecstatic about their victories as the winners of 1976 were about theirs. Killanin's assessment
does, however, say a good deal about *his* state of mind. His ineptitude
as IOC president caused a number of the older members to become
nostalgic for Avery Brundage. Conscious of the urgent need for strong
leadership, the members selected a Brundage protégé, Juan Antonio
Samaranch, as their next president. Samaranch received forty-four
votes; Switzerland's Marc Hodler had twenty-one; Canada's James
Worrell, seven; and Willi Daume, a mere five. It was clear that Daume
was being punished for his inability to persuade his own national Olympic committee to send a team to Moscow. Samaranch, a sixty-year-
old Spanish diplomat, proved to be every bit as insightful and decisive
as his colleagues hoped.

In the fall of 1981, there was an important Olympic congress in
Baden-Baden, the first to be convened since the one held in Varna,
Bulgaria, in 1973. Police were everywhere, security was tight, and there
was an atmosphere of crisis, but there was also the realization, which
grew stronger every day, that Samaranch was the right choice as Killanin's successor. There were resolutions about what the IOC intended
to do if future boycotts threatened the games. There was deep concern
about drugs. There were attempts to listen to what the athletes had
to say. And there was the election of the first two female members of
the IOC. According to Geoffrey Miller, Killanin had offered an IOC
seat to the American skater Tenley Albright, but she had declined the
opportunity. Flor Isava Fonseca of Venezuela and Pirjo Haggman of
Finland were elected at Baden-Baden, breaking the eighty-six-year-old
male monopoly. (They were followed by Britain's Mary Alison Glen-
Haig [1982] and Princess Nora of Liechtenstein [1984].)

Observers with a sense of history were bemused by the choice of
Sarajevo, in Yugoslavia, as the site of the next winter games. It was
there that a Serbian patriot had assassinated Archduke Franz Ferdinand
of Austria and set off the chain reaction that led to World War I. In
fact, commentators on the games were able to draw a happy contrast
between the murderously nationalistic hatreds of 1914 and the more
pacific national rivalries of 1984. Although the Soviet Union and East
Germany dominated most of the events at the 1984 Winter Games

and collected a total of forty-nine medals (compared with eight for the United States), they were unable to compete with the Americans and Swiss in Alpine skiing nor with the Scandinavians in Nordic skiing. (In these fifteen events, the Soviet Union was victorious only in the men's 30-kilometer cross-country race.) In the public's favorite competition, figure skating, Elena Valova and Oleg Vasiliev defeated an American pair, Kitty and Peter Carruthers, while Britain's Jayne Torvill and Christopher Dean overwhelmed their Russian rivals in ice dancing. Katarina Witt (GDR) outscored Rosalynn Summers (USA) in the women's singles competition, but Witt's moment of extraordinary fame was not to come until 1988.

None of these marvelous performances caught the attention of the American television audience as the victory in ice hockey had done four years earlier. The A. C. Nielsen Company reported a decline from the ratings attained in 1976 and 1980. On the average, only 28 percent of the viewers watched the skiers and the skaters (as compared to 37 percent for the Lake Placid Games in 1980). ABC-TV, which had paid $92 million for the American rights, lost money.

In the chilly air of Sarajevo, the cold war was more or less in abeyance. In the smog of Los Angeles, the ghosts of absent athletes were oppressively present. The prospect of Soviet retaliation was discussed from the moment that President Carter first announced his intention to force a boycott of the 1980 Games. The question of Soviet participation was definitively settled on May 8, 1984, when the Russian National Olympic Committee issued the following statement:

> Chauvinistic sentiments and an anti-Soviet hysteria are being whipped up in the United States. Extremist organizations and groupings of all sorts, openly aiming to create "unbearable conditions" for the stay of the Soviet delegation and performance by Soviet athletes, have sharply stepped up their activities. . . . Washington has made assurances of late of the readiness to observe the rules of the Olympic charter. The practical deeds by the American side, however, show that it does not intend to ensure the security of all athletes, respect their rights and human dignity and create normal conditions for holding the games. . . . In these conditions, the National Olympic Committee of the USSR is compelled to declare that participation of Soviet sportsmen in the Games is impossible.

There was no mention of retaliation as a motive. Marat Gramov, president of the Soviet Union's national Olympic committee, presented this decision as if it had been made by the committee and not by the Central Committee of the Communist Party, but Gramov's credibility was diminished by the fact that he had previously served as propaganda chief for the Central Committee. He was clearly a political appointee and just as clearly subject to political controls.

Although some had predicted this decision, most commentators were caught by surprise. Certainly the Soviet Union gave few signs of dissatisfaction with the arrangements in Los Angeles in the autumn and winter of 1983-84, not even when the California state legislature, angered by the Soviet destruction of an off-course Korean Air Lines jet on September 1, had voted unanimously that Soviet athletes should be barred from entering the United States. Indeed, Gramov remarked on December 7 that he saw no reason for the Soviet team to stay away from the games. Visiting Los Angeles, he seemed satisfied with arrangements (which included special permission for Aeroflot flights to land at the airport and for a Soviet cruise ship to dock at Long Beach). On February 6, at the winter games in Sarajevo, Andrianov opined that the Los Angeles Olympic Organizing Committee (LAOOC) was doing an excellent job. His younger colleague, Valentin Smirnov, indicated that *he* was not worried about the safety of Soviet athletes.

Shortly thereafter, Soviet President Yuri Andropov died and was replaced by Konstantin Chernenko. Whether this change in leadership made a difference is difficult to determine. The LAOOC chairman, Paul Ziffren, thought it did. Given the secretive nature of the pre-*glasnost* Soviet regime, we cannot know exactly when the Kremlin decided on a tit-for-tat strategy, nor can we gauge what opposition there might have been to this strategy within the Politburo, the Soviet National Olympic Committee, or the governments and national Olympic committees of the Soviet Union's allies. As late as April 24, Samaranch was able to announce, after meeting with Soviet and American officials in Lausanne, "We may say that the black clouds that accumulated in the Olympic sky have vanished or are very soon going to vanish." After the black clouds re-formed and released the thunderstorm of Russian anger, the IOC's Comte Jean de Beaumont defended Samaranch against those who thought that he should have been able to avert the disaster: "Have you been to Moscow? Could you handle those people? Nobody can."

Speculation on the internal debates within the Politburo is idle for anyone but Kremlinologists, and perhaps for them too, but one must at least venture an opinion on the motivation behind the decision to boycott the 1984 Summer Games. Although the Los Angeles police and the FBI did not always work well together, there seems to be no reason to think that security was inadequate or that Soviet worries about the safety of their athletes should have been taken at face value. There was the threat of agitation by part of the local emigré community, but a demonstration at LAOOC headquarters had drawn fewer than one hundred persons and a petition that was supposed to have one million names on it actually garnered one tenth of 1 percent of that number. Soviet authorities must have been well enough informed about American political conditions to have expected some kind of agitation, and it is inconceivable that they had not realized the possibility of protest before May 8, when their decision was announced. For decades international sports events have been occasions for athletes from the Warsaw Pact nations to defect to the West, but there was no reason to fear an exodus of the sort that occurred in Melbourne in 1956. Ziffren called the Soviet statements of concern over security "transparently absurd."

Charges of petty harassment by the U.S. State Department have always been a part of East-West relations, but an incident of some importance had occurred on March 1 when the Reagan administration denied a visa to the Soviet Union's proposed Olympic attaché, Oleg Yermishkin, whom American officials identified as a KGB operative. There seems little doubt that Yermishkin was in fact an intelligence officer who had been given a hurried course in sports administration. Although even a very perceptive KGB spy was unlikely to learn much about American defenses while driving up and down the Los Angeles freeway, LAOOC Director Peter Ueberroth had failed to sway the administration on this matter. He was, however, more successful in a related effort. When the East Germans complained about the wording of the standard United States visa application, Ueberroth persuaded the State Department to alter the language of the questionnaire.

Some people have speculated that the Soviet Union might have feared athletic humiliation at the hands of an American team with the home-court advantage. This was Ueberroth's opinion, but a comparison of world records and personal bests in various disciplines where contests are decided by times and distances indicates that the Americans were not likely to have done much better against the Soviet Union than they had in Montreal in 1976. In short, there seems little doubt that the Soviet decision was motivated mainly by the desire to retaliate for the damage done in 1980. As Ueberroth commented after the games were over, "I knew how bitter hurt they were [in 1980]." Thinking of 1980 as well as 1984, the LAOOC director termed Carter and Chernenko a pair of political hacks.

Quite apart from politics, there was anxiety about Los Angeles as a venue: twenty-three separate sites scattered over 4,500 square miles; events at Lake Casitas, 84 miles north of the city, and at the Fairbanks Ranch, 110 miles south. Furthermore, in a metropolitan area notorious for its lack of public transportation, the potential for freeway gridlock was enormous. In fact, traffic flowed more smoothly than usual, no doubt because many Angelinos parked their cars in their garages and themselves before their television sets.

Another fear proved groundless—that adequately financing the games would be impossible. Frightened by the debts incurred by the city of Montreal and the province of Quebec in 1976, no government body was willing to guarantee the financial resources of the 1984 Games. Los Angeles was the only candidate to host the games in 1984 and the Californian group that made the bid was a private body. Killanin's first reaction was to insist that this private group be replaced by the city of Los Angeles, in accord with the Olympic Charter, but Mayor Thomas Bradley's response, on July 18, 1977, was to recommend that the bid be withdrawn. On August 31, the executive board of the International Olympic Committee bit the bullet and revised Rule 4 of the Olympic Charter. Having made its point about financial responsibility, the city then ratified the accords between the IOC and the LAOOC, prompting voters to amend the *city's* charter to prohibit public reimbursement in the event that the LAOOC lost money.

This precaution proved to be unnecessary. Led by the dynamic and ingenious Ueberroth, the LAOOC sold television rights to ABC for $225 million; the European networks, Eurovision and Intervision, together paid another $22 million, and the Japanese added some $11 million to the coffers. The LAOOC raised another $130 million from thirty corporate sponsors, including American Express, Anheuser-Busch, Canon, Coca-Cola, Levi's, IBM, Snickers, and Sanyo. Noting that Lake Placid's 381 sponsors had brought in only $9 million, the LAOOC demanded that *its* sponsors make a minimum pledge of $4 million each. In addition, the Southland Corporation built a velodrome for the cyclists, the Atlantic-Richfield Company refurbished the Los Angeles Coliseum, General Motors donated Buick automobiles, and Xerox gave copiers.

There were also forty-three companies licensed to sell "official" Olympic products. McDonald's, for instance, marketed the official hamburger of the 1984 Olympics, and the Mars Bar was the official snack food. Dutiful believers in Olympism were also expected to drink Coca-Cola and shop at 7-11 stores. Although Anheuser-Busch was a sponsor, Schlitz, not Budweiser, was the official domestic beer and Kirin the official import. The Miller Brewing Company, not wanting to be left out in the cold, sponsored the U.S. Olympic Training Center in Colorado Springs. When the USOC objected to Miller's slogan ("Let's Win the Games Again"), the objections were brushed aside. As a Miller spokesman said, "We felt it would be easier to raise money if we worked the national pride angle."

How much damage to the Olympic movement was done by the boycott of 1984? The Soviet Union and sixteen of its allies stayed away, but the LAOOC hosted 140 teams, including one from Romania (which was greeted with wild enthusiasm by the spectators and whose expenses were shared by the IOC and the LAOOC, each of which contributed ⅓ of the costs). With fifty-three medals, the Romanian athletes provided significant competition for the American and West German teams. The People's Republic of China also rejected the call for a boycott and made its debut as an Olympic power, winning fifteen gold medals. Li Ning, competing in men's gymnastics, was the only athlete at the games to win six medals. The athletes from Taiwan competed as "Chinese Taipei." (When the local Chinese community invited both teams to a luncheon, the Communists accepted and the Nationalists refused.)

American spectators were apparently delighted with the show-biz approach to the opening ceremony. President Ronald Reagan certainly seemed in his element as eighty-four grand pianos sounded with music by George Gershwin. And then there was the spectacle of covered wagons carrying brave pioneers from California to New England. The sociologist Alan Tomlinson was not impressed with "the world according to Disney." He condemned the "heights, depths, and breadths of shallowness, oversimplification, superficiality," but most people probably inclined to Reagan's uncritical acceptance of patriotic kitsch. The IOC members were generally discreet about the opening and closing ceremonies.

The sports dominance of the home team was, however, an embarrassment for anyone who recalled Pierre de Coubertin's dream of international harmony and good will. To the spectators' chants of "USA! USA!" American athletes won 174 medals, including 83 golds. In their jubilation, the spectators were obviously unperturbed that the Soviet media labeled the games a complete farce. IOC Director Monique Berlioux was as repelled by partisan American spectators as her countryman Charles Maurras had been in 1896. In fact, she used the same comparison he had: "They are like children. . . . We have in French a word for this—*chauvinistes.*" Writing for *Sports Illustrated,* Frank Deford voiced the same reaction, referring to "Large Boor Freestyle Jingoism." It should, however, be pointed out that there were no episodes of spectator violence of the sort that has disfigured soccer matches in Europe and Latin America.

For the American public, polled just before the opening of the games, Mary Decker Slaney was the best-known athlete on the American team. If recognition of her surpassed that for such stars as Carl Lewis, Edwin Moses, and Greg Louganis, it was probably because of the controversy involving Zola Budd, an Afrikaaner from Bloemfontein who was declared eligible to compete after the hasty award of British citizenship (on the grounds that her grandfather was British). Budd, who looked much younger than eighteen, had set an unofficial world record while still in South Africa. Running in bare feet at Stellenboesch's Coetzenburg Stadium, she did 5,000 meters in 15:1.83. That was 7 seconds faster than Slaney's official mark. Track-and-field enthusiasts expected to be thrilled by a Budd-Slaney matchup in the 3,000-meter race, but no one predicted the bizarre outcome. At the 1,600-meter point, Budd passed Slaney. Two-hundred meters later, as she attempted to block Slaney's bid to become the front runner, her left leg was struck by Slaney's right foot. The contact caused Slaney to lose her balance and sustain a serious injury as she fell to the ground in anguish. When the race was over, Romania's Maricica Puica had outsprinted Britain's Wendy Sly. Budd, psychologically shaken by the mishap, finished in seventh place, wrongly blamed not only by the spectators but also by many of the journalists who had not yet studied the videotape of the race.

If this was the saddest moment of the games, the most joyous (at least for American spectators) may have been the victories of Mary Lou Retton in women's gymnastics and Joan Benoit in the first-ever women's marathon. (A Greek woman, Melpomone, is sometimes said to have run unofficially in the first marathon and to have finished in 4.5 hours, but there is no evidence to support the claim.) Benoit bore the California heat better than her Norwegian rivals Greta Waitz and Ingrid Kristiansen. "I might have run faster," commented Waitz, "but I was afraid of dying." That Retton edged Romania's Ecaterina Szabo was sweet revenge for her coach, Romanian-born Bela Karolyi. Once the coach of Nadia Comaneci, he had been virtually driven into exile by rivals favored by the dictatorial regime. The stars of men's gymnastics were China's Li Ning and Japan's Koji Gushiken, the all-round winner.

In swimming, Tiffany Cohen, Mary Meagher, and Tracy Caulkins led the American team to a near-sweep of the women's events. Germany's Michael Gross, Canada's Alex Baumann, and Rick Carey of the United States were all multiple winners in men's swimming. Greg Louganis was the victor in both platform and springboard diving.

Equally expected were the four gold medals won by Carl Lewis (100 meters, 200 meters, 4 × 100–meter relay, long jump) and the first-place finish of Edwin Moses in the 400-meter hurdles. Sebastian Coe defeated Steve Cram with a new Olympic record for the 1,500 meters (3:32.53). Britain's Daley Thompson also set an Olympic record, winning the decathlon ahead of three German rivals. In the men's marathon, Carlo Lopes won the first gold medal ever for a Portuguese athlete.

One of the most dramatic contests was the first-ever women's heptathlon. On the first day the athletes competed in the 100-meter hurdles, the high jump, the shot put, and the 200-meter sprint; the second day was for the long jump, the javelin throw, and the 800-meter race. Australia's Glynis Nunn won with a score of 6,390 points. America's Jackie Joyner and Germany's Sabine Evert were second and third with 6,385 and 6,383 points. Had Joyner or Evert been a second faster in the 800-meter race, the gold medal would have gone to one of them.

Robert G. Meadows has calculated that American athletes received 44.7 percent of ABC's television coverage. Track-and-field events, which Americans dominated, were prominently featured (as they have been in the various media since 1896), with the men's events consuming 65.6 percent of the 1,089 minutes devoted to track and field. The next most thoroughly televised sports were boxing and gymnastics. In the latter, women appeared 45.2 percent of the time.

Despite the overrepresentation of American victors, or perhaps because of it, ABC was able to hold the television audience. On the first day of the games, the network garnered 54.7 percent of the viewers while CBS and NBC together had only 18 percent. ABC earned a profit of approximately $435 million despite the $225 million dollars it had paid for American rights and the further millions it had expended for the costs of production. The network did this by charging as much as $250,000 for a thirty-second prime-time advertisement. McDonald's alone spent $30 million for its commercial spots.

When the books were closed on the 1984 Games, the Los Angeles Olympic Organizing Committee had raised so much money from the sale of television rights and from its phalanx of sponsors that it had a surplus of over $200 million. It was only the second time since 1932 that the games had not run a deficit. Peter Ueberroth thanked the loyal volunteers for their altruism and awarded himself a bonus of $475,000. The organizers were able to crow about the glories of capitalism and the critics of the games were free to sermonize about the horrors of capitalism. For any television viewer who preferred sports to hamburger commercials, the critics had a point.

Grenoble, 1968. Jean-Claude Killy (France). *International Olympic Committee.*

Mexico City, 1968. George Foreman (USA) celebrates his gold medal in heavyweight boxing. *Corbis Images.*

Mexico City, 1968. The black-power salute of Tommie Smith (USA) and John Carlos (USA). To the left of Smith is Australia's Peter Norman; below Smith is the Marquess of Exeter, president of the International Amateur Athletic Federation. *AP/Wide World Photos.*

Munich, 1972. Olga Korbut (USSR) in the floor exercise. *International Olympic Committee.*

Munich, 1972. Vassily Alexeev (USSR), heavyweight champion. *International Olympic Committee.*

International Olympic Committee Executive Board, 1971-72. Standing (*left to right*): Juan Antonio Samaranch (Spain), Konstantin Andrianov (USSR), Sir Adetokunbo Ademola (Nigeria), Sylvio de Magalhães Padilha (Brazil), Prince Tsuneyoshi Takeda (Japan); seated (*left to right*): Hermann van Karnebeek (Holland), Lord Killanin (Ireland), Avery Brundage (USA), Comte Jean de Beaumont (France). *International Olympic Committee.*

Moscow, 1980. Steve Ovett (279) and Sebastian Coe (254) of Great Britain and East Germany's Jürgen Straub (338) in the 1,500 meters. *AP/Wide World Photos.*

Los Angeles, 1984. Carl Lewis (USA) wins the 100 meters. Ray Stewart (Jamaica) comes in sixth. *Corbis Images.*

Calgary, 1988. Katerina Witt (GDR) as "Carmen." *Nationales Olympisches Komitee der DDR.*

Seoul, 1988. Florence "Flo-Jo" Griffith-Joyner (USA) wins the 200 meters. *Corbis Images.*

11

Calgary and Seoul—
But Not Pyongyang

The decision to return to an Asian site for the games of the Twenty-fourth Olympiad was made at the Olympic congress held in Baden-Baden in the fall of 1981. Seoul was clearly a risky choice. Not only was South Korea ruled by an authoritarian government, it was also the capital of a divided nation. And South Korea was still technically at war with its Communist neighbor to the north. The International Olympic Committee members representing the Soviet Union and its allies were extremely unhappy with the choice, but there was only one other candidate, the Japanese city of Nagoya, and a number of Japanese had journeyed to Baden-Baden to plead with the IOC *not* to choose their city. Their argument was that the construction required for the games would forever destroy the remnant of park space still to be found in the densely populated metropolis. The IOC was also the target of an anti-Olympic letter-writing campaign organized by Nagoya's citizen-activists. Finally, it may be that some of the IOC members were not unhappy about an opportunity to outvote unpopular colleagues like the Soviet Union's Konstantin Andrianov.

The rulers of North Korea were angered by the success of their ideological foes, but they responded cleverly. From Pyongyang came not merely threats of a possible boycott but also the demand that half the events on the Olympic program take place north of the thirty-eighth parallel (the border between the two countries). This request put the IOC in an awkward position. While the committee had always urged Seoul and Pyongyang to cooperate, in 1981 thirty-seven nation-states with recognized national Olympic committees did not have diplomatic relations with North Korea. IOC president Juan Antonio Samaranch decided, despite this impediment, to seek a compromise. Negotiating with the North Koreans, he offered them a chance to host all the competitions in archery and table tennis (both very popular sports in the Far East) and some of the competitions in cycling and soccer.

The offer greatly displeased the South Koreans and failed to satisfy the North Koreans, who stayed away from Seoul as they had from Los Angeles. Had Leonid Brezhnev, Yuri Andropov, or Konstantin Chernenko been the general-secretary of the Communist party of the Soviet Union, the IOC might have been afflicted by the fourth major boycott in a row, but Mikhail Gorbachov was the unchallenged leader in the Kremlin and he made it clear that the Russians intended to rejoin the Olympic movement. In what looked rather like a quid pro quo, the president of the Soviet National Olympic Committee, Marat Gramov, was rewarded by election to the IOC. To the chagrin of the North Koreans, Cuba was the only athletically significant state to boycott the 1988 Games.

In the summer of 1985, at the IOC's ninetieth session in East Berlin, Samaranch ousted Monique Berlioux from her post as IOC director. One issue that had separated them was her opposition to a contract with International Sports, Culture, and Leisure Marketing (Lausanne), but it had been clear for several years that Berlioux was too strong willed a person to work easily with her boss. She was replaced by Françoise Zweifel, who was appointed IOC secretary-general. By all accounts, Zweifel has served with great efficiency and without illusions about the extent of her authority.

By 1986, Samaranch's power within the IOC was so great that it was relatively easy for him to persuade committee members to select Barcelona as the site for the 1992 Summer Games. (At the same IOC session, in Lausanne, Anita DeFrantz, an Afro-American woman who had rowed in the bronze-medal eight in 1976, was elected to the committee. She was followed, at two-year intervals, by Britain's Princess Anne and by Carol Anne Letheren of Canada.)

As early as 1981, Samaranch had advocated open games and an end to the Byzantine convolutions of the amateur rule. At Sapporo in 1972, IOC president Avery Brundage had waged a last-ditch campaign to stop the juggernaut of commercialization that threatened to overrun the Olympics. As we have seen, he lashed out at the skiers, most of whom seem to have had not-very-secret contracts with the ski manufacturers, and he made a scapegoat of Austria's Karl Schranz, who was expelled from the games by a vote of 28-14. By the standards of 1988, Schranz was an economic naïf unable to look out for his own best interests. By the 1988 Games, practically no one was ineligible—except for professional boxers, NBA basketball players, and soccer players over the age of twenty-three. (In 1992, even the NBA players became eligible.) The tennis tournament had almost the same cast of characters as Wimbledon and the U.S. Open. Olympic athletes were free, at last, of the hypocritical need to pretend that they were really just ordinary blokes who trained a bit after work. Journalists who had covered earlier Olympics marveled at the new acceptance—call it realistic, call it cynical—of undisguised professionalism. Since open games posed a threat to the dominance of "state amateurs" from the Soviet bloc, Gramov's anguished protests were no surprise: "We cannot accept those people leading us off the fine avenue of Olympism onto the backstreets of commercialism."

Gramov had a point, one that most of Samaranch's predecessors would have granted. Negotiations for television rights have become almost as much a part of the pre-Olympic story as speculations about the probability of a boycott. The negotiations were certainly salient in the minds of the IOC and the organizing committees for the 1988 Games. They ended happily for Calgary's organizers, who received $309 million from ABC, and much less happily for Seoul's, who had dreamed of a billion-dollar contract and had to settle for a mere $300 million from NBC. (To recoup this sum, NBC had to charge as much as $285,000 for a thirty-second commercial.) That NBC outbid ABC can be attributed to the sale of the latter network to Capital Cities Communications in March 1985 for $3.5 billion. Dennis Swanson, who replaced the legendary Roone Arledge, felt that the bidding had become economically unrealistic.

The network's realism, and the organizers' willingness to accommodate the network's needs, was demonstrated in the scheduling of events. Since the charges for advertisements are calculated on the basis of the A. C. Nielsen Company's audience ratings for the month of February, the 1988 Winter Games were not allowed to continue into March. The duration of the games was, however, extended from twelve days to sixteen in order to span three weekends rather than two. The opening ceremony was moved from Wednesday to Saturday. Events at the summer games were scheduled to permit prime-time reception rather than to maximize the athletes' performances. The convenience of the American viewer-consumer was utmost in the media managers' minds. Since NBC's $309 million was over 90 percent of all television contributions to the Olympic till, American track-and-field fans were able to watch the runners, jumpers, and throwers at 9:00 P.M. (Eastern Standard Time) when it was already 1:00 A.M. in London, 2:00 A.M. in Frankfurt, and even later in Moscow.

ABC had paid the unprecedented sum of $309 million for the winter games in Calgary because the network counted on a large North American audience composed principally of men (who are more likely than women to be sports fans and who are also more likely to purchase the advertisers' "big ticket" items like automobiles, copiers, and computers). They were surprised to learn from the Nielsen Company that the prime-time audience was 56 percent female and that female viewers outnumbered male viewers for almost every event except ice hockey. Since there was little diminution in the number viewing the competing telecasts of NBA and NCAA basketball, one surmises that the audience for the Olympics consisted largely of women who would not otherwise have watched a sports event. This was one disappointment (from ABC's point of view). Another was that there simply were not enough viewers, male or female, for the network to fulfill its promises to the advertisers. As a result, ABC lost some $65 million.

The initial audience ratings reported by the Nielsen Company for the 1988 Summer Games were also much lower than had been anticipated, placing NBC in the same predicament ABC had been in a few months earlier: namely, the network was unable to deliver the audience it had promised when its advertising rates were set. Rather than refund money to the disappointed sponsors, NBC reran the commercials at no extra cost. This tactic alienated viewers whose interest in sports was greater than their interest in junk food.

No one could blame the performances of the skaters and skiers in Calgary for the paucity of male viewers in the United States. The athletes were spectacular. The excitement engendered by the downhill and slalom and ski-jump specialists was intense, but it seemed low key in comparison to that accompanying women's figure skating. Debbie Thomas, an Afro-American, had won the world championship in 1987. Her strongest rival, East Germany's Katarina Witt, was the gold medalist from the 1984 Olympics. Midori Ito of Japan was the first Asian skater with a real chance for a first-place finish. It was a close contest won by Witt after an inspired and overtly erotic dance to the music of Bizet's *Carmen*. Witt was not unaware of her physical attractiveness. "I rather think every man prefers looking at a well-built woman [rather] than someone built in the shape of a ball." Neither Thomas nor Ito looked like balls, but they failed to impress the judges as Witt did. Ito was fifth, Thomas third, behind Canada's Elizabeth Manley.

At the Seoul Games, the American boxers failed to reestablish their former supremacy. Kennedy McKinney (119 pounds), Andrew Maynard (179 pounds), and Ray Mercer (201 pounds) were the only Americans to win a final bout. It was not always the lack of pugilistic skill that defeated the Americans. In a replay of the fiasco in Munich in 1972, Anthony Hembrick's coaches misread the schedule and he was disqualified for a late arrival in the arena. In another bout, Roy Jones battered a nearly helpless Park Si-Hun from one side of the ring to the other, but the judges from Morocco, Uganda, and Uruguay awarded the medal to the Korean boxer. Perhaps they interpreted it as a consolation prize. The other winners came from seven different countries.

The Soviet weight lifters won six of ten events and the Soviet wrestlers won eight of twenty. (In two final bouts, the American wrestlers overcame their Russian rivals.) In men's gymnastics, China's Lou Yun's gold medal for vaulting was the only one to escape Russian hands. Although three of the four women's gymnastics events were won by the Romanians, the Soviet team outscored them and Yelena Shoushunova was the all-around champion. The American women probably never had a chance for a medal, but they were further handicapped by the unfairness of Ellen Berger, the East German head of the FIG's technical committee. Berger interfered frequently and blatantly in the scoring and was consistently upheld by Yuri Titov, the Russian head of the international gymnastics federation. It was a sign of *glasnost* that the Soviet news agency reporter on the scene did not automatically defend Berger and Titov against their "capitalist" critics. Instead, he referred disgustedly to the "judging mafia."

As had been the case in 1984, the German women turned out to be the best fencers, while the men from France, Germany, Hungary, Italy, and the Soviet Union divided up most of the medals for foil, saber, and épée. In swimming, too, a number of different flags were raised in the victory ceremonies, including that of Surinam, whose Anthony Nesty won the 100-meter butterfly. Led by Kristin Otto, easily the most impressive swimmer in Seoul (she won four individual medals), the East German women took ten of the fifteen events. Americans consoled themselves with replays of the diminutive Janet Evans splashing her way to gold medals in the 400-meter, the 800-meter, and the 400-meter individual medley.

As always, the track-and-field competitions attracted the most attention. The most successful, the most flamboyant female athlete of these Olympics was Florence Griffith-Joyner. She won the 100-meter race ahead of 1984 winner Eveyln Ashford (USA) and Heike Drechsler (GDR) and she repeated in the 200-meter race (ahead of Jamaica's Grace Jackson and Drechsler). She also anchored the winning 4 × 100–meter relay, overcoming Drechsler's significant lead. Meanwhile, Griffith-Joyner's sister-in-law, Jackie Joyner-Kersee, won the long jump and the heptathlon. Since the 400-meter hurdles, the high jump, and the marathon were won by Debra Flintoff-King (Australia), Louise Ritter (USA), and Rosa Mota (Portugal), it seemed that the East European domination of women's track-and-field events might be drawing to an end.

Athletes from the Soviet Union and East Germany won most of the men's field events (shot put, high jump, hammer throw, pole vault, discus). The Kenyans were especially strong in the middle distances, winning the 800 meters (Paul Ereng), the 1,500 meters (Peter Rono), the 5,000 meters (John Ngugi), and the steeplechase (Julius Kariuki). When Canada's Ben Johnson finished the 100 meters in 9.79 seconds, it seemed that Carl Lewis had been dethroned as the world's best sprinter. As it turned out, Lewis was able to add the 100-meter title to his long-jump victory and his second-place finish over 200 meters because Johnson tested positive for anabolic steroids and was disqualified. The medal went to Lewis by default.

Later investigations implicated Johnson's coach, Charles Francis, and a certain Dr. George Mario Astaphan, who seems to have been taken in by Bulgarian claims that the doctors in Sofia had discovered a way to foil the drug testers in Seoul. Since the Bulgarian weight lifters Mitko Grablev and Angel Guenchev were disqualified for steroid use, after which the whole Bulgarian lifting team departed hastily for Sofia, it seems that Astaphan was too gullible. Francis later confessed that thirteen of the male and female athletes he coached had taken steroids. How many other athletes had halted their intake of steroids in time for the traces of the artificial hormone to be washed from their systems will never be known. Had Griffith-Joyner also used anabolic steroids to transform her body? Among those hinting that she had was her teammate Carl Lewis. She was never formally accused of any transgression, nor is it possible for her or any of the other athletes to prove conclusively that such accusations were groundless. Unless the drug testers can devise some definitive proof of innocence, which seems to be unlikely, wisps of suspicion and distrust are bound to linger in the air. It is a gloomy prospect.

12

Juan Antonio Samaranch as CEO

In assessing the leadership of Lord Killanin, Richard Kevan Gosper, one of Australia's IOC members, remarked, "We were lucky to survive his presidency." When Gosper and his IOC colleagues made Juan Antonio Samaranch their president, they clearly hoped for stronger and more imaginative leadership than they had had from Samaranch's limited and indecisive predecessor. As history has shown, their hopes were fulfilled. Samaranch has been, in the words of the historian Alfred Senn, "a more flexible, determined, and forceful presence than Killanin had been." Samaranch was re-elected by acclamation at the 95th Session of the IOC in San Juan, Puerto Rico, in 1989 and again at the 101st Session in Monaco in 1993. Four years later, he expressed the desire to continue in office for a fourth term. To make that possible, the IOC extended the age of mandatory retirement from seventy-five to eighty, a change of policy that caused some unease among the members.

Until the scandals of 1998, opposition to Samaranch within the IOC was muted, but there was no lack of criticism in the press and in that small corner of the academic world inhabited by sports historians. The most serious accusations were contained in *The Lords of the Rings,* published in 1992 by two British journalists, Vyv Simson and Andrew Jennings. They indicted Samaranch for his support of General Francisco Franco's fascist regime. "He remained loyal," they asserted, "until [Spanish] fascism died." They also condemned Samaranch for his determination, as president of the IOC, to exploit the commercial potential of the Olympic Games, for his alleged indifference to the plague of performance-enhancing drugs, and for what his accusers saw as a shameless—although cleverly disguised—lust for power.

No one can deny that Samaranch was an important figure in sports administration during the Franco regime, as evidenced by his election to the National Olympic Committee in 1956 and his service as Spain's Minister of Sports from 1966 to 1970. The facts are clear, but what to make of them is not. Although David Miller asserts in *The Olympic Revolution* (1994) that Samaranch was able "to rise above any criticism of his involvement in administration during Franco's time," this airy dismissal of the charge is much too easy. It seems more honest to say that complicity with dictatorship was, to one degree or another, the price paid by every ambitious Spaniard who made his or her public career—in politics, in the economic realm, or in the academic world—during the fascist era. Unfortunately, Samaranch has never availed himself of this argument. On the contrary, he asserted in a 1998 televised interview with CBS that he was proud of his past. Whatever one might now think of Samaranch's suitability for the mantle worn by Pierre de Coubertin, he was not judged harshly by his Spanish contemporaries. After his country's transition from dictatorship to democracy, he continued to play an important role in sports administration. In addition, in 1977 Spain's socialist government chose him to be its ambassador to the USSR.

Whatever Samaranch's politics might have been before he came to the IOC in 1966, he has done a great deal as president of the committee to democratize the Olympic movement. He brought Jean-Claude Ganga, one of the foremost African critics of racial segregation, into the IOC as a representative of the Republic of the Congo. Another prominent African sports adminstrator, Louis Guirandou-N'Diaye, an IOC member from Côte d'Ivoire, has praised Samaranch to the skies: "When Samaranch arrived, he opened all the windows." The reinstatement of post-apartheid South Africa on July 7, 1991, was clearly a victory for democracy secured by decades of exclusionary sanctions. Greeting Nelson Mandela, who visited the IOC's Lausanne headquarters in 1992, Samaranch exclaimed, "We've been waiting for you for a long time." Although Samaranch cannot claim all the credit for what looks like a conclusive solution to the "two Chinas" problem that baffled Brundage and Killanin, it is nonetheless true that it was during his presidency, in 1992, that the People's Republic of China finally entered the Olympic movement. None of these actions suggests an IOC president nostalgic for a fascist past.

Nor does Samaranch's approach to women's sports suggest a president mired in traditions of inequality. Since he assumed office in 1980, there has been a transformation of women's roles within the Olympic movement. At the 1980 Moscow Games, 18 percent of the athletes were women; by 1996, at the Centennial Games in Atlanta, that percentage had doubled. Today, women compete in a number of sports, such as soccer, ice hockey, and weightlifting (introduced in 1996, 1998, and 2000, respectively), that in 1980 were reserved for men.

The number of women in the IOC has also continued to grow, albeit gradually. In 1995, five years after the election of Canada's Carol Anne Letheren, the Czech Republic's famed gymnast, Vera Caslavska, became the committee's eighth female member. In 1996, Mary Allison Glenn-Haig retired from the IOC, but Sweden's Gunilla Lindberg and China's Shengrong Lu were added to the committee. Women have also made modest gains within the national Olympic committees and the international sports federations. Samaranch told the IOC Executive Board, at its December 1994 meeting in Atlanta, that there was a moral obligation to "enhance women's access to positions of responsibility in the management of sport at the national and world level." In 1995, only 5 of 196 NOCs and 2 of 34 ISFs were headed by women. At the 105th Session of the IOC, just before the Atlanta games, the committee resolved that by December 31, 2000, the NOCs and ISFs should reserve at least 10 percent of their legislative and executive positions for women and should double that percentage by December 31, 2005.

Proposals to punish national Olympic committees that fail to include female athletes in their Olympic teams were made some months before the 1996 Games. They failed to win broad support because they were offensive to many Islamic nations, whose religious principles require women to hide their bodies from what Western feminists castigate as "the male gaze."

The accusation that under Samaranch's leadership the Olympic movement has been commercialized and sold to the highest corporate bidder is more difficult to answer than allegations about residual fascism on the part of the IOC president. Economic factors, like those that motivated the choice of Atlanta over Athens as the venue for the Centennial Games, now play a greater role in Olympic affairs than political factors, like those that favored Sydney over Beijing for the 2000 Games.

The IOC's initial agreement with International Sports, Culture, and Leisure Marketing, signed in 1985, generated $95 million by the end of 1988. The nine multinational corporations that participated in what came to be called TOP I ("The Olympic Program I") grew to twelve for TOP II. Eight of the original nine continued as "worldwide sponsors" (Coca-Cola, Kodak, Visa, Time, Matsushita, Brother, Philips, and 3M), one dropped out (Federal Express), and four new corporations joined the program (UPS, Bausch & Lomb, Mars, Ricoh). Hundreds of other corporations paid smaller amounts to become sponsors of the winter games in Albertville or the summer games in Barcelona. All in all, TOP II raised some $175 million. TOP III reduced the number of "worldwide sponsors" to ten (the original five plus UPS, Bausch & Lomb, Xerox, IBM, and John Hancock). The price for sponsorship ranged from $25 million to $40 million. With the addition of four official suppliers (John Hancock, Lufthansa, Mercedes, Ricoh), some $350 million was raised by the end of 1996. For TOP IV, which carried the program through the year 2000, there were twelve "worldwide sponsors" and total sponsorship revenues in excess of $350 million.

One result of this aggressive marketing program has been the achievement of one of Samaranch's most important goals—a reduction of the IOC's previous near-total dependence on the sale of television rights—despite the fact that income from these rights has continued to escalate. The Canadian IOC member in charge of media negotiations, Richard Pound, has been as effective as his predecessor, France's Comte Jean de Beaumont. After a slight dip in revenue from the $325 million received for the Calgary games to $292 million for Albertville, the winter games in Lillehammer brought in more than $350 million. For the right to telecast the Nagano games, CBS paid $375 million, and contracts with the European and Japanese networks brought the total to more than $500 million. The rights to televise the summer games in Barcelona and Atlanta were sold for $636 million and $900 million, respectively. After securing the American rights to the 2000 Summer Games in Sydney and the 2002 Winter Games in Salt Lake City for $1.2 billion, NBC contracted in December 1996 for the rights to the 2004 and 2008 Summer Games and the 2006 Winter Games for an incredible $2.3 billion. These amounts might seem fiscally insane but for the fact that the $456 million that NBC paid to televise the games in Atlanta brought in more than $600 million in advertising revenue.

Despite the huge increases, network contracts accounted for only 47 percent of the IOC's 1993–96 income (the sale of sponsorships accounted for 20 percent). In the course of these often protracted negotiations over television rights, the IOC achieved another goal, which was to increase its income from the European and Japanese networks and thus to decrease the relative importance of money it received from U.S. networks. Of the $636 million that was paid for television rights to the Barcelona games, $416 million came from NBC, $90 million from Eurovision, and $62.5 million from Japan's NHK. For the rights to the games in 2004, 2006, and 2008, the Europeans and Japanese have agreed to pay nearly $2 billion.

In their official history of these years, *The Presidencies of Lord Killanin (1972–1980) and Juan Antonio Samaranch (1980–) (1996)*, Fernand Landry and Magdeleine Yerlès speak of the International

Olympic Committee's newly achieved economic "autonomy." While it is certainly true that Killanin and Samaranch vastly increased the funds available to the IOC, "autonomy" may not be the appropriate word to describe the present situation. The IOC can now pay its bills and even distribute millions of dollars to the national Olympic committees of less-affluent nations (under "Olympic Solidarity"), but the "worldwide sponsors" and the television networks expect something in return for their generous support. Cynics have noted that Atlanta, which is the headquarters of Coca-Cola, was chosen for the 1996 Centennial Games over Athens, site of the first modern Olympic Games one hundred years earlier.

The influence of the mass media on the duration of the games and on the time of day for each event is obvious to every observer. And then there is the familiar problem of advertisements. Commercial breaks made the complex pageantry of the opening ceremony of the 1992 Barcelona Games unintelligible to American TV viewers. NBC's offer of $456 million for the Atlanta games was accompanied by requests for an extension of the diving and gymnastics competitions, both very popular with viewers, and for more finals in the first half of the games. The sheer number of commercial breaks and the annoying obtrusiveness of corporate logos (often superimposed over panorama shots of the sports venues) alienated so many viewers of the 1998 Winter Games in Nagano that ratings plummeted, which motivated NBC to increase the number of commercial breaks in order to fulfill its obligations to the advertisers, which drove away even more viewers.

The decline in ratings was even more severe during the Sydney Olympics. The advertisements were only part of the problem. NBC telecast taped versions of events that had actually been contested many hours earlier. Viewers who had listened to the radio or read their morning newspapers already knew the results of the competition. The network's commentators added insult to injury by chattering incessantly, assuring viewers—among other things—that it was difficult for a gymnast to win a gold medal if she fell off the balance beam.

One effect of the Los Angeles games was to dispel the spectre of debt that had haunted the Olympic scene since the financial debacle of 1976. After 1984, many metropolitan centers were dazzled by the twin suns of prestige and profit. In 1986, six cities bid for the 1992 Games. By 1997, there were eleven candidates eager to act as Olympic hosts in 2004. Presentations became increasingly elaborate and expensive. Barcelona, for instance, employed some 750 people to produce a six-volume promotional dossier. In this frantic atmosphere, urban delegates courted IOC members and showered them with costly inducements, including—according to the IOC's critics—the nocturnal company of some of the world's most welcoming women. In response to credible rumors that some committee members were soliciting material and other favors, the Executive Board voted to limit the number of presentations and the value of the gifts offered to IOC members.

Failure to accept these limits led to the worst bribery scandal in Olympic history. On June 16, 1995, Salt Lake City, Utah, won the bid to hold the 2002 Winter Olympics by a vote of 54 to 35. On November 24, 1998, station KTVX in Salt Lake City reported that the local organizing committee had paid for a "scholarship" for Sonia Essomba, daughter of the late IOC member René Essomba of Cameroon. That story released what the *New York Times* later referred to as a "cascade of disclosures." In addition to "scholarships" that totaled nearly $400,000, various IOC members or their relatives had received lavish vacations, costly medical treatments, expensive gifts, and direct cash payments. According to a report released by the organizing committee's Board of Ethics on February 9, 1999, Jean-Claude Ganga (Congo) and various members of his family had been given $115,000 in travel expenses; Ganga was treated for hepatitis, his mother-in-law underwent knee replacement surgery, and his wife had cosmetic surgery; and Ganga received $70,010 in "unexplained payments."

While insisting that there was "no possibility" that the 2002 Winter Games might be taken away from Salt Lake City, Samaranch promised a prompt investigation and a purge of those found guilty. On December 15, 1998, he announced the formation of an ad hoc commission under the chairmanship of Canada's Richard Pound. During the commission's investigation, Pirjo Haggman (Finland), Bashir Mohammed Attarabulsi (Libya), Charles Mukora (Kenya), and David Sikhulumi Sibandze (Swaziland) resigned from the committee. Six other members were expelled when the IOC met in special session on March 17, 1999: Agustin Arroya (Ecuador), Zein El Abdin Abdel Gadir (Sudan), Jean-Claude Ganga (Congo), Lamine Keita (Mali), Sergio Santander Fantini (Chile), and Seiuli Paul Wallwork (Samoa). Nine other members received warnings.

The "bad guys" were not the only ones to suffer. Switzerland's Marc Hodler, who had asserted to the press that corruption had also tainted the bids for Atlanta and other sites, found that he was now persona non grata in the eyes of many of his colleagues. When the IOC selected Turin, Italy, as the site of the 2006 Winter Games, many commentators surmised that the committee had rejected the front-runner—Sion, Switzerland—in order to express their anger at Hodler.

Noting that two-thirds of those who lost their seats were Africans or Pacific Islanders, critics charged the International Olympic Committee with racist scapegoating. They alleged that Australia's Phillip Coles and Guatamala's Willi Kaltschmitt Lujan (and their families) had been treated to a trip to Florida for the Super Bowl at a cost of nearly $20,000. Why were Coles and Kaltschmitt Lujan merely warned and not asked to resign? Another of those who escaped with a warning, South Korea's Kim Un-yong, was said to have solicited a sham job for his son. He managed to retain his seat on the IOC's Executive Board and his position as president of the General Association of the International Sports Federations (GAISF). Was this because Kim was a member of Samaranch's coterie? Critics, demanding that Samaranch accept full responsibility for the entire mess, called for his resignation. He refused and received a nearly unanimous vote of confidence from the IOC.

The Salt Lake City scandal was a direct consequence of the billions of dollars that now pour into and out of Olympic coffers. There is also a somewhat less obvious relationship between the commercialization of the Olympics and the final demise of the amateur-professional dichotomy (except in the hypocritical world of American intercollegiate sports). This relationship requires some discussion.

While material gain has never been the only motive sending athletes down the rocky road to Olympia, its growing importance cannot be denied. The lure of material benefit cannot be banished—unless one is ready and able to demolish the entire structure of Olympic sports. When the material gain that followed an Olympic victory took the form of an endorsement contract for a million dollars (rather than a shiny new automobile), more and more athletes were motivated to make sports their vocation rather than their avocation (as required by the amateur rule). Sprinter Leroy Burrell was unabashedly candid about his motivation when he remarked, "We're not in this sport because we like it or [because] we want to earn our way through school. We're in it to make money." One reason that the IOC finally discarded the anachronistic amateur rule was precisely this realization that Olympic sports are no longer an avocation. By 1980, when Samaranch took office, Rule 26, which limited the Olympics to "amateur athletes," had become an international joke. As Germany's Willi Daume put it, in a single laconic sentence, "It was a system of lies." To call for a return to some imagined paradise of pure amateurism, which is the position taken by Simson and Jennings in *The Lords of the Rings,* is naïve. The alternative to quixotism was obvious. The only realistic solution to rampant hypocrisy was to open the Olympics to the world's best athletes—and, simultaneously, to increase the flow of revenue from the television networks to the IOC.

Although there was opposition from some of the Communist members of the IOC, who preferred that their professionals continue to compete against American collegians, the reformers prevailed. Athletes such as Michael Jordan, Wayne Gretzky, and Steffi Graf were welcomed to the Olympics—and their loyal fans were lured to their television sets. More viewers meant higher prices for TV commercials, which meant that the networks were motivated to pay more for the right to cover the games—which, in the end, meant more money for the IOC.

This happy state of affairs was not reached from one day to the next. As noted in the previous chapter, the trend toward completely "open games" that began under Killanin accelerated under his successor. In 1984, the international sports federations were allowed, within some limits, to set the rules for eligibililty to participate in the Olympics. In 1986, a commission chaired by Germany's Willi Daume proposed an Athlete's Code to replace Rule 26 (which defined eligibility). In November 1987, the IOC voted to welcome openly professional tennis players to the Olympic Games. At the 95th Session of the IOC, in San Juan in 1989, the welcome was extended to other openly professional athletes. The following year, the IOC approved the Athlete's Code as Rule 45. The next edition of the Olympic Charter, which appeared in 1991, explained eligibility in a single sentence: "To be eligible for participation in the Olympic Games a competitor must comply with the Olympic Charter as well as with the rules of the international federation concerned as approved by the International Olympic Committee, and must be entered by his National Olympic Committee." After sixty-seven years of controversy, the IOC was back to where it had been in 1924, when the Olympic Charter read, "The definition of an amateur in each sport is established by the International Federation governing that sport." The door that had been ajar was flung completely open.

The IOC's policy toward performance-enhancing drugs is another cause for contention. Samaranch's critics, with Simson and Jennings foremost among them, have strongly implied that his repeated statements against the use of anabolic steroids and other banned substances have been a rhetorical smokescreen. His critics acknowledge that Samaranch may indeed have spoken out against drugs and "the creation of artificial athletes," but they cite the epidemic of drug use as proof of the insincerity of such statements.

It is very difficult to counter such accusations. There is no doubt about the prevalence of drug use among Olympic athletes. For example, East German women such as Marita Koch and Bärbel Wöckel were given anabolic steroids at twice the level taken by Ben Johnson. There is no evidence, however, that the IOC in any way encouraged the epidemic of drug use. Quite the contrary. In 1966, the IOC established a Medical Commission, headed by New Zealand's Arthur Porritt, and in 1968 drug tests were conducted at both the winter games in Grenoble and the summer games in Mexico City. A prohibition of drug use was introduced into the Olympic Charter in 1972. Led by Samaranch and by Belgium's Prince Alexandre de Mérode, who has chaired the Medical Commission since 1967, the IOC has sponsored a number of international conferences on banned substances, the most important of which was the Ottawa Conference in June 1987. The laboratories accredited by the IOC analyze approximately 100,000 urine samples a year, of which about 1.25 percent test positive.

While no informed observer believes that these tests are good enough to detect drug use in each and every athlete who resorts to steroids or to human growth hormone, it is important to note that the IOC has taken action against many of the world's most famous athletes. The examples of the Canadian sprinter Ben Johnson (Seoul, 1988) and the Irish swimmer Michelle Smith (Atlanta, 1996) come quickly to mind. It is very difficult to believe that these and other champions have been selected as mere scapegoats while the IOC has turned a blind eye toward thousands of other athletes. What possible motive does the IOC, a transnational organization, have for dissimulation? The desire to enhance *national* prestige certainly tempts the NOCs to cheat. The systematic state-supervised use of banned substances by East German athletes and others is a dramatic example of this. But Samaranch and Mérode have always deplored this kind of nationalism and condemned it as a violation of the international spirit of Olympism.

In short, although the IOC's efforts to eliminate drugs have proven ineffective, there is no reason to doubt Samaranch's sincerity or to accuse him of subterfuge and disingenuousness. Indeed, if he were the cynical representative of realpolitik that his critics have portrayed him to be, he might well argue, as some academic scholars have, that anabolic steroids and other banned substances should be "decriminalized" and made freely available, with appropriate medical supervision, to all athletes willing to accept the risks to their health. Ironically, Samaranch seems too idealistic to argue for that version of an "open" Olympics.

Of all the charges brought against Samaranch, the most difficult to assess is the claim that he has worked constantly to consolidate and increase his personal power within the world of international sports. The suave Catalan, claim his critics, is a sophisticated version of the bruskly authoritarian Brundage. There is some evidence to support this claim. As noted earlier, Samaranch was responsible for the dismissal of Monique Berlioux from her position as IOC director. At the end of the Brundage years, and during all of Killanin's eight years in office, Berlioux had become too powerful to be tolerated by a man determined to rescue an organization that seemed adrift. Nor is there reason to doubt that Samaranch used his influence to bring the 1992 Games to Barcelona, his native city, just as Coubertin used his prestige to have the 1924 Games awarded to Paris.

Behind the scenes, Samaranch has worked closely with a group of powerful men whom critics refer to as "The Club." At one point, members of "The Club" allegedly included Horst Dassler, the owner of Adidas, whom a former partner, Patrick Nally, characterized as "the puppet-master of the sporting world." Dassler invested in International Sports, Culture, and Leisure Marketing, which markets the Olympics to Coca-Cola and other "worldwide sponsors." Through Adidas, Dassler was allied with Primo Nebiolo, the Italian head of the International Amateur Athletic Federation whom Samaranch brought into the IOC, where he is now among the most influential members. Nebiolo also rose to become head of the Association of Summer Olympic International Federations. In addition, Dassler was closely allied with another influential IOC member, João Havelange, the Brazilian head of the Fédération Internationale de Football Association. Other influential IOC members identified as stalwarts of "The Club" were Mexico's Mario Vázquez Raña, president of the Association of National Olympic Committees, South Korea's Kim Un-yong, president of the General Association of the International Sports Federations, and Robert Helmick, head of the United States Olympic Committee.

That Samaranch worked closely with all six of these men, and with Mahtar M'Bow during his term as secretary-general of UNESCO, is no secret. Samaranch relied on them for support and they, in turn, supported him. The most dramatic instance of their mutually beneficial relationship came in Budapest in August 1995 when Samaranch sought to have the age of mandatory retirement raised from seventy-five to eighty so that he could stand for re-election in 1997. The motion failed—at first. Three days later, there was a second vote and the rephrased motion passed. Canada's Richard Pound, who opposed the change, thought that the sequence of events had made the IOC a "laughing stock." Nebiolo, Havelange, and Vázquez Raña had all used their influence to sway members in Samaranch's direction.

It is difficult to say whether, in Budapest or elsewhere, "The Club" violated the Olympic Charter or conspired to control the IOC by shady means. Accusations abound, especially against Nebiolo and Havelange, but Helmick and Kim Un-yong were the only members of "The Club" against whom conclusive evidence was brought. Helmick is no longer a member of "The Club," having left the IOC and the USOC in December 1991 in the wake of conflict-of-interest charges.

For the sake of fairness, it must also be acknowledged that during Samaranch's presidency IOC membership has been granted to a number of men closely connected with undemocratic regimes. Kuwait's unsavory Sheik Fahd Al-Ahmad Al-Jabar Al-Sabah and Saudi Arabia's rather more respectable Prince Faisal Fahd Abdul Aziz come to mind. The number of such members is, however, almost certainly lower now than at any time in the last fifty years. One further observation is in order. If "The Club" was in control of the IOC, it is hard to see why Sydney was chosen for the 2000 Summer Games when Beijing had the support of Havelange, Nebiolo, and Vázquez Raña. Future historians may characterize Samaranch as a Machiavellian figure who survived by means of bribery and corruption, but it is premature to conclude that on the basis of rumor and innuendo.

It is curious that one of the charges leveled against Samaranch is that he was passionately involved in the creation of the Olympic Museum. He campaigned for the project and raised most of the money from private donors. Designed by Jean-Pierre Cahen and IOC member Pedro Ramirez Vázquez, officially opened on June 23, 1993, the museum, which stands near the IOC's headquarters at the Château de Vidy in Lausanne, is a handsome structure that looks out from Quai d'Ouchy over Lake Geneva to the Alps. Its permanent exhibits, which consist largely of video presentations, present a rather sanitized history of the Olympics—a celebration rather than a critique of Olympism—but it seems unreasonably idealistic to expect otherwise. Scholars with a more skeptical view of the past and present are welcome at the Olympic Study Centre, which is part of the museum complex.

Samaranch has also been ridiculed for his February 1994 visit to Sarajevo, where, on the tenth anniversary of the 1984 Winter Games, he appealed for an end to the bloody ethnic conflict that had, only three days earlier, taken the lives of scores of people in the city's crowded marketplace. While this gesture, like Samaranch's frequent appeals for an "Olympic Truce," may have been naïve, it is hard to see it as harmful to the cause of peace and international reconciliation which, after all, was the principal reason for Pierre de Coubertin's inspired invention of the modern games.

Whatever Samaranch's colleagues may have thought of him in his role as peacemaker, they did not challenge his position when, in the wake of the Salt Lake City scandal, they voted to reform the governance of the Olympic movement. In December 1999, the eighty-two-member IOC 2000 Commission, whose majority consisted of non-IOC members, brought fifty recommendations to an Extraordinary Session of the IOC, which proceeded to accept them. With Salt Lake City clearly in mind, it was agreed that the sites of future games will be evaluated by a special committee. IOC members not serving on the Evaluation Committee are prohibited from visiting cities that are bidding to host the games. After the Sydney games, future Olympics will have no more than 280 events and every national Olympic committee will have the right to send at least six athletes to the games. The latter decision benefits NOCs whose athletes are objectively unable to meet qualifying standards.

Reform did not stop with these changes. It was also voted that the IOC would eventually have a maximum of 115 members. (Current members have been "grandfathered" for eight years, after which time they must stand for re-election.) Among the 115 members will be 70 individual members plus 15 NOC presidents, 15 ISF presidents, and 15 athletes who must have participated in the games within four years of their election. Except for the athletes, who will serve four-year terms, members will be elected to eight-year terms. The age of mandatory retirement was set at seventy, with current members "grandfathered." Future presidents will be elected to one eight-year term and may be re-elected to a four-year term. Under these new guidelines, Juan Antonio Samaranch continued in office. His successor, Jacques Rogge of Belgium, was elected IOC president in 2001.

Albertville, 1992. Bonnie Blair (USA) wins the 500-meter speed-skating race.
AP/Wide World Photos.

Barcelona, 1992. "Dream Team" star Michael Jordan (USA) passes the ball between two Puerto Rican players in the quarter-final game. *AP/Wide World Photos.*

Lillehammer, 1994. Johann Koss (Norway), winner of the 1,500-meter, 5,000-meter, and 10,000-meter speed-skating races. *Corbis Images.*

Lillehammer, 1994. Nancy Kerrigan (USA) practices. *AP/Wide World Photos.*

Atlanta, 1996. Medal winners in the women's marathon (*left to right*): Fatuma Roba (Ethiopia), gold; Arimori Yuko (Japan), bronze; and Valentina Yegorova (Russia), silver. *AP/Wide World Photos.*

Sydney, 2000. Ian Thorpe (Australia) wins the 400-meter freestyle in a world-record time of 3:40.59. *AP/Wide World Photos.*

13

After the Cold War

The opening ceremony of the 1992 Games, celebrated in Barcelona, included not only an Olympic flame lit by a fiery arrow but also what was probably the most elaborate pageant ever staged in an Olympic stadium. To the music of the Japanese composer Sakamoto Ryuichi, a gigantic metal figure representing Hercules moved its arms to symbolize the formation of the Straits of Gibraltar, through which the waters of the Atlantic flowed to create the Mediterranean Sea. Across this sea, represented by hundreds of blue-clad dancers, the good ship *Barca Nona* made its perilous way to the shores of Spain, where its crew founded the city of Barcelona. Unfortunately, most spectators were mystified by what they saw. Although the organizers had provided the television networks with a detailed explanation of the allegorical pageant, few journalists bothered to read the explanation, which meant that they were unable to help viewers make sense of what they saw. Instead of explanation, viewers were offered the affable chit-chat that seems to be the sportscaster's stock-in-trade. The traditional parade of national teams, beginning with Greece and ending with the host nation, was easy to understand and appreciate—except for American viewers, who were subjected to a seemingly endless series of commercial breaks.

Between the closing ceremony in Seoul in 1988 and the opening ceremony in Barcelona in 1992, the cold war had come to an end. Some 498 athletes from the "former Soviet Union," representing twelve newly independent nations, comprised a "Unified Team" that was formidable but not quite the juggernaut that had dominated the games four years earlier. In track and field, the Unified Team was able to win only seven events, including the pole vault—in which Maxim Tarassov soared higher than the famed Sergei Bubka. Their teammates won two events that rarely make headlines: the hammer throw and the 50-

kilometer walk. The women on the Unified Team took home four medals: Elena Romanova won the 3,000-meter race; Valentina Egorova finished the marathon eight seconds ahead of Japan's Arimori Yuko; the 400-meter specialists won the relay; and Svetlana Kriveleva was victorious in the shot put with a throw of 21.06 meters.

The track-and-field specialists of the Unified Team were overshadowed by the men and women of African descent. Britain's Linford Christie won the 100 meters in 9.96 seconds. Black runners were also victorious in the men's 200-meter, 400-meter, and 800-meter races as well as the 4 × 100–meter and the 4 × 400–meter relays. Gail Devers and Gwen Torrence were the stars of women's track and field, winning the 100-meter and 200-meter races. Devers triumph came two years after doctors, while treating her for a severe reaction to thyroid medication, considered amputating both of her legs. Torrence joined three other African Americans (Evelyn Ashford, Esther Jones, and Carlette Guidry) to win a gold medal in the 4 × 100–meter relay, and she might well have won a third gold in the 100-meter hurdles had she not stumbled over the last hurdle. When France's Marie-José Pérec won the 400-meter race, it was impossible not to notice that female runners of African descent now represented many European countries as well as the United States and the islands of the Caribbean.

Equally noteworthy were victories by three women from African nations. In the grueling 10,000-meter contest, Ethiopia's Derartu Tulu defeated her white South Africa rival, Elana Meyer. Algeria's Hassiba Boulmerka, the first Islamic woman to become a world-class runner, was victorious in the 1500-meter race—a remarkable feat given that she had received numerous death threats from Islamic fundamentalists (because her refusal to wear a track suit that covered her arms and legs violated Islamic religious doctrine).

There were also moments of glory for Spanish, German, and Korean runners. Spain's Fermín Cacho spurted to the lead in the last 250 meters of the 1,500-meter race. Germany's Dieter Baumann finished ahead of his Ethiopian and Kenyan rivals in the 5,000 meters. And Korea's Young-Cho Hwang won the marathon.

American swimmers and divers, who once dominated their sports, won thirteen events, including solo and duo synchronized swimming, but they were individually less impressive than the Hungarians and the members of the Unified Team. The former included Krisztina Egerszegi, the only swimmer to win three gold medals. She was first in the 100-meter and 200-meter backstroke and third in the 400-meter individual medley. Her teammate Tamas Darnyi repeated his double victory of 1988, winning the men's 200-meter and 400-meter individual medleys.

The Unified Team also had a pair of multiple winners: Alexander Popov (50- and 100-meter freestyle) and Evgeny Sadovii (200- and 400-meter freestyle, 4 × 200–meter relay). Chinese divers won the men's springboard competition and both of the women's diving competitions.

Vitali Chicherbo of the Unified Team was supreme among the male gymnasts. He won the vault, the rings, and the parallel bars, tied for first on the pommel horse, and was the unchallenged individual champion. Shannon Miller, America's star female gymnast, managed a silver medal on the balance beam and bronze medals on the uneven bars and in the floor exercises, which was enough to place her second in the overall competition. Although the Eastern European women took seven of eight gold medals for gymnastics, the competition ended, in the words of the IOC's official history, "without a queen."

The Cuban women defeated the United Team to win the volleyball tournament, which was a surprise, and the Cuban boxers won seven of the twelve weight categories in boxing, which was perhaps an even greater surprise. Oscar de la Hoya was the only American champion. In judo, Miriam Blasco defeated the European lightweight champion, Britain's Nicola Fairbrother, en route to the first gold medal ever won by a Spanish woman.

None of these athletes, not even Carl Lewis (who won gold medals in the long jump and the 4 × 100–meter relay) or Jennifer Capriati (who defeated Steffi Graf for the tennis title), aroused the enthusiasm of basketball's "Dream Team," which consisted of Larry Bird, Michael Jordan, Earvin "Magic" Johnson, and a constellation of slightly less brilliant stars such as Moses Malone and Patrick Ewing. The Americans defeated the Croatian team by a score of 117 to 85, which was closer than expected. The American women came in third, behind the Unified Team and the Chinese.

The winter games celebrated in Albertville were the last to take place in the same year as the summer games. Slovenia and Croatia made their Olympic debut as independent nations. After complicated negotiations, the United Nations Security Council permitted the International Olympic Committee to invite Yugoslavia, then subjected to UN sanctions, to send individual athletes, but not members of teams, to Albertville. The IOC also offered war-torn Bosnia-Herzogovina a chance to participate as an "Independent Team," with Olympic colors and the Olympic anthem, but the government in Sarajevo refused the opportunity.

When the competitions began, American speed-skater Bonnie Blair, whose first Olympic triumph came in Calgary when she won a gold medal in a world-record time of 39.10 seconds over 500 meters, won two more golds (500 and 1000 meters). American figure skater Kristi

Yamaguchi achieved fame (and fortune) when she outperformed Ito Midori (Japan) and Nancy Kerrigan (USA). Natalia Mishkutenok and Artur Dmitriev won the pairs competition, and the men's title went to their teammate Viktor Petrenko.

The star of Alpine skiing was clearly Italy's flamboyant Alberto Tomba, who won the giant slalom and came in second in the slalom (both of which he had won in 1988). The most remarkable skier may have been forty-year-old Raisa Smetanina of the Unified Team. Appearing in her fifth consecutive Olympics, she added a gold medal in cross-country skiing to the three golds, five silvers, and one bronze she had already accumulated.

There were also indications that the winter games were no longer a monopoly of Europeans and North Americans. Speed-skaters Qiaobo Ye and Li Yan won China's first-ever winter medals (the former for the 500- and 1000-meter races, the latter for the 500-meter short-track contest). With a second-place finish in the slalom, New Zealand's Annelise Coberger became the first winter medalist from Oceania.

The 1994 Lillehammer Games were the first to be celebrated *between* the summer games rather than in the same year. Memorable for the atmosphere of good will created by their generous Norwegian hosts, they were also the first winter games at which the women rather than the men were unquestionably the focus of media attention. No athlete, male or female, received more adulation than Nancy Kerrigan, the bronze medalist in figure skating from 1992. Already immensely popular, Kerrigan basked in the world's sympathy in the aftermath of a brutal physical assault, carried out several weeks earlier, by an acquaintance of rival skater Tonya Harding (whom the media had already cast as the "tough girl" of the sport). That Kerrigan, a tall and graceful beauty, was finally (and perhaps unfairly) judged second to the child-like Ukrainian skater Oksana Baiul seemed only to enhance her popularity (and her endorsement income). Under a cloud of suspicion, Harding later pled guilty to a felony and was ordered to pay $110,000 in fines and fees. The cloud had the proverbial silver lining. According to *Sports Illustrated,* she was offered $400,000 for interviews with the CBS tabloid show "Inside Edition," and the All-Japan Women's Professional Wrestling Association reportedly offered her two million dollars to grapple as a "baddie."

Not quite forgotten in the glare of publicity were the men's and the pairs competitions. In the former, Russia's Aleksei Umanov was judged slightly above Canada's Elvis Stojko. In the latter, the demise of the amateur rule enabled Ekaterina Gordeyeva and Sergei Grinkov of the USSR, who had turned professional after they won the gold medal in

1988, to return to Olympic competition. They forced Albertville's winners, Artur Dmitriev and Natalya Mishkulenok, to settle for the silver medal.

Nearly as popular, at least with the American commentators, was Bonnie Blair, who sped to victory once again in the 500- and 1000-meter races, bringing her Olympic medal total to five golds and a bronze. Among the most-decorated athletes at the games was Italy's cross-country skier Manuela DiCenta, who was first in the 15- and 30-kilometer races, second in the 5-kilometer and the pursuit, and third in the 4 × 5–kilometer relay.

The most spectacular male athlete of the Lillehammer games was a member of the home team: speed-skater Johann Koss. He repeated his 1992 win in the 1500-meter race, setting a world record of 1:15.29. He set another record (6:34.96) en route to victory in the 5,000 meters. Next came the 10,000-meter race. As David Wallechinsky notes in *Complete Book of the Winter Olympics* (1998), Koss then "demoralized his opponents . . . by reeling off 24 straight sub-33-second laps to break his own world record by 12.99 seconds." After the games, Koss returned to Eritrea, which he had visited as a supporter of the Olympic Aid project, and delivered twelve tons of sports equipment to that nation's impoverished children. In a sports world that sometimes seems appallingly bereft of role models, Koss was a true hero.

At the Centennial Olympics in Atlanta, the women's program expanded to include soccer, softball, and beach volleyball as well as new events in previously contested sports. Swimming, which began in 1912 with two events, and track and field, which began in 1928 with five events, now had nineteen and twenty events, respectively. There was a record number of female athletes at the 1996 Games—3,779, or 36.4 percent of the 10,361 Olympians, which was a far cry from the handful of women who participated in 1900.

Once again, the United States dominated the men's track and field events. Led by Michael Johnson, who won both the 200- and 400-meter sprints, the former in a world-record time of 19.32 seconds, the Americans captured ten of twenty-four gold medals. That all eight finalists for the 100 meters were men of African descent was no longer a surprise. Two false starts cost Britain's Linford Christie the chance to defend the title he had won in Barcelona. Canada's Donovan Bailey was the winner in 9.84 seconds, a new world record.

American men swam to victory in all three relay races, but they won only three of the other thirteen events. Russia's Alexander Popov and Denis Pankratov took home two medals each (50- and 100-meter freestyle; 100- and 200-meter butterfly), while New Zealand's Danyon

Loader doubled in the 200- and 400-meter freestyle. The Chinese were clearly the best divers: Ni Xiong won the men's springboard competition, and Fu Mingxia won both of the women's events. The Chinese also took eight of twelve medals in table tennis.

Although the American women's total of seventeen victories was nearly twice that of their Chinese rivals, who had nine, female athletes from twenty-seven other nations collected one or more gold medals. Great athletes such as the sprinter Marie-José Pérec (200 and 400 meters) and the swimmer Krisztina Egerszegi (200-meter backstroke) repeated earlier Olympic successes, and there were some new stars, including Ireland's Michelle Smith, who swam to three golds and a bronze. The 1996 Games were also remarkable for victories by athletes from small countries that had rarely, if ever, had their national anthems played during the medal ceremonies. Among the women, gold medals went to Chioma Ajunwa (Nigeria) in the long jump, Ghada Shouaa (Syria) in the heptathlon, Claudia Poll (Costa Rica) in the 200-meter freestyle, and Lai-Shun Lee (Hong Kong) and Kristine Roug (Denmark) in sailing. In addition, the Danish women won the handball tournament, and a Brazilian pair finished first in beach volleyball. Smaller nations were less successful in men's sports, but Denmark's Poul-Erik Hoyer-Larsen did manage to win the men's badminton title, Burundi's runner Venuste Niyongabo was first in the 5,000-meter race, and Nikolaos Kaklamanakis sailed to victory in the mistral 9 class.

The most memorable athletes from the Atlanta games were probably two track-and-field "old-timers." Ending an Olympic career that stretched from 1984 to 1996, Carl Lewis (USA) won the long jump and mounted the victor's platform to receive his ninth gold medal. On the women's side, Merlene Ottey (Jamaica) sprinted to two silver medals and capped a career that began in Moscow in 1980. Although she never achieved her lifetime goal of winning Olympic gold, she came away from ten Olympic finals with two silver and five bronze medals.

Environmental battles, which usually ended in a compromise, preceded the 1998 Winter Games in Nagano. When the games finally began, the dramatic contest in figure skating was not between Good and Evil, which is how the media had tended to portray the earlier Kerrigan-Harding rivalry. It was between womanly grace (Michelle Kwan was all of seventeen) and childlike energy (Tara Lipinski was fifteen). Kwan, the favorite, arrived after the games had begun and stayed at a hotel in order to concentrate on the task before her. Lipinski lived in the Olympic Village, posed with the massive sumo wrestler Akebono, and quickly became the most widely recognized spectator at the games. Although Kwan skated beautifully, she came in second to Lipinski, who spun and jumped like a symbolic embodiment of youthful energy. In the pairs competition, Artur Dmitriev, who had won gold and silver medals with Natalya Mishkutenok in 1992 and 1994, partnered Oksana Kazakova for a second gold. It was the tenth consecutive pairs victory for the USSR/Russia.

In the alpine events, Austria's Hermann Meier survived a spectacular crash in the slalom and stormed back to win both the giant and the super-giant slaloms. Germany's Katja Seizinger triumphed in the combined event and the downhill and was third in the giant slalom. America's Picabo Street failed to win a medal in the downhill, her specialty, but then surprised the experts with a win in the super-giant slalom. Russian skiers took all five gold medals in the Nordic events.

To the delight of traditionalists, who lamented the eligibility of National Hockey League stars, the American and Canadian teams were eliminated from the finals of men's hockey. While the Czechs were defeating the Russians, some of the NHL's highly paid poor losers were venting their anger on the furniture. Playing as roughly as the men, the American women defeated their Canadian rivals in the first-ever women's Olympic ice hockey tournament. Canadians took comfort in the tamer excitements of a win in curling, which also had its Olympic debut in Nagano.

Thanks to the "klap" skates introduced a few years earlier by Dutch speed-skaters and adopted by nearly everyone else, world records were broken and rebroken at almost every distance. It was fitting that the Dutch skaters were the most successful. Ids Postma and Jan Bos were first and second in the men's 1000-meter race and second and third over 1500 meters (won by Norway's Adne Sondral). Gianni Romme and Rintje Ritsma won gold and silver medals over 5,000 meters, and a trio of Dutch skaters—Romme, Bob de Jong, and Ritsma—swept the men's 10,000-meter race. The Dutch women were not as successful, but Marianne Timmer did manage to add gold medals for the 1,000- and 1,500-meter races to the Dutch total. Canadian speed-skating fans also had reason to rejoice when Catriona LeMay Doan and Annie Perrault won the women's 500 and short-track 500 races, respectively, and the men's 5,000-meter relay team took a third gold. In addition, Canadian skaters garnered two silver and four bronze medals. The Japanese, who had more to cheer about at these games than they had had since their swimmers stunned the world in 1932, screamed their support for Shimizu Hiroyasu and Nishitani Takafumi, who won the gold in the men's 500 and short-track 500, respectively. (There was also a trio of bronze medals.)

In Nagano, Japanese *seishin* (fighting spirit) appeared most dramatically in the form of a skier the American sportscasters dubbed "Happy Harada" (because of his trademark smile). At the Albertville games, Harada Masahiko and his teammates had the fourth-best combined score in the large-hill ski-jump competition. At the Lillehammer games, after the seventh of their eight jumps, the Japanese quartet had an apparently insurmountable lead of 54.9 points. Then the last German jumper—Jens Weissflog—soared 133.5 meters, which tied the record for the longest jump in Olympic history. Harada, who needed a mere 105 meters to ensure victory for the Japanese team, mistimed his takeoff and touched down at 97.5 meters. He and his teammates—Okabe Takanobu, Nishikata Jinya, and Kasai Noriaki—had to be content with silver medals. Four years later, history threatened to repeat itself. Harada and Okabe, joined now by Saitô Hiroya and Funaki Kazuyoshi, were engaged in a close contest with the German team. Harada's first jump, in the middle of a blizzard, was a paltry 79.5 meters. For his second jump, under improved conditions, Harada came down the hill and took off—in Steve Rushin's words—"as if at Kitty Hawk." Stretching forward, nearly parallel to the V of his skis, Harada flew 137 meters to his redemption. He wept with joy as Funaki's second jump secured the gold. All in all, the Japanese had every right to smile as they bid *sayônara* to their guests.

During the months that preceded Sydney's seventeen days of glory in 2000, there were times when Australian smiles were somewhat strained. When the Pound Commission reported to an Extraordinary Session of the IOC in March 1999, Sydney's organizers were much less severely criticized than Salt Lake City's, but Phillip Coles was warned that he had crossed the line into unacceptable behavior. Immediately before the Sydney games, another problem loomed. Australia's aboriginal community planned massive protests to draw attention to past and present injustice. The majority of the protesters decided, however, that interference with the games was more likely to damage than to further their cause. In the words of Andrew Donnelley, an aboriginal leader, "We don't wish to disrupt the games." Many of those who were originally disaffected were assuaged when one of their own, Cathy Freeman, was chosen to light the Olympic flame at the opening ceremony. Others were won over when Freeman triumphed in the 400-meter race and carried the aboriginal flag as well as the Australian national banner on her victory lap.

Freeman shared the hometown headlines with swimming sensation Ian Thorpe, the towering (6'5") "Torpedo," who set a new world record in the 400-meter freestyle (3:41.3). Italy's Massimiliano Rosolino, who was second, had a simple comment: "He does amaze me."

(Rosolino had a triumph of his own to celebrate: victory in the 200-meter individual medley.) Thorpe then anchored Australia's 4 × 100 freestyle relay team to victory over their arrogant American rivals, who had predicted that they would "break the Australians like guitars." The winning time of 3:13.67 was another world record. Thorpe was upset in the 200-meter freestyle by Pieter Van den Hoogenband of the Netherlands, who was also first in the 100-meter freestyle. Journalists who asked Thorpe how he felt about the setback were told, politely, "You have to be happy with what you do." Lenny Krayzelburg, an immigant from Odessa, was the only American swimmer whose feats were comparable to Thorpe's and van den Hoogenband's. He splashed to victory in the 100- and 200-meter backstroke races but had to settle for a silver medal in the 50-meter freestyle when a pair of Americans, Gary Hall, Jr., and Anthony Ervin, finished with identical times: 21.98 seconds.

In the women's events, American swimmers triumphed in all three relay races (4 × 100, 4 × 200, 4 × 100 medley). Brooke Bennett (USA) and Diana Mocanu (Romania) were double winners, but the women's aquatic star was unquestionably van den Hoogenband's teammate, twenty-seven-year-old Inge De Bruijn, who won the 50- and 100-meter freestyle and the 100-meter butterfly, all in world-record time.

As the swimmers, who competed in thirty-two events, swam their last races on the ninth day of competition, the track-and-field specialists began their thirty-six events. The focus of media attention was, for once, on the women's rather than the men's competition. Before the games began, Marion Jones (USA) had announced her goal of an unprecedented five gold medals. In the 100- and 200-meter races, her combined margin of victory—0.37 and 0.43 seconds, respectively—was the second largest in Olympic history. Merlene Ottey, the veteran Jamaican runner, sighed, "I wish I were ten years younger so I could try to chase her, but it's useless now. It's useless for all of us." Ekaterini Thanou of Greece, second in the 100 meters, acknowledged that she had set her sights on a silver medal because the gold was clearly out of reach. A third gold medal for Jones came, as expected, in the 4 × 100-meter relay. The 4 × 400 was a different story. Although she had seldom run a 400-meter race, Jones ran the third leg of the 4 × 400 in an amazingly fast 49.59 seconds. It was not enough to make up for two bad baton passes; the team finished in third place. In her fifth event, the long jump, Jones was outperformed by Germany's Heike Drechsler. With three gold and two bronze medals, Jones was probably the most successful "failure" in Olympic history.

As for the men, Maurice Greene (100 meters) and Michael Johnson

(400 meters) continued American dominance of their events, but there was a real surprise in the 200-meter race, which was won by Konstantinos Kenteris of Greece, the first Greek runner to win an Olympic race since Spiridon Louys took gold in the marathon in 1896. Over 800 meters, Nils Schumann of Germany edged Wilson Kipketer, running for Denmark, but in the longer races, East African runners overwhelmed their rivals. Except for two silvers and two bronzes taken by North African men, the East Africans swept every race. Kenyans were first and third in the 1,500-meter race, first and second in the 3,000-meter steeplechase, and second in both the 10,000-meter race and the marathon. Ethiopian runners won the 5,000-meter race and captured gold and bronze medals in the 10,000-meter race and the marathon.

Confronted with an Olympic extravaganza that now included thirty-one different sports, television networks responded—as always—nationalistically. NBC, which has seldom, if ever, lingered among the Greco-Roman wrestlers, showed its prime-time American viewers the heavyweight match in which Rulon Gardner defeated the "invincible" Alexander Karelin of Russia, the most successful wrestler in the history of the sport. Japanese spectators were offered coverage of their judo team, which won four golds, two silvers, and two bronzes, while South Koreans watched their tae kwon do team, which was restricted by the IOC to four of the eight events, win three golds and a silver. Chinese TV viewers were shocked when Laura Wilkinson (USA) came from fifth place to upset Li Na in the finals of platform diving, but they exulted in the first-ever victory of their men's gymnastics team.

Women's gymnastics, which draws billions to their television sets, provided the usual drama as the Russians and the Romanians competed for team and individual honors. An inexplicable blunder on the part of the officials shattered Svetlana Khorkina's dream of victory in the all-around competition. The vaulting block was installed at 120 cm rather than 125 cm, a small difference in height that made a huge difference in performance. Khorkina ended her vault on her hands and knees. Romania's diminutive (4'10") Andreea Raducan was less disadvantaged than her much taller rival by the height of the block and scored well enough to finish as the all-around champion. Her joy was short-lived. She was summarily stripped of her title when she failed the mandatory drug test. The IOC's decision was controversial because of the circumstances: Raducan had a cold and was given medication by an obviously incompetent doctor who failed to notice that it contained pseudoephedrine, a banned substance. While acknowledging that the young gymnast had not intentionally violated the rules, the IOC remained adamant. She was allowed to keep the silver medal she had won in the vault, but the all-around title devolved to her teammate, Simona Amanar. As for Khorkina, her trademark smile reappeared when she was awarded a gold medal for her stellar performance on the uneven bars.

The gold medals for ballgames were shared by a number of countries:

Sport	Men	Women
Baseball/softball	USA	USA
Basketball	USA	USA
Handball	Russia	Denmark
Soccer	Cameroon	Norway
Volleyball	Yugoslavia	Cuba
Beach volleyball	USA	Australia

The excitement was particularly intense in the men's basketball semifinals, when Lithuania came within three points of upsetting the Dream Team, and in women's soccer, when Norway defeated the United States by a score of 3 to 2 in the twelfth minute of a sudden-death overtime. Curiosity may have been most intense when Denmark played Norway in women's handball. Denmark's Camilla Andersen was legally married to Norway's Mia Hundvin—the first intramarital contest in Olympic history. (Norway won 19-17.)

* * *

This seems a fitting time to raise the question of "cultural imperialism," which I have discussed at length in *Games and Empires* (1994). At the summer games of 1996, gold medals were more widely distributed than ever before. Athletes from fifty-three different countries received gold medals, and athletes from another twenty-six countries won at least one silver or bronze medal. Of the 265 gold medals that were awarded, however, 70 went to American and Russian athletes, the Germans took 20, and other Europeans captured 91. The Chinese, now the dominant Asian athletic power, accounted for 16 gold medals, while Cuban athletes took 9 and the rest of Asia and Latin America had to be satisfied with just 32. African athletes won only 11 events.

The distribution of medals at Sydney in 2000 was, if anything, even more unequal. Athletes from fifty-two different countries shared 298 gold medals. The United States (39), Russia (32), China (28), and Australia (16) led the count. Germany (14), France (13), and Italy (13) accounted for nearly a third of the 132 European victories, while

twenty-two Asian nations won a combined total of only 40 events—
and the Chinese were the victors in 28 of them. Cuba took 11 of the
14 gold medals won by athletes from Latin America and the Caribbean, and African athletes, though highly visible on the track and in the
marathon, captured just 9 events. Another way to think about this is
to consider that the Europeans and North Americans who invented the
modern games continue to claim over three-fourths of all the gold, silver, and bronze medals. In short, while the disparities among nations
are certainly much reduced from what they were twenty years earlier,
the men and women—especially the women—of Asia, Latin America,
and Africa continue to play ancillary roles on the Olympic stage. For
them, Olympic commonplaces about the superior importance of participation will have to suffice.

In the unlikely event of an absolutely even distribution of medals—
one gold medal for every 25,000,000 people—a critic might still speak
of cultural imperialism. If the dream of Pierre de Coubertin is ever to
be realized, the Olympic *program* must be revised to equalize the number of events for men and women and also to include sports of non-Western origin in which the nations of the Third World have some kind of
natural or cultural advantage. An enlarged and diversified program will
not, however, automatically guarantee success to third-world athletes.
Although judo was invented by the Japanese, they returned from Atlanta
with only three of that sport's fourteen gold medals. Finally, no matter
what the origin of an Olympic sport, it is now conceptualized in specifically modern (i.e., Western) terms. In other words, the root difficulty is
that modern sports, like the universalistic political ideals institutionalized in the Olympic Games, are themselves a product of Western civilization. Paradoxically, the success of the baron's dream is one of the things
that prevents the dream's full and complete realization.

Appendix

Table A.1. Participation in the Summer Olympic Games

Year	Male Athletes	Female Athletes
1896	295	0
1900	1,066	11
1904	548	6
1908	1,998	36
1912	2,447	57
1920	2,527	64
1924	2,939	136
1928	2,681	290
1932	1,204	127
1936	3,652	328
1948	3,677	385
1952	5,349	518
1956	2,958	384
1960	4,785	610
1964	4,903	683
1968	5,845	781
1972	6,595	1,299
1976	4,938	1,251
1980	4,835	1,088
1984	5,429	1,626
1988	6,941	2,476
1992	6,648	2,715
1996	6,582	3,779
2000	6,582	4,069

Table A.2. Olympic Sites

Olympiad	Year	Site
1	1896	Athens
2	1900	Paris
3	1904	St. Louis
4	1908	London
5	1912	Stockholm
6	1916	(games not held)
7	1920	Antwerp
8[a]	1924	Chamonix
		Paris

Appendix

Table A.2. Olympic Sites

Olympiad	Year	Site
9	1928	St. Moritz
		Amsterdam
10	1932	Lake Placid
		Los Angeles
11	1936	Garmisch-Partenkirchen
		Berlin
12	1940	(games not held)
		(games not held)
13	1944	(games not held)
		(games not held)
14	1948	St. Moritz
		London
15	1952	Oslo
		Helsinki
16	1956	Cortina d'Ampezzo
		Melbourne
17	1960	Squaw Valley
		Rome
18	1964	Innsbruck
		Tokyo
19	1968	Grenoble
		Mexico City
20	1972	Sapporo
		Munich
21	1976	Innsbruck
		Montreal
22	1980	Lake Placid
		Moscow
23	1984	Sarajevo
		Los Angeles
24	1988	Calgary
		Seoul
25	1992	Albertville
		Barcelona
	1994	Lillehammer
26	1996	Atlanta
	1998	Nagano
27	2000	Sydney
	2002	Salt Lake City
28	2004	Athens
	2006	Turin

a. Beginning in 1924, and until 1992 when the pattern changed, winter games were held several months before the summer games for that year.

Bibliographical Essay

Thousands of books in dozens of languages have been written about the Olympics. Although much of the best published scholarship is in French, German, and Italian, the materials available in English are ample enough to satisfy most nonacademic readers. Most books on the Olympics are devoted to the athletic contests that in this study are subordinated to the political, economic, and social aspects of the games. Readers who desire a one-volume general account of the sports competitions per se might well begin with the third edition of Dick Schaap's *Illustrated History of the Olympics* (New York: Knopf, 1975) or with *The Olympic Games,* ed. Lord Killanin and John Rodda (New York: Macmillan, 1976). There is no satisfactory narrative account that brings the story to the present, but the International Olympic Committee and the U.S. Olympic Committee both publish detailed official reports of the summer and winter games. Readers famished for statistical information should consult Erich Kamper and Bill Mallon, *The Golden Book of the Olympic Games* (Milan: Villardi, 1992), or David Wallechinsky, *The Complete Book of the Olympics* (Boston: Little, Brown, 1992).

The most detailed account of the political, economic, and social aspects of the modern games can be found in the massive three-volume history published by the IOC: *The International Olympic Committee: One Hundred Years* (Lausanne: International Olympic Committee, 1996). These volumes, which were written by a team of distinguished sports historians, have numerous photographs, multicolored figures, and statistical tables. Their drawback is that the accounts of the Killanin and Samaranch years are somewhat sanitized. John E. Findling and Kimberly Pelle's *Historical Dictionary of the Modern Olympic Movement* (Westport, Conn.: Greenwood Press, 1996) is not only informative but also much more readable than its title suggests. Robert K. Barney and Klaus V. Meier have edited two valuable collections of Olympic essays: *Proceedings of the First International Symposium for Olympic Research* (London, Ont.: University of Western Ontario, 1992) and *Critical Reflections on Olympic Ideology* (London, Ont.: Centre for Olympic Studies, 1994). *The Olympics at the Millennium*

(New Brunswick, N.J.: Rutgers University Press, 2000), edited by Kay Schaffer and Sidonie Smith, also contains thoughtful criticism, much of it from a feminist perspective.

Christopher R. Hill's *Olympic Politics* (Manchester: Manchester University Press, 1992) is excellent. Alfred E. Senn's *Power, Politics, and the Olympic Games* (Champaign, Ill.: Human Kinetics, 1999) is reliable but bland. Some older histories on the topic of politics and the Olympics remain useful. David B. Kanin's *Political History of the Olympic Games* (Boulder, Colo.: Westview Press, 1981) contains good information but is marred by an unusually large number of factual errors. John Lucas combines sports history in the narrower sense with a broad view of the Olympic Games as a social movement in *The Modern Olympic Games* (Cranbury, N.J.: A. S. Barnes, 1980). Lucas's book is especially good on the personal conflict between Pierre de Coubertin and James E. Sullivan. Richard Espy's *The Politics of the Olympic Games* (Berkeley: University of California Press, 1979) is an excellent study of the international political context for the postwar games (1948–76). Its chief limitation is that Espy worked almost exclusively from sources available in English.

There are many histories of national participation, including a few in English. Most of them emphasize sports per se. Among the best is Max and Reet Howell's *Aussie Gold* (Albion, Queensland: Brooks Waterloo, 1988). The Howells discuss each of the games in some detail and then provide sketches of the Australian athletes. Canadian athletes are the subject of Frank Cosentino and Glyn Leyshon's *Olympic Gold* (Toronto: Holt, Rinehart & Winston, 1973). Explanations for the athletic successes of the Soviet Union and East Germany are offered by Yuri Brokhin in *The Big Red Machine* (New York: Random House, 1978) and by Doug Gilbert in *The Miracle Machine* (New York: Coward-McCann, 1979). The latter is weakened by its author's inability to read or speak German. The Rhodesian controversy is discussed by John Cheffers in *A Wilderness of Spite* (New York: Vantage, 1972). Richard E. Lapchick analyzes the South African controversy in great detail in *The Politics of Race and International Sport* (Westport, Conn.: Greenwood Press, 1975). The crisis provoked by the Asian Games and the Games of the New Emerging Forces is the topic of Ewa T. Pauker's short study *GANEFO: Sports and Politics in Djakarta* (Santa Monica, Calif.: Rand Corp., 1964). Since American and British historians and journalists tend to focus on their compatriots, who have in fact been central players in the Olympic drama, there has been little incentive to publish special histories entitled *Uncle Sam at the Olympics* or *John Bull Gathers the Gold.*

Biographies and autobiographies of the presidents of the IOC are an important source of information. Coubertin's autobiography, which orginally appeared in 1931, has been translated into English and published as *Olympic Memoirs* (Lausanne: International Olympic Committee, 1979). None of the many French biographies of Coubertin has been translated into English. Neither Henri Baillet-Latour nor Sigfrid Edstrøm left an account of his years as IOC president. Heinz Schöbel's *Four Dimensions of Avery Brundage* (Leipzig: Edition Leipzig, 1968) is beautifully illustrated but otherwise undistinguished. Portions of Brundage's unpublished autobiography have appeared in German but not in English. His manuscript, part of the voluminous Avery Brundage Collection at the University of Illinois at Urbana-Champaign, was an important source for one of my books, *The Games Must Go On: Avery Brundage and the Olympic Movement* (New York: Columbia University Press, 1984). Lord Killanin's *My Olympic Years* (London: Secker & Warburg, 1983) provides insights into its author's opinions and contains numerous photographs of the jovial Irishman in the company of Queen Elizabeth and other heads of state, but it cannot be relied upon for accurate information. The years of Killanin's presidency are better surveyed in Geoffrey Miller's *Behind the Olympic Rings* (Lynn, Mass.: H. O. Zimman, 1979). Juan Antonio Samaranch is treated as if he were a candidate for sainthood in David Miller's *Olympic Revolution* (London: Pavilion Books, 1992) but is demonized in Vyv Simson and Andrew Jennings's *The Lords of the Rings: Power, Money, and Drugs in the Modern Olympics* (New York: Simon & Schuster, 1992). Jennings continues the attack in *The New Lords of the Rings* (London: Pocket Books, 1996). The most balanced account of Samaranch's presidency is Fernand Landry and Magdeleine Yerlès's contribution to the IOC's official three-volume history (mentioned above), but even they tend toward canonization.

Many past and present members of the International Olympic Committee have written about their experiences. Unfortunately, none of these memoirs seems to have been translated into English.

If one turns from the administrators to the athletes, one finds a plethora of autobiographies (often written with the help of sports journalists) and biographies. The problem for the historian is that these books rarely deal with the larger contexts of the games.

The majority of the books available in English focus on track-and-field sports. Among the best of these—in the order of the games at which the athletes participated—are Ellery H. Clark's *Reminiscences of an Athlete* (Boston: Houghton Mifflin, 1911); Robert W. Wheeler's *Jim Thorpe*, rev. ed. (Norman: University of Oklahoma Press, 1979);

Babe Didrikson's *This Life I've Led* (New York: A. S. Barnes, 1955); William Oscar Johnson and Nancy P. Williamson's *"Whatta Gal": The Babe Didrikson Story* (Boston: Little, Brown, 1977); Susan E. Cayleff's *Babe: The Life and Legend of Babe Didrikson Zaharias* (Urbana: University of Illinois Press, 1995); William J. Baker's *Jesse Owens, an American Life* (New York: Free Press, 1986); Marty Glickman and Stan Isaacs's *The Fastest Kid on the Block* (Syracuse, N.Y.: Syracuse University Press, 1996); Herb McKenley et al.'s *Herb McKenley* (Kingston: Institute of Jamaica, 1974); Olga Connolly's *The Rings of Destiny* (New York: David McKay, 1968); Roger Bannister's *The Four Minute Mile* (New York: Dodd, Mead, 1955); Vincent Matthews and Neil Amdur's *My Race Be Won* (New York: Charter House, 1974); Jim Scott's *Bob Mathias* (Englewood Cliffs, N.J.: Prentice-Hall, 1952); Gordon Pirie's *Running Wild* (London: W. H. Allen, 1961); Dorothy Hyman's *Sprint to Fame* (London: Stanley Paul, 1964); Wilma Rudolf's *Wilma* (New York: New American Library, 1977); Frank Shorter and Marc Bloom's *Olympic Gold* (Boston: Houghton Mifflin, 1984); Mary Peters and Ian Woodbridge's *Mary P.* (London: Stanley Paul, 1974); and Sebastian Coe's *Running Free* (New York: St. Martin's, 1981).

Other sports are much less well represented. For swimming and diving, see Dawn Fraser and Harry Gordon's *Below the Surface* (New York: William Morrow, 1965); Don Schollander and Duke Savage's *Deep Water* (New York: Crown Publishers, 1971); and Greg Louganis and Eric Marcus's *Breaking the Surface* (New York: Random House, 1995). For gymnastics, see Mary Lou Retton et al.'s *Mary Lou* (New York: Dell, 1986). For skating, see Jean-Claude Killy and Al Greenberg's *Comeback* (New York: Macmillan, 1974). For figure skating, see Dorothy Hamill and Eva Clairmont's *On and Off the Ice* (New York: Knopf, 1983). For rowing, see David Halberstam's *The Amateurs* (New York: Viking, 1985) and Heather Clarke and Susan Gwynne-Timothy's *Stroke* (Toronto: James Lorimer, 1988).

A good deal of lively biographical information appears in William O. Johnson's *All That Glitters Is Not Gold* (New York: G. P. Putnam's Sons, 1972). Women's Olympic participation is discussed in Adrianne Blue's *Faster, Higher, Further* (London: Virago Press, 1988) and in my own *Women's Sports* (New York: Columbia Unversity Press, 1991). Doris H. Pieroth's *Their Day in the Sun* (Seattle: University of Washington Press, 1996) is concerned exclusively with the female athletes at the 1932 Games. Gina Daddario's *Women's Sport and Spectacle* (Westport, Conn.: Praeger, 1998) focuses on the media's presentation of female athletes. There is also a great deal of information in the *International Encyclopedia of Women and Sport,* ed. Karen Christensen,

Allen Guttmann, and Gertrud Pfister, 3 vols. (New York: Macmillan Reference, 2001).

A number of valuable studies concentrate on a single period or even a single Olympiad. John J. MacAloon's *This Great Symbol* (Chicago: University of Chicago Press, 1981) deftly places Coubertin in his social and intellectual context. Influenced by Émile Durkheim and Victor Turner, MacAloon offers an excellent analysis of the Olympic Games as a social ritual; with considerably less success, he subjects the baron to psychoanalytical scrutiny. A more traditional account of these same years can be found in Richard Mandell's *The First Modern Olympics* (Berkeley: University of California Press, 1976). The same author has written a classic account of the 1936 Games, *The Nazi Olympics*, 2d ed. (Urbana: University of Illinois Press, 1987). Duff Hart-Davis's *Hitler's Games* (New York: Harper & Row, 1976) is also valuable, especially for the British perspective. Of the many books on Leni Riefenstahl and her documentary film *Olympia,* the best (in English) are probably Glenn B. Infield's *Leni Riefenstahl* (New York: Crowell, 1976) and Cooper C. Graham's *Leni Riefenstahl and Olympia* (Metuchen, N.J.: Scarecrow Press, 1986). Riefenstahl's fascinating but untrustworthy autobiography has been translated into English as *Leni Riefenstahl: A Memoir* (New York: St. Martin's, 1993). Richard Mandell's *The Olympics of 1972* (Chapel Hill: University of North Carolina Press, 1991) is based on a diary kept during the 1972 Games. In it he combines the alert observer's eye with the trained historian's retrospective imagination, and the result is fascinating. For the tragedy that befell the Israeli team at the hands of Palestinian terrorists, one must consult Serge Grousset's *The Blood of Israel,* trans. Harold J. Salemson (New York: William Morrow, 1975). Economic miscalculation rather than political terror is the theme of Nick Auf der Maur's severely critical account of the 1976 Games in Montreal, *The Billion-Dollar Game: Jean Drapeau and the 1976 Olympics* (Toronto: James Lorimer, 1976). Jack Ludwig's version of these games, *Five Ring Circus* (Toronto: Doubleday, 1976), is superficial.

The games of the Twenty-second and Twenty-third Olympiads were badly damaged by the boycotts led by the United States in 1980 and the USSR in 1984. There is a fairly extensive collection of books devoted to these boycotts: Dereck L. Hulme, Jr.'s *The Political Olympics: Moscow, Afghanistan, and the 1980 U.S. Boycott* (New York: Praeger, 1990); Baruch Hazan's *Olympic Sports and Propaganda Games: Moscow, 1980* (New Brunswick, N.J.: Transaction Books, 1982); Christopher Brooker's *The Games War: A Moscow-Journal* (London: Faber & Faber, 1981); and Bill Shaikin's *Sport and Politics* (New York:

Praeger, 1988). Kenneth Reich's *Making It Happen: Peter Ueberoth and the 1984 Olympics* (Santa Barbara, Calif.: Capra Press, 1986), which includes a good deal more than the immediate story of the boycott, is good journalism. The impact of the mass media on more recent games is covered by *The Olympic Movement and the Mass Media,* ed. Roger Jackson (Calgary: Hurford Enterprises, 1989). Olympic ceremony and its transmission by the mass media are central themes of two collections: *Olympic Ceremonies,* ed. Miquel de Moregas, John MacAloon, and Llines Montserrat (Lausanne: Olympic Museum–International Olympic Committee, 1996), and *Television in the Olympics,* ed. Miguel de Moregas Spa, Nancy Rivenburgh, and James F. Larson (London: John Libbey, 1995).

There are two English-language journals that specialize in scholarly studies of the Olympic Games: *Olympika* and *Journal of Olympic History* (formerly *Citius, Altius, Fortius*). Interested readers will frequently find essays on the Olympics in the *Journal of Sport History, Sport History Review, Sporting Traditions,* and the *International Journal of the History of Sport.*

Index